Applications for reproductions should be made in writing to:
MOD copyright Unit, Intellectual Property Rights Group, Poplar 2 #2218, MOD Abbey Wood, Bristol, BS34 8JH

AIR FORCE LEADERSHIP: BEYOND COMMAND?

Edited by   John Jupp
                   Keith Grint

Compiled by   Katherine Slater

© Crown Copyright 2005
Published by the Royal Air Force Leadership Centre
ISBN: 0-9552189-0-X
ISBN: 978-0-9552189-0-3

CONTENTS

Title	**Page**
Contents	iii
Acknowledgements	v
Introduction *Air Chief Marshal Sir Jock Stirrup*	1
Chapter 1 **Keynote Address**	3
What is Leadership? Beyond Command, Management & Contingency Theory *Professor Keith Grint*	4
Chapter 2 **Leading A Downsizing Air Force**	23
'If you do what you've always done…' Leadership Challenges in a Downsizing RAAF *Professor Stephen Mugford and Wing Commander Bob Rogers*	24
Chapter 3 **Leadership In Adversity**	41
Leading Change: The Defence Aviation Repair Agency *Air Vice-Marshal Peter Dye*	42
The Air Surveillance and Control System: Changing Mindsets to Realise Effect *Group Captain Malcolm Crayford and Brian Howieson*	48
Public Value and Adaptive Leadership *Professor John Benington*	59
Public Value and Adaptive Leadership in the Policing of 'Drumcree' in Northern Ireland *Assistant Chief Constable Irwin Turbitt*	65
Chapter 4 **Leadership In The Air**	73
The Art of Leadership in the Air *Group Captain John Jupp*	74
Leadership From Today's Cockpit *Squadron Leader Harvey Smyth*	84

Chapter 5	**Historical Address**	91
	Historical Perspective of Air Force Leadership Post WWI and WWII *Mr Sebastian Cox*	92
Chapter 6	**Operational Leadership**	105
	Leadership: Force Development Processes for the Command and Control of Airpower *Major General Stephen M. Goldfein*	106
	Command or Control? Leadership in the Battle of Britain *Doctor Stephen Bungay*	115
Chapter 7	**Leadership Throughout The RAF**	129
	Exposed Leadership *Sergeant 'Tomi' Tomiczek and Corporal Brendan McGarrity*	130
	Followership: The Anvil of Leadership *Professor Keith Grint*	135
Chapter 8	**Transformational Leadership**	151
	Leadership: What Helps and What Hurts *Air Commodore Steve Abbott*	152
	Transformational Leadership: Unlocking Human Potential *Professor Alan Hooper*	157
Chapter 9	**Closing Address**	165
	Air Chief Marshal Sir Brian Burridge	166
Biographies		173

ACKNOWLEDGEMENTS

The editors are most grateful to the authors of the various chapters in this volume for their written submissions, and for the enthusiasm with which they embraced the Conference on which this book is based. It is axiomatic that the book could not have occurred without their efforts. We are particularly grateful for the effort taken to produce these papers after the Conference by such busy people.

The organisation of the Conference itself, without which this book could not have been published, involved considerable effort by all those at the RAF Leadership Centre. We would like to mention particularly Squadron Leader Rhys Cowsill, Flight Lieutenant Toria Fuller, Warrant Officer Mick Stuart and Mrs Carole Ross whose indefatigable efforts before and during the Conference made it happen and whose advice and proof reading afterwards enabled this publication.

Production of the book would not have been possible without the assistance of Mr Richard Dixon, and his team at Media Services, Training Group Defence Agency at RAF Innsworth.

INTRODUCTION

Air Chief Marshal Sir Jock Stirrup

I have the great pleasure of welcoming you to the first of a continuing series of Leadership and Air Power conferences within the Royal Air Force. You may be asking yourself "what am I doing here?" You may feel, as I do, that the need for leadership should be self-evident in any organisation, let alone a military service. So what is it that we aim to get out of the presentations which follow?

I think the answer to that depends very much on your own approach to leadership and to what you consider to be the key attributes of a military leader. Good leadership is at the very core of whom and what we are. It is the bedrock of military success and to my mind winning is its only measure. But what is leadership? How is it measured? Can it be taught? These are all complex questions to which there are no set answers. There is no algorithm which, when applied will result in effective leadership. In my view leadership qualities are essentially personal. They relate to the individual; and individuals differ widely in their characteristics as illustrated by these two stark examples from WWII.

Firstly, General Bill Slim; very much a soldier's soldier who knew his men well. Known as "Uncle Bill," he visited and spoke with his troops frequently and had what we might describe as the common touch. He engendered respect and affection and led his people through bad times as well as good. A likeable human being, he was a highly successful leader.

In contrast, Air Chief Marshal Arthur Harris was a difficult and abrasive character. Except when on business in London, he rarely left his office at High Wycombe. He hardly ever visited his groups, stations and squadrons and yet, he secured a high degree of devotion from his people. I doubt that he won much affection, but he inspired respect from a group that suffered the highest casualty rate of any organisation in the British Armed Forces during the Second World War. Harris too was a very successful leader.

There is of course, something of the caricature in those examples. The full picture is inevitably more complex but, as with all good caricatures, it draws out the salient features, even if, in doing so, it exaggerates them slightly. The key point is that two very different men in different situations found different ways to succeed as leaders. Perhaps Harris's methods would never be encouraged, but we can see that it worked for him in those circumstances. We must realise that even a style that works for one individual in one situation may not always be appropriate. The environment will change, and so may some of the actors. Robert E. Lee's loose style of leadership worked well for him at Second Manassas and Chancellorsville because it made use of Stonewall Jackson's talents. However, at Gettysburg after Jackson's death, it was a key factor in the Confederate debacle.

Personalities and their interaction are key issues and individual relationships can be tricky. For example, even in this electronic age the impact of personal presence can be important. In late 1997 one of the more serious disputes with Saddam Hussein over weapons inspectors built towards a major confrontation and there were fears that Saddam might move south again. Both the Americans and ourselves started to increase force levels. We deployed aircraft to Kuwait and a ground force was assembled under Lieutenant General Tommy Franks. As pressure increased the Chief of Joint Operations, Christopher Wallace, found it increasingly difficult to stay abreast of developments at United States Central Command. I was summoned from my job as Air Officer Commanding No1 Group to become the inaugural Senior British Military Advisor to the Commander-in-Chief (CinC) United States Central Command in Florida. The CinC, General Zinni, intended to run the joint operation from his Headquarters (HQ) in Florida, linking electronically with his Component Commanders. It soon became clear, however, that this would not be possible. Zinni's major challenge, as it turned out, was to keep his Component Commanders focused on fighting Saddam's forces, rather than each other. This demanded his personal presence at key moments. The response was to deploy a small element of his Command HQ to Bahrain. In this situation, leadership was not just a matter of individual style, but also of personal presence.

All of these examples demonstrate the importance of individual character in leadership and underline the fact that it is very much a bespoke issue. Leadership that is not based on someone's own personality, that does not take and build upon their own individual strengths and gifts, will not withstand the stresses and strains of the military environment.

So does this imply that leadership cannot be developed; that you either have it or you don't? Of course it doesn't. My point is that each individual has to find his or her own solutions to the challenge of leadership. Examples and techniques can be extremely useful in reaching those solutions, but they have to be applied intelligently. That means thinking deeply, not just about the problem, but also about yourself.

The Royal Air Force certainly recognises this challenge. That is why we are adapting both officer and NCO training. Why we are making a considerable investment in our Force Development Squadrons. Why we have produced an anthology of writings and interviews from leaders of the past. Why the RAF Leadership Centre was established two years ago and why you are attending this conference. The presentations which follow will not give you a template for leadership. They won't give you that magic algorithm because it doesn't exist. What they will do is give you a great deal to think about in the context of your own character and personality; thoughts on which you can base your own development as a leader. Just as important, they will give you some clear ideas about how to develop such leadership in your subordinates.

CHAPTER ONE

KEYNOTE ADDRESS
WHAT IS LEADERSHIP?

WHAT IS LEADERSHIP? BEYOND COMMAND, MANAGEMENT & CONTINGENCY THEORY [1]

Professor Keith Grint

Some problems are so complex that you have to be highly intelligent and well informed just to be undecided about them.

Attributed to Laurence J. Peter

Abstract

This paper suggests we might usefully rethink what leadership is by differentiating it from both Management and Command. An alternative model is developed that adapts the Tame and Wicked problem analysis of Rittell and Webber, in association with Etzioni's typology of compliance, to propose an alternative analysis that is rooted in social constructivist approaches. It then suggests that decision-makers are much more active in the construction of the context than conventional contingency theories allow: in particular, that a persuasive rendition of the context legitimizes a particular form of action which often relates to the decision-maker's preferred mode of engagement, rather than what 'the situation' ostensibly demands.

Introduction

Conventionally leadership theories that eschew the dominant and proactive role of the individual leader in favour of more social or structural accounts tend to assume that the context or situation should determine how leaders respond, thus in terms of contingency or situational theories (Bratton et al, 2005: 162-78; Fiedler, 1967; Grint, 2000: 2-3; House and Dessler, 1974), situation X requires leadership X to ensure an appropriate response. But contingency and situational theories are premised upon an 'essentialist' notion of the context: in other words, that we can render the context or situation transparent through scientific analysis. In what follows I suggest that this is a naïve assumption because it underestimates the extent to which the context or situation is actively constructed by the leader, leaders, and/or decision-makers. In effect, decision-makers are involved in the construction of a context that both legitimates a particular form of action and constitutes the world in the process. If that rendering of the context is successful – for there are usually contending and competing renditions – the newly constituted context then limits the alternatives available such that those involved begin to act differently. Or to put it another way, we might begin to consider not what the *situation* is but how it is *situated*. Shifting the focus from noun to verb facilitates the reintroduction of the proactive role of leadership in the construction of context, not in the sense that individual leaders are independent agents, able to manipulate the world at will, as in Carlyle's 'Great Man' theory, but in the sense that the context is not independent of human agency, and cannot be objectively assessed in a scientific form.

In what follows I first introduce some of the theoretical background to the areas of problem definition, power and uncertainty and then apply this heuristic to several examples, including the war on terrorism. My argument, in short, is that contingency theories that are premised on securing independent and objective accounts of the context, situation, leader and followers – essentialist approaches – are fundamentally flawed and we should pay much more attention to the role of leaders and decision makers in the construction of contexts that legitimates their intended or executed actions and accounts.

Problems, Power & Uncertainty

Much of the writing in the field of leadership research is grounded in a typology that distinguishes between Leadership and Management as different forms of authority – that is legitimate power in Weber's conception – with leadership tending to embody longer time periods, a more strategic perspective, and a requirement to resolve novel problems (Bratton et al, 2004: 58-85; Zaleznik, 1977). But in most cases the leader or manager is charged with solving the problem that faces them, the only difference tends to relate to the analysis of the situation. Another way to put this is that the division is rooted partly in the context: management is the equivalent of *déjà vu* (seen this before), whereas leadership is the equivalent of *vu jàdé* (never seen this before) (Weick, 1993). If this is valid then the 'manager' is simply required to engage the same requisite process that was used to resolve the problem the last time it emerged. In contrast, the 'leader' is required – somehow – to reduce the anxiety of his or her followers who face the unknown, but this cannot be simply rolling out a known process to a previously experienced problem.

But the division between Management and Leadership, rooted in the distinction between known and unknown, belies the complexity of the relationship between problem and response. Oftentimes the simple experience of déjà vu does not lend itself to the application of a tried and trusted process because it is really 'déjà vu all over again': in effect, the 'certain process' has not solved the same problem because it isn't the same problem. And sometimes the situation is interpreted as too complex, too divisive and too immediate to allow the leader the time to facilitate a collaborative solution to the problem.

Perhaps the first thing we need to do is consider a contextualized typology of problems. Management and Leadership, as two forms of authority rooted in the distinction between certainty and uncertainty, can be related to Rittell and Webber's (1973) typology of **Tame** and **Wicked** Problems. A **Tame** Problem may be complex but is resolvable through unilinear acts because there is a point where the problem is resolved and it is likely to have occurred before. In other words, there is only a limited degree of uncertainty and thus it is associated with Management. The manager's role, therefore, is to engage the appropriate processes to solve the problem. Examples would include: timetabling the railways, building a nuclear plant, training the army, planned heart surgery, a wage negotiation, refuelling a plane in the air – or enacting a tried and trusted policy for fighting an air war. A **Wicked** Problem, on the other hand, is complex and often intractable, there is no unilinear solution, moreover, there is no 'stopping' point, it is novel, any apparent 'solution' often generates other 'problems', and there is no 'right' or 'wrong' answer, but there are better or worse alternatives. In other words, there is a huge degree of uncertainty involved and thus it is associated with Leadership. The leader's role with a Wicked Problem is to ask the right questions rather than engage the appropriate responses because the answers may not be self-evident and will require a collaborative process to make any kind of progress. Examples would include: developing a transport strategy, an energy strategy, a defence strategy, a national health system or an industrial relations strategy; considering what to do about the impending collapse of France in 1940 or developing a strategy for air warfare in the next decade. This kind of issue implies that techniques such as Appreciative Enquiry may be appropriate for Leadership (Cooperrider and Whitney, 1999).

However, there is a third set of problems that do not fit these criteria and hence fall outside the Leadership/Management dichotomy. This third set of problems I will refer to as Critical. A **Critical** Problem, e.g. a 'crisis', is presented as self-evident in nature, as encapsulating very little time for decision-making and action, and it is often associated with authoritarianism – Command (Howieson, B. and Kahn, H. (2002); Cf. Watters, 2004). Here there is virtually no uncertainty about what needs to be done – at least in the behaviour of the Commander, whose role is to take the required decisive action – that is to provide the answer to the problem, not to engage processes (management) or ask questions (leadership). Of course, it may be that the Commander remains privately uncertain about whether the action is appropriate or the presentation of the situation as a crisis is persuasive, but that uncertainty will probably not be apparent to the followers of the Commander. Examples would include the immediate response to: a major train crash, a leak of radioactivity from a nuclear plant, a military attack, a heart attack, an industrial strike, the loss of employment or a loved one, or the immediate response to a terrorist attack such as the September 11th or the July 7th London bombings.

That such 'situations' are constituted by the participants rather than simply being self-evident is best illustrated by considering the way a situation of ill-defined threat only becomes a crisis when that threat is defined as such. For example, financial losses – even rapid and radical losses – do not constitute a 'crisis' until the shareholders decide to sell in large numbers, and even then the notion of a crisis does not emerge objectively from the activity of selling but at the point at which a 'crisis' is pronounced by someone significant and becomes accepted as such by a significant others.

It is also the case that 'the problem' is often constituted as fluid. On the morning of 7th July 2005, for instance, I was stranded in Edgware Road London as the tube system was shut down because of what appeared to be a 'power-failure'. It was only after the mobile network had returned that I became aware that the 'tame' problem of a power-failure was actually a 'critical' problem after the Scotland Yard Commissioner, Sir Ian Blair, had announced that the cause was a series of bombs and that people should stay where they were. Subsequently the crisis was managed into a tame problem as the emergency services deployed their standard emergency plans – but there is still a case to be made that the problem is actually 'wicked' because while the symptoms can be 'managed', the causes need 'leadership' because they are encased in a wicked problem.

The nature of the 'problem' is also often disputed: in the winter of 1979, James Callaghan, then the British Prime Minister, returned from an economic conference in the West Indies as strikes in the British public services mounted. Asked how he was going to solve 'the mounting chaos' by journalists at the airport Callaghan responded "I don't think other people in the world would share the view [that] there is mounting chaos." But the headlines in the Sun newspaper the following day suggested he had said 'Crisis – what Crisis?' In this case the formal political leader was unable to counter 'the critical situation', as constituted by the news media, and Labour lost the subsequent general election [2].

Similarly, it would be difficult to state objectively at what point the Battle of Britain became a crisis and when it ceased to be one because that definition rested upon the persuasive rhetoric of various parties involved. As Overy (2000: 267) suggests,

> Many of those 'decisive strategic results' became clear only with the end of the war and the process of transforming the Battle into myth. The contemporary evidence suggests that neither side at the time invested the air conflict with the weight of historical significance that it has borne in the sixty years since it was fought.

And if the notion of a crisis requiring a Commander thrust Churchill into the limelight in 1940 so too the requirement for a system to deal with the Tame problem of Luftwaffe raids over southern England pulled Keith Park into his own. Of course, to suggest that Luftwaffe raids were manifestations of something 'Tame' is to risk misunderstanding the nature of the label: a Tame problem is one which may be complex but is resolvable and for which a solution already exists. Keith Park's contribution to the war effort, among other things, was to develop such a system of squadron-based defences, contrary to Leigh Mallory's opinions, but supplemented by the usual array of managerial performance metrics to measure time into the air, interception rate and so on (Bungay, 2001).

The crucial value of asking the right question in an attempt to generate the collaborative approach necessary to engage with a Wicked problem is best exemplified by Hugh Dowding's famous warning letter to the Under Secretary of State at the Air Ministry on 16th May 1940. Here, as a military subordinate of a political master, Dowding was not in a position to Command or even Manage a resolution to the problem of retaining sufficient fighter strength to protect Britain as France teetered towards collapse – but he could, and did, ask a crucial question that forced his political superiors to make a decision that reflected his evident concerns.

> … it is necessary to retain some minimum fighter strength in this country and I must request that the Air Council will inform me what they consider this minimum strength to be, in order that I may make my dispositions accordingly…. I would remind the council that the last estimate which they made as the force necessary to defend this country was 52 squadrons, and my strength has now been reduced to the equivalent of 36 squadrons…. Once a decision has been reached as to the limit on which the air council and the Cabinet are prepared to stake the existence of the country, it should be made clear to the Allied Commanders on the continent that not a single aeroplane from Fighter Command beyond the limit will be sent across the channel, no matter how desperate the situation may become…. I must point out that within the last few days the equivalent of 10 squadrons has been sent to France…. I must therefore request that as a matter of paramount urgency the Air Ministry and the Cabinet will consider and decide what level of strength is to be left to the Fighter Command for the defence of this country, and will assure me that when this level has been reached, not one fighter will be sent across the channel however urgent and insistent the appeals for help may be (quoted in Finn, 2004: 178).

Note here the method by which a subordinate in the decision-making hierarchy 'leads' his superiors to make a decision: through a powerful question – not an assertion: Not 'I must have 52 squadrons' (Commander), not even 'I know how to do it with 52 squadrons' (Manager) but 'You tell me how many fighters you will stake our survival on – and then stick to that number' (Leadership).

Finally, we might recall how Churchill reversed the relationship between political leader and military follower in his voluntary – if recalcitrant – subordination to military experts with regards to military decisions. As Cohen noted about the relationship between Churchill and his military advisers (as perceived by Ismay),

> Not once during the whole war did [Churchill] overrule his military advisers on a purely military question…. He exercised control of events, rather by incessant questioning of the staffs (Cohen, 2002: 118).

Whilst Churchill and Dowding used questions to secure collaborative consent, others in authority in the military have embodied the ideals of leadership in their most radical guise. In October 1940 Keith Park, for example, encouraged open debate about fighter tactics amongst all his officers, especially the younger ones with the most recent combat experience (Bungay, 2005). Even more radical, Lt Col. Evans F Carlson, CO of the 2nd Marine Raider Battalion, literally inverted US Marine culture by demanding honest feedback from his subordinates after each training and combat mission. The removal of rank insignia, the priority of soldiers before officers in terms of food and shelter, and the radical decentralization of command both mirrored some of the aspects of Mission Command deployed by the German Army in its philosophy of Auftragstaktik and also proved extraordinarily successful in inflicting the first defeats against the Japanese army in the Pacific theatre. Indeed, the 2nd Marine Raider Battalion held the highest kill ratio of any US combat unit throughout the Pacific War following their famous 31 day patrol in 1942 behind Japanese lines in Guadalcanal which generated 488 Japanese dead for 16 Raider deaths and 18 Raider wounded.

In 1943 Carlson took part in the Battle of Tarawa and, on his return to Camp Pendleton in the US, spoke to a meeting of 1,000 officers about his experiences:

> Tarawa was won because a few enlisted men of great courage called out simply to their comrades, 'Come on, fellows. Follow me!' And then went on, followed by men who took heart at their example, to knock out, at great sacrifice, one Jap position after another, slowly, until there were no more. Tarawa is a victory

because some enlisted men, unaffected by the loss of their officers, many of whom were casualties in the first hour, became great and heroic commanders in their own right. But ... But with all that courage and fortitude and willingness to die on the part of some of the men, too many others lacked initiative and resourcefulness. They were not trained to understand the need for sacrifice. Too many men waited for orders and while they waited they died. What if they had been trained not to wait for orders?" [3]

Needless to say many in the Marines regarded Carlson's maverick Leadership style as more dangerous than the Japanese and, against his explicit wishes, he was promoted to a desk job in 1943 (Zimmerman, forthcoming). The links between Command and the military are clear, and may well explain why discussion of non-military leadership has tended to avoid the issue of command or explain it as authoritarian leadership that may be appropriate for the military but not in the civilian world (Howieson and Kahn, 2002). These three forms of authority – that is legitimate power – Command, Management and Leadership are, in turn, another way of suggesting that the role of those responsible for decision-making is to find the appropriate Answer, Process and Question to the problem respectively.

This is not meant as a discrete typology but an heuristic device to enable us to understand why those charged with decision-making sometimes appear to act in ways that others find incomprehensible. Thus I am not suggesting that the correct decision-making process lies in the correct analysis of the situation, but that decision-makers tend to legitimize their actions on the basis of a persuasive account of the situation. In short, the construction of the problem legitimizes the deployment of a particular form of authority. Moreover, it is often the case that the same individual or group with authority will switch between the Command, Management and Leadership roles as they perceive – and constitute – the problem as Critical, Tame or Wicked, or even as a single problem that itself shifts across these boundaries. For example, constructing a situation as Critical – thus enabling a Commander's approach – but failing to resolve the crisis may make it easier for the Commander's enemies and competitors to define the new situation as Wicked – in some ways more difficult than a Crisis because it requires a longer time frame and a more collaborative solution than does a Crisis.

Nor am I suggesting that different forms of problem construction restrict those in authority to their 'appropriate' form of power. In other words, Commanders, for example, having defined the problem as critical – do not only have access to coercion but coercion is legitimated by the constituting of the problem as critical in a way that Managers would find more difficult and Leaders would find almost impossible. In turn, Commanders who follow up on their constitution of the problem as Critical by asking followers questions and seeking collaborative progress (attributes of Leaderships) are less likely to be perceived as successful Commanders than those who provide apparent solutions and demand obedience. In effect, the situation does legitimate particular forms of decision-making – but that situation is itself interpreted, constituted and contested by the various actors involved. Or, as George Bernard Shaw's Vivie responds to her mother's (Mrs Warren) denial of choice in the circumstances she found herself in:

> Everybody has some choice mother. The poorest girl alive may not be able to choose between being Queen of England or Principal of Newnham; but she can choose between rag-picking and flower-selling, according to her taste. People are always blaming their circumstances for what they are. I don't believe in circumstances. The people who get on in this world are the people who get up and look for the circumstances they want, and, if they can't find them, make them (Shaw, 2000: 246).

That persuasive account of the problem partly rests in the decision-makers access to – and preference for – particular forms of power, and herein lies the irony of 'leadership': it remains the most difficult of approaches and one that many decision-makers will try to avoid at all costs because it implies that:

(1) the leader does not have the answer,
(2) the leader's role is to make the followers face up to their responsibilities (often an unpopular task) rather than shoulder the responsibility of decision-making and provide the answer (see Heifetz, 1998),
(3) the 'answer' to the problem is going to take a long time to construct and that it will only ever be 'more appropriate' rather than 'the best', and
(4) it will require constant effort to maintain. It is far easier, then, to opt either for a Management solution – engaging a tried and trusted process – or a Command solution – enforcing the answer upon followers – some of whom may prefer to be shown 'the answer' anyway. This latter approach, of course, assumes that the decision-maker can persuade the followers that the situation is, indeed, one of either Tame or Critical format.

The notion of 'enforcement' suggests that we need to consider how different approaches to, and forms of, power fit with this typology of authority, and amongst the most useful for our purposes are Etzioni's (1964) typology of compliance, and Nye's distinction between Hard and Soft Power. Nye (2004) has suggested that we should distinguish between power as 'soft' and 'hard'. 'Soft', in this context, does not imply weak or fragile but rather the degree of influence derived from legitimacy and the positive attraction of values. 'Hard' implies traditional concepts of power such as coercion, physical strength, or domination achieved through asymmetric resources rather than ideas. Thus the military tend to operate through 'hard' power in war, while political authorities tend to operate through ideological attraction – 'soft power'. Of course, these are not discrete categories – the military has to 'win hearts and minds' and this can only be achieved through 'soft power', while politicians may need to authorise coercion – hard power. Indeed, as Nye (2004: 1) recognizes 'The Cold War was won with a strategy of containment that used soft power along with hard power.'

If we return to some of the early modern theorists on power, like Dahl (1961), Schattschneider (1960), and Bachrach and Baratz (1962), all summarized in Lukes' (1974) 'Three Dimensions of Power', then we can see how the very denial of Soft Power is – in itself, and ironically, an example of Soft Power – or what might be called Agenda Setting – the Second Dimension of Power, or Non-Decision-Making – where certain aspects of the debate are deemed irrelevant and thus subordinated by those in power. In other words, and to adopt Nye's terminology again, to deny that any other option exists (e.g. soft power) is itself an ideological claim – e.g. soft power, and not simply a claim to the truth. While Soft Power seems appropriate to Leadership with its requirement for persuasion, debate and ideological attraction, Hard Power clearly fits better with Command, but Management sits awkwardly between the two rooted in both or neither, because coercion is perceived as inappropriate within a free labour contract, while ideological attraction can hardly explain why all employees continue to turn up for work.

The limits of using an analysis based on Hard and Soft Power might be transcended by considering Etzioni's (1964) alternative typology. Etzioni distinguishes between Coercive, Calculative and Normative Compliance. Coercive or physical power is related to total institutions, such as prisons or armies; Calculative Compliance is related to 'rational' institutions, such as companies; and Normative Compliance is related to institutions or organizations based on shared values, such as clubs and professional societies. This compliance typology fits well with the typology of problems: Critical Problems are often associated with Coercive Compliance; Tame Problems are normally associated with Calculative Compliance and Wicked Problems are traditionally associated with Normative Compliance.

Again, none of this is to suggest that we can divide the world up objectively into particular kinds of problems and their associated appropriate authority forms, but that the very legitimacy of the authority forms is dependent upon a successful rendition of a phenomenon as a particular kind of problem. In other words, while contingency and situational theories suggest precisely this (rational) connection between (objective) context (problem) and (objective) leadership style (authority form), I am suggesting here that what counts as legitimate authority depends upon a persuasive rendition of the context and a persuasive display of the appropriate authority style. In short, success is rooted in persuading followers that the problematic situation is either one of a Critical, Tame or Wicked nature and that therefore the appropriate authority form is Command, Management or Leadership, in which the role of the decision-maker is to provide the answer, or organize the process or ask the question, respectively.

This typology can be plotted along the relationship between two axes as shown below in figure 1 with the vertical axis representing increasing uncertainty about the solution to the problem – in the behaviour of those in authority – and the horizontal axis representing the increasing need for collaboration in resolving the problem. Again, it should be recalled that the uncertainty measure used here is not an objective element of the situation but the way the situation is constituted by those in authority. Of course, that authority and problem may be disputed by others but the model assumes that successful constitution of a problem as Wicked, Tame or Critical provides the framework for particular forms of authority. The model also represents the most likely variant of authority model, but note again, that while, for example, Commanders may use the resources more commonly adopted by Leaders, or Managers, and the most prevalent is likely to be that of coercion.

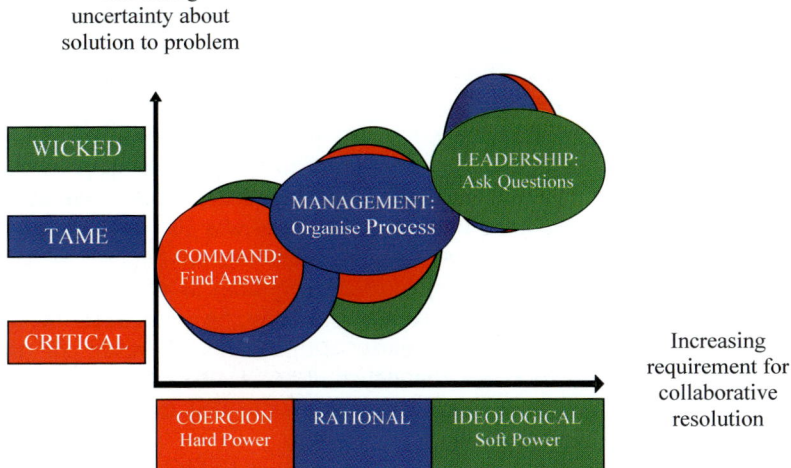

Figure 1: A Typology of Problems, Power and Authority

What might also be evident from this figure is that the more decision-makers constitute the problem as Wicked and interpret their power as essentially Soft or Normative, the more difficult their task becomes, especially with cultures that associate leadership with the effective and efficient resolution of problems. In other words, were a military chief to suggest that the problem facing him or her is a Wicked Problem that requires long term and collaborative leadership processes with no easy solutions, and where everyone must participate and share the responsibility, that chief's enactment of Leadership – rather than Command or Management – may be perceived as illegitimate or weak by the followers; hence the Irony of Leadership: it is often avoided where it might seem most necessary. Instead such a military chief may well be persuaded to act decisively – as a Commander – even if the resultant action makes the situation worse; or at least act competently – as a Manager – even if the resultant action fails to resolve the problem.

Where most people are uncertain about what needs to be done to resolve what appears to be a Critical problem – for example, a road traffic accident or an aircraft crash – they are often willing to comply with a categorical Command by those perceived to have the requisite knowledge and authority to resolve the problems: usually the police, the fire service and the ambulance service. We will, therefore, normally allow ourselves to be commanded by such professionals in a crisis. However, when the problem is not an emergency but, for instance, the planned phasing of an urban traffic light system, we are less likely to comply with a flashing blue light than with a traffic management expert – at least as long as the procedures work. Even more difficult is rethinking a traffic strategy that balances the needs of the environment with those of rural dwellers, those without private transport, and those whose houses would be demolished if private roads or public railways were to be built. In effect, as the level of uncertainty increases so does our preference for involvement in the decision-making process. The implication of this is that political leaders might well seek to construct political scenarios that either increased or decreased assumptions about uncertainty in order to ensure sufficient political support. For example, it might not be in the interests of political leaders to equivocate about the threat posed by terrorism but to imply that the threat was obvious and urgent such that any necessary measure was taken – including pre-emptive strikes. However, though the temptation to categorize everything as a crisis may be strong – because the inclination to Command may be embedded in the organizational culture – there are clearly dangers if the result of the Commander's decision is to make the situation worse: to generate greater support for terrorism or to undermine the very culture that the terrorists are seeking to destroy in the first place.

The shift from Command through Management to Leadership also relates to degree of subtlety necessary for success. For instance, a sergeant with a gun standing over a squad of soldiers facing an attack does not need to be very subtle about his or her Command to stand and fight. Similarly, a police officer coming upon a train crash need not spend a lot of time, effort or rhetorical skill in persuading on-lookers to move away; she or he may simply Command them to move. However, for that same sergeant to operate as a Manager in an air force training academy requires a much more sophisticated array of skills and behaviours in order to train cadets in the skills needed to maintain an air force; and many of these techniques and processes are already well known, tried and tested. But to develop a new air strategy for countering air-terrorism might mean more than Commanding civilians or military personnel and more than simply training up military cadets through Management processes.

For example, if the problem is perceived to be self-evident and Critical – a plane has been hijacked and it looks like its heading for London – then it probably is possible to Command pilots to shoot it down. If the problem is perceived to be Tame – i.e., the possibility is that at some point terrorists will attempt to highjack another plane – it should be possible for a Manager to deploy the process for ensuring the terrorists are prevented from achieving their aim. But if the problem is perceived to be Wicked – that is high-jacking is regarded as a symptom of a much deeper malaise to which there is no simple or existing solution – then the Leader needs to initiate a collaborative process of discussions with all interested parties to try and solve the problem itself or at least render its effects minimal. In the next section I use this triple typology to explore the War on Terror and the insurgency in Iraq to see whether the framework does facilitate different ways of understanding the problem.

The War on Terrorism and the Insurgency in Iraq

The definitional quagmire that surrounds 'terrorism' – aka 'freedom-fighter', 'separatist', 'rebel', 'guerrilla', 'fighter', and increasingly in Iraq –
'insurgent', was raised by Sir Jeremy Greenstock, Chair of the UN Security Council's Committee on Terrorism on 28 October 2001. He suggested that terrorism should be considered as: 'The indiscriminate use of violence, particularly against civilians, to further a political aim.' In fact, the original use seems to have been recorded by the Académie Français in 1789, as 'a system or rule of terror' – an interesting definition since it includes the use of terror by a state against its own citizens. Indeed, for much of the post 1945 era the UN has failed to agree a definition of terrorism precisely because such a definition may implicate some member states, and because some definitions imply a justification of terror. Since 1963 twelve international conventions on terrorism have been drawn up against specific acts of terrorism: hijacking and hostage taking and so on but no definition has ever been agreed (Roberts, 2002: 18-19), though resolution 1373 (2001) on terrorism was adopted by the Security Council at its 4,385th meeting, on 28 September 2001 [4]. The nearest thing to a consensus on the definition of terrorism talks of:

> '... criminal acts intended or calculated to provoke a state of terror in the general public, a group of persons or particular persons for political purposes.... [these are] in any circumstances unjustifiable whatever the considerations of a political,

philosophical, ideological, racial, ethnic, religious or other nature that may be used to justify them' (quoted in Roberts, 2002: 19).

Honderich (2002:95-105) however, is unhappy with such an indiscriminate account of what can be a discriminate act. For example, he suggests that 'political violence' should be differentiated from 'terrorism' because the former can be directed at political leaders rather than at entire populations. Thus an assassination of Hitler would be both an example of 'political violence' and justifiable, while the attack on the twin towers was both 'terrorism' and unjustifiable.

Fisk (2001) insists that linguistic gyrations around the word 'terrorism' are common and contemptible on the part of all involved in such conflicts. In other words, the problem is not using the word 'terrorist' to say what we mean, but that competing groups try to delineate their 'legitimate' acts in contrast to the 'terrorism' imposed by the other side. In most cases both sides seem to be involved in acts of terrorism. As Fisk, (2001: 444) suggests, 'Terrorists" are those who use violence against the side that is using the word.' Under any of these definitions 9/11 in the USA, the Madrid bombings on 11 March 2004 and July 7 bombings in London 2005 were acts of terrorism, acts of violence perpetrated against non-combatants for political and religious ends.

In order to understand the role of leadership in this we need to consider what kind of problem political leaders say terrorism is, and then what kind of power is constituted through that account as necessary to try and resolve that problem. As should become clear, the temptation of leaders is to define the problem in such a way that it becomes more tractable, such that a quick fix is the most viable option, and intriguingly to turn what may be a problem of Leadership first into a problem of (military) Command and then into a problem of Management.

It is not as if terrorism (as defined by the coalition) is – at least as yet – a significant threat to human life, especially compared to other 'traditional' killers. For example, as the graph in figure 2 over the page suggests, the annual global death rate from road traffic accidents (RTA), HIV/AIDS, breathing problems, diarrhoea and smoking are all hugely more significant than terrorist incidents. Indeed, more people committed suicide in 2000 (around 1 million) than were killed in all the global wars combined in the same year. In Europe more people kill themselves than are killed in road traffic accidents – but we do not appear to have instigated a Global War on Suicide, still less a Global War on diarrhoea or road traffic accidents [5]. Indeed, for many political leaders, the real threat to humanity is not terrorism but global warming.

Source: Reconstructed from the 2004 World Health Organization Report, World Report on Violence and Health, available from:
http://www.who.int/violence_injury_prevention/violence/world_report/en/

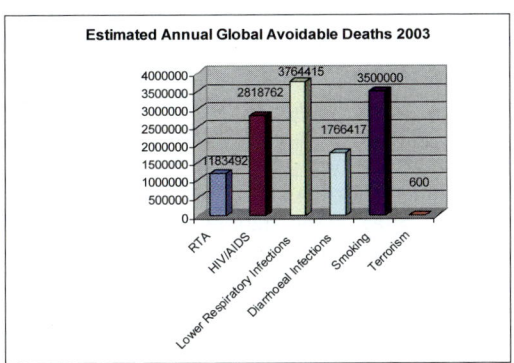

Figure 2: Estimated Annual Global Avoidable Deaths

Clearly, however, the political significance of terrorism is deemed to outweigh its social cost in some morbid scale of death, and that really is the point: do decision-makers respond to contexts or seek to constitute them in particular ways to legitimate particular forms of action? In effect, if the problem of terrorism is perceived as critical and as one that is deteriorating because of the action or inaction of political leaders then, in a democracy, those leaders may well be perceived as failing and be replaced. However, if the crisis is regarded as something that only the incumbent leadership can resolve, then they may well defeat any political opponent. And by definition the threat embodied in the crisis relates to uncertainty: we are all mortal and thus the threat of death in and of itself is less critical than the uncertainty about its timing: the more uncertain we are, the more likely we may be to turn to those who profess certainty. Or, as Pyszczynski et al (2002) have suggested in their Terror Management Theory, external threats to life necessarily tend to generate greater loyalty towards one's culture. In fact, the situations facing senior leadership teams generally are typically perceived as highly ambiguous/uncertain and very risky (Eisenhardt and Kahwajy, 1997). In that sense the continuing insurgency in Iraq can be configured in a multitude of other ways, all of which support the contention that it is a critical problem requiring the authority of a Commander. For instance, it can be read as evidence that terrorism was already there and thus needed to be stamped out, or that even if there were no terrorists in Iraq before the invasion, it is now a significant danger and needs resolving. In the words of Ben Johnson commenting on Bush re-election in November 2004, 'The American people have given George Bush an unprecedented mandate to win the war on terrorism' (Johnson, 2004: 25, my emphasis).

George W. Bush's appropriation of Command authority legitimated by a Critical Problem may also explain the quandary that has led some political analysts to query his approach. But the issue is that Bush has been relatively successful, at least in political terms, and this might be better explained not by 'luck', or labelling his supporters as mindless, but by suggesting that Bush's rendition of the problem of terrorism as both the most important and critical problem facing the USA predisposes him – and his supporters – to adopt a Command approach; and this approach in turn becomes the default category for decisions – everything is defined as a crisis requiring Command. As Gergen suggests, 'That [Command] approach worked in rallying the country and then winning conflicts in Afghanistan and Iraq, but seems peculiarly inappropriate for winning the peace in those same regions.' Again, the issue is not really 'What is really the problem facing the USA?' but what is the successful rendition of that problem that facilitates a particular kind of authority?

The Bush-Blair coalition has also been accused of provoking a Critical problem from what was a Tame problem (the Blix led UN search programme for WMD) and thus causing a Tame Problem to degenerate into a Wicked Problem – but without providing the necessary means to resolve it. In fact, in the perception of many critics that problem has moved not just from Tame (the search for WMD) to Critical (45 minutes to deploy weapons of mass destruction) but on to Wicked (Iraq as the new [post-war] breeding ground for international terrorism). If it is the latter then there is no real stopping point, it is unclear what the solution is, any solution is likely to generate further problems, there is no longer a right and wrong answer – even if there ever was – but there may still be better or worse scenarios to consider. Under this approach some form of collaborative leadership seems crucial to stabilizing Iraq, securing collective consent and preventing a deterioration of security and conditions for all Iraqis; but collaboration is not something Commanders tend to be very interested in.

Certainly, the UN's approach to the Iraq problem was that it was not embedded in, or even linked to, the War on Terror. Furthermore, that the problem of Saddam Hussein was essentially Tame; of course it was complex but there was a technical solution rooted in tried and tested managerial processes – using embargoes, weapons inspectors, oil for food programmes, no-fly zones and so on and so forth. The compliance system was ultimately rooted in Calculation: Saddam Hussein knew he could not invade anywhere again; those sympathetic towards Iraq could not afford to upset the fragile balance of power at the UN; and those wary of Saddam recognized that eliminating him carried the unnecessary risk of escalating the conflict and generating support for the very terrorism that Saddam was accused of.

The vigorous attacks upon John Kerry by the Bush camp in the run up to the November 2004 election on the basis of his alleged indecisiveness and 'flip-flopping' are witness to this approach, particularly Kerry's early attempts to configure the problem of terrorism as one of Wicked status, requiring deep thought, questions and collaborative solutions: in effect Leadership. In contrast, Bush always represented himself as the 'Commander-in-Chief', whose unwavering determination in the face of an overt threat, and whose readiness to provide 'the answer' to the problem of terrorism, nestles the problem as one of Crisis where Command is appropriate.

However, if defining a problem as Critical with its requisite Command undermines the political legitimacy of Leadership which is deemed to be 'indecisive', it remains difficult for political leaders to maintain a constant state of public anxiety so as to facilitate support for their Command activities: by definition, and pace Orwell, the crisis of war cannot be maintained indefinitely without damaging democratic support. The solution, therefore, might be to displace the anxiety into a more manageable form by encasing it in tried and tested procedures. In other words, by establishing a protective boundary around the threat, the political leadership of the coalition might try and shift the threat from one of Crisis – where Command is required – to one of Tame where Management is required. This shift prevents the problem emerging as one of a Wicked nature – where Leadership and collaboration is required but maintains the level of control because it is constituted as a technical problem requiring expert resolution. The Iraqi elections in January 2005 provide one such form of problem shift because the Critical problem of terrorism will – in theory – be Tamed by the tried and tested Management process of democracy.

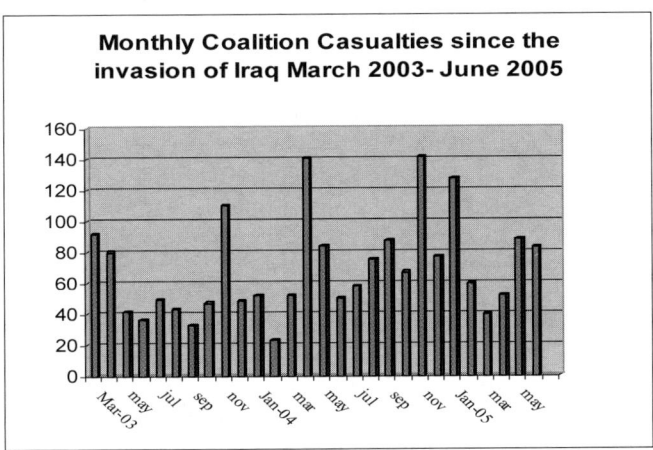

Figure 3: Monthly coalition casualties since the invasion of Iraq
Source: Reconstructed from Iraq Coalition Casualty Count at http://icasualties.org/oif/

Yet as the coalition casualties and those of the Iraqi population mount steadily after the election there is clearly a question mark about what this comprises – the last days of the insurgents or the intensification of an unwinnable war.

Conclusion

I began by suggesting that one way of understanding the War on Terror and the insurgency of Iraq was to combine a typology of problems with a typology of power. The increasingly divisive nature of the War on Terror, at least in its manifestation in Iraq, is usually explained – by all sides – as rooted in a basic misunderstanding of the nature of reality and/or rooted in the self-interest of those involved heavily disguised to retain support. But a more useful approach may be to reconfigure the active construction of the problem by various parties that are based upon legitimating their preferred or available sources of power. The combination of problem analysis and resource availability or preference generates a typology of authority that repositions Leadership as the authority form most suited for the collective negotiation of Wicked problems, while Management is more suited to the deployment of tried and tested processes to resolve Tame Problems. A third category, Critical problems, generates a compelling case for using some form of coercion used by a Command form of authority.

The critical points, then, are two. First, it is not which accurate representation of the context should determine what form of problem exists and what kind of authority is appropriate, but what kind of persuasive account of the context renders it as a specific kind of problem that, in turn, legitimates a certain form of authority. Second, that Leadership may be an appropriate form of authority for coping with Wicked problems which are perceived as intractable, but this is often constituted as indecisiveness by the opponents of the formal leader(s) and generates what may be considered the Irony of Leadership: it is so difficult to achieve that even where the formal leader(s) may be consider it appropriate and even necessary, they may be very unwilling to attempt it.

I then used this typology as a heuristic device to try and understand the War on Terror and the insurgency in Iraq. This was composed of two key problems: the danger of uncertainty and the avoidance of collaboration. Both, in theory, could be managed through a reliance on Coercion or Hard Power: the overwhelming military strength of the USA dominated coalition would be used, in isolation if necessary, to coerce Iraq into submission, thus creating the space for a problem transition from Critical to Tame that could be solved through the managed process of a democratic election. The difficulty is that, ironically, any perceived 'failure' of a Command solution actually facilitates the constitution of the very Wicked problem they have been trying to avoid; in effect it compounds rather than resolves the problem. The difficulty for their opponents relates to a different irony, the Irony of Leadership, because to configure the problem as Wicked implies a long term collaborative approach to the issue that their opponents in turn, and successfully in the US November Presidential Election, configure as the indecisiveness fatal to a Commander in a Crisis.

Endnotes

1. This chapter was first published in Human Relations Vol 58 No. 11
2. http://news.bbc.co.uk/1/hi/uk_politics/921524.stm
3. http://www.angelfire.com/ca/dickg/carlson.html
4. Resolution 1373 (2001) on terrorism was adopted by the Security Council at its 4385th meeting, on 28 September 2001. It can be viewed at: http://www.un.org/Docs/sc/committees/1373/
5. http://www.who.int/mediacentre/news/releases/2004/pr61/en/

Bibliography

Bachrach, P. and Baratz, M.S. *The Two Faces of Power*. American Political Science Review, 1962, 56 (4), 942-952.

Blumenthal, S. *'Far Graver than Vietnam'*, Guardian, 16 Sept 2004.

Bratton, J., Grint, K, and Nelson, D. *Organizational Leadership*. Thomson/Southwestern, 2004.

Bungay, S. *The Most Dangerous Enemy: A History of the Battle of Britain* London@ Aurum Press, 2001.

Bungay, S. *'Command or Control? Leadership in the Battle of Britain'* paper delivered at the RAF Leadership Centre Conference: Beyond Command? RAF Hendon, 13-14 July 2005.

Cohen, E. *Supreme Command: Soldiers, Statesmen and Leadership in Wartime London*. Simon & Schuster, 2002.

Cooperrider, D. and Whitney, D. *Collaborating for change: appreciative enquiry*. San Francisco, CA. Berrett Koehler, 1999.

Dahl, R.A. *Who governs?* New Haven, CT. Yale University Press, 1961.

Eisenhardt, K.M. and Kahwajy, J.L. *Conflict and Strategic Choice: How Top Management Teams Disagree*. Californian Management Review, 1997, 39.2. 42-62

Etzioni, A. *Modern organizations*. London: Prentice Hall, 1964.

Fielder, F.E. *A theory of leadership effectiveness*. New York McGraw Hill 1967.

Finn, C.J. *A Brief History of the Royal Air Force*. London: HMSO, 2004.

Fisk, R. *Pity the nation*. Oxford: Oxford Paperbacks, 2001.

Hall, S. Norton-Taylor, R. and MacAskill, E. *Blair: We must win this new conflict*, Guardian, 20 Sept 2004 @
http://www.guardian.co.uk/Iraq/Story/0,2763,1308349,00.html.

House, R. and Dessler, G. *The Path-Goal theory of Leadership*, in Hunt, J.G. and Larson, L.L. (eds.), *Contingency approaches to leadership*. Carbondale, IL.: Southern Illinois University Press, 1974.

Gergen, D. *'Stubborn Kind of Fellow'* Key Note speech at the International Leadership Association Conference in Seattle, Nov 2002. Reproduced in Compass: A Journal on Leadership 2003 available at:
http://www.ksg.harvard.edu/leadership/COMPASS_Fall2003.html.

Grossman, D. *Israel Has Won For Now But What Is Victory When It Brings No Hope?* Guardian Unlimited, 30 Sept 2002

Grint, K. *The Arts of Leadership*. Oxford: Oxford University Press 2000.
Heifetz, R. *Leadership without easy answers*, Cambridge, Mass: Harvard University Press, 1998.
Hinsliff, G. *'Iraq leak has Blair back in the firing line'*, Observer, 19 Sept 2004.
Honderich, T. *After the terror*. Edinburgh: Edinburgh University Press, 2002.
Howieson, B. and Kahn, H. *Leadership, Management and Command: The Officer's Trinity* in Gray and Cox (eds.) *Air power leadership: theory and Practice*. Norwich: HMSO, 2002.
Johnson, B. *Now we can sleep easy*. Guardian, 4 Nov 2004.
Lukes, S. *Power: a radical view*. London: Macmillan, 1974.
Mitroff, I. I. and Anagnos, G. *Managing crises before they happen*. New York: Amacon, 2000.
Mitroff, I.I. *Grading bush: the president's job performance as the chief crisis manager of the nation*, 2004, available at:
http://www.mitroff.net/documents/Grading_President_Bush.pdf.
Norton, A. *Leo Strauss and the politics of American empire*. London: Yale University Press, 2004.
Norton-Taylor, R. *Axis of failure*. Guardian, 3 November 2004,
Nye, J.S. *Power in the global Information age: from realism to globalization*. London: Routledge, 2004.
Overy, R. *How significant was the battle?* in Addison, P. and Crang, J.A. (eds.), *The burning blue: a new history of the battle of Britain*. London: Pimlico, 2000.
Pyszczynski, T., Sheldon, S. and Greenberg, J. *In the wake of 9/11: the psychology of terror*. Washington DC: APA, 2002.
Rittell, H., Webber, M. *Dilemmas in a general theory of planning*. Policy Sciences, 1973. 4, 155-69.
Roberts, A. *Can we define terrorism?* Oxford Today 2002. 14, 2 ,18-19.
Schattschneider, E.F. *The semi-sovereign people: a realist view of democracy in America*. New York: Reinhart and Winston, 1960.
Shaw, G.B. *Mrs Warren's Profession*. London: Penguin, 2000.
Smith, M. *Black Watch senior officers question No 10 Iraq strategy*. Daily Telegraph, 29 Oct 2004.
Steele, J. *The cheers were all ours*. Guardian, 11 Feb 2005.
Watters, B. *Mission Command: 'Auftragstaktik'*. Paper at the Leadership Symposium, RAF Cranwell, 13 May 2004
Weick, K.E. *The Collapse of Sensemaking in Organizations: The Mann Gulch Disaster.* Administrative Science Quarterly 1993, 38: 628-652
Younge, G. *'President was told in July of Civil War risk in Iraq'*. Guardian, 17 Sept 2004.
Zaleznik, A. *Managers and Leaders: Are They Different?* Harvard Business Review 1977, 55, 5 67-80.
Zimmerman, P. (forthcoming): *The First Gung Ho: Evans Carlson and the 2nd Marine Raider Battalion*.

CHAPTER TWO

LEADING A DOWNSIZING AIR FORCE

© Stephen Mugford & Robert Rogers 2005

"IF YOU DO WHAT YOU'VE ALWAYS DONE ... ":
LEADERSHIP CHALLENGES IN A DOWNSIZING RAAF

Professor Stephen Mugford &
Wing Commander Bob Rodgers RAAF

The views expressed in this paper are the personal views of the authors and not an official view from the RAAF.

Introduction

The RAAF was faced with a difficult challenge in the late 1990s and met this challenge by finding new ways to do business at the senior levels. This paper tells the story, covering five main issues: the context, the challenge, the story of what happened, the outcomes and the lessons.

The process experienced was like a fairground ride – perhaps the "Tunnel of Adventure" – but hindsight and 'narrativity' produce a 'smooth' story. Rationales and logics described may sound clear and compelling, but often the reality was more intuitive and emergent in character. One thing that everyone involved knew, however, was that unless 'something different' was found the Air Force would end up back where it started.

The Context

In the 1990s a number of broad, global trends were affecting developed nations including:
- A belief that governments, especially 'Welfare States' had gone too far, that the freedom of individuals and markets was blanketed by excessive regulation, stifling initiative and competition;
- A linked belief that government should be 'reeled in', with lower demands for taxation, more opportunity for entrepreneurialism and outsourcing or privatisation of many functions to private enterprise;
- The rise of 'economic rationalism';
- The belief that by 'downsizing' organisations could become lean, mean and competitive; and

- A triumphalist feeling that the Cold War had been won, proving the value of the capitalist way and generating a 'Peace Dividend.

Where the Australian Defence Organisation (ADO) was concerned, these and other forces came together in a series of initiatives such as the Civilian Support Program (CSP) and Defence Reform Program (DRP)

Commercial Support Program

The CSP was introduced in 1991 following a review entitled, 'The Defence Force and the Community', which proposed greater use of civilian infrastructure and national resources to achieve best value for money in the acquisition of support services and to give the private sector an opportunity to participate in the provision of those support services. CSP harvested significant savings costs for the Australian Defence Organisation, and contributed to the introduction of a more far-reaching initiative – the DRP.

Defence Reform Program

Based on the report of the Defence Efficiency Review, in 1997, DRP was designed to enable Defence resources to be focused more efficiently and effectively on core functions by:
- maximising the **focus** of the Defence organisation and its resources on achieving the Defence mission;
- having a Defence organisation **organised for war and adapted for peace** with a clear command and management structure and better long-term planning and decision making;
- increasing the **efficiency** of support and administrative functions; and
- **maximising the resources** available to sustain and enhance the operational capabilities of the Australian Defence Force (ADF).

Defence implemented DRP for three years and brought it to an accounting close on 30 June 2000. Under DRP, the proportion of ADF personnel in combat or combat-related positions increased from about 40 to 60 per cent. It challenged the existing culture and broke down many functional stovepipes. The changes were essential precursors to an organisational renewal agenda which sought to engender a culture of continuous improvement within the Defence organisation. CSP and DRP led to important, large scale changes *but these were not balanced and harmonised*.

Joyce (*Megachange*, 1999) offers a useful model for large scale change, see figure 1 over the page, arguing that successful adaptation involves balancing structure, strategy and systems with aspects of the workforce. Frequently, organisations change only some of the areas and hope that somehow the others will come into line.

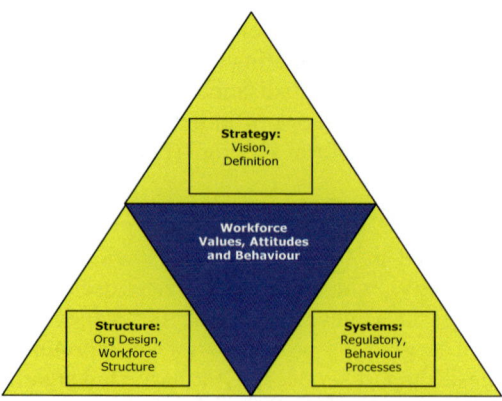

Figure 1: Joyce Model for Large Scale Change

In complex organisations like the ADF, however, 'hope is not a method'. If one changes, say, a major structural component but leaves systems – such as posting, promotions and training – unchanged, *major dislocations occur*.

In the ADF case dislocation is *exactly* what resulted with numerous 'unintended consequences of purposeful action' arising. In the Air Force these included:

- 'Stove-piping' was exacerbated, not reduced, by down-sizing;
- Down-sizing meant that people were pushed to leave and/or not replaced, with numerous side effects:
- People were treated as 'resources', demeaning them and 'breaking the psychological contract' for many;
- Certainty was reduced, undermining loyalty;
- There was devaluation of some roles and functions – 'soft' skills were seen as expendable while 'hard' skills were deemed essential and retained;
- Task rotation was created to manage overload but in ways that devalued and de-motivated people;
- Informal networks were threatened and damaged, often without the consequential loss being understood; and
- The structure was attacked, but systems and people were not reformed, so there was no real positive strategy for change;
- Morale declined (through loss of institutional trust levels);
- Wastage rose;
- Recruitment fell; and
- Negative perceptions of Defence senior leaders by lower ranks increased, senior leaders being seen as:
    - remote;

- not caring for the well-being of their people;
- expecting loyalty but not giving it in return; and
- not to be trusted.

Serious dissatisfaction was expressed by senior Defence leaders with the way things were going, and the (then) Secretary of the Defence Department described the ADO culture as one of *destructive tribalism* and *hierarchical dependence*. In 1996/97 an internal RAAF paper examined issues of ethos and suggested that:
- there were perceived deficiencies in junior officer standards.
- there were perceived deficiencies in SNCO standards.
- there were perceived deficiencies in standards of airmen and airwomen graduates.
- there were inappropriate attitudes towards ground defence; and
- the prevalence of inappropriate workplace behaviour was unacceptably high.

These perceived deficiencies were the symptoms of the dislocations referred to above but initially the 'condition' was not correctly diagnosed, being seen as requiring increased discipline and training.

The RAAF Culture Assessment Project (RAAFCAP), using external consultants, was another response, surveying all personnel force in the RAAF over a three-month period, to map the extant culture and identify the alternative, desired culture. Important gaps emerged between the kind of Air Force people worked in and the kind of Air Force they wanted to work in and believed important for future effective functioning. Three important elements were:
- feedback and comment are restrained and conservative, but it was believed that people should be able to speak out and have emotions valued as data;
- control is imposed rigidly and from above, but people believed that they needed more control over processes at the organisational and individual level;
- the main focus was on the 'now' and the immediate, but people believed that there needed to be a better balance of past, present and future time frames.

These results were not well received, and RAAFCAP slowly sank with few traces. However, other, broader cultural factors were also at work, including:
- generational change, with differing expectations among the young people recruited to the Air Force;
- changes in the world strategic environment, with a rising operational tempo for the ADF (for example, the East Timor deployment commenced in 1999); and

- resource constraints that increased the pressure to ensure that people and their skills were best utilised.

In the specifically military area, other pressures included:
- the changing nature of the technologies being used, with more emphasis upon skilled personnel and less on 'obedient dummies';
- the challenges of network centric warfare;
- the need to become an 'expeditionary Air Force'.

These general factors intersected with the dislocations outlined to create a serious challenge for the RAAF.

The Challenge

When we started the culture change journey in late 1999, the overall objective was not articulated, but soon we came to phrase it as creating:

> *"An Air Force which is attuned to its environment and which acts purposefully and strategically to effect its objectives."*

To achieve this, it was necessary to build an adaptive culture key attributes being:
- Shared sense of purpose.
- Open.
- Understands and values relationships.
- Values learning.
- Applies a systems thinking approach to organisational decision-making at all levels.

This required a wide range of purposive actions. Central to the plan was the role of senior leaders, because:
- Senior leaders needed to be seen in a positive light by the rest of the Air Force, so that people would want to follow their lead and be proud to do so.
- Many of the changes could not emerge 'bottom up', because unless the culture at the top was to change, it would stifle change from below.

Clearly, there is an important difference between directed change and innovation although both types call for purposive action from leaders. Directed change is 'top down' and leaders call the shots in the familiar command and control model. In contrast, with innovation the leader role is 'facilitative' – to open spaces for subordinates to create innovation. We coined the following maxim:

> *Commitment is a liquid – it trickles down from the top.*
> *Innovation is a gas – it bubbles up from the bottom. Commit to*

change and let that trickle down, while making room for innovation to bubble up.

Behavioural attributes sought from the senior leaders were:
- Decreased Tribalism; Increased Collaboration and Collegiality and the need to take a Stewardship role for Air Force.
- Decreased Hierarchical Dependence; Increased Empowerment/Autonomy.
- Decreased Blame Culture; Increased Learning Culture.

Not every senior leader immediately agreed with this direction, sometimes because they had not thought about the issues, sometimes because they had a different analysis – often predicated on a 'rear-view mirror' perspective. There was a tendency to believe things were rosier than they were and/or that one should "command one's way of the situation". There was also an absence of some subtle aspects of organisational trust, the group exhibiting instead a mild form of *cordial hypocrisy*:

> ... the strong tendency of people in organizations, because of loyalty or fear, to pretend that there is trust when there is none, being polite in the name of harmony when cynicism and distrust are active poisons, eating away at the very existence of the organization. (Solomon & Flores, 2001, Building Trust, Oxford UP, p.4)

Cordial hypocrisy was highlighted at an early SLT meeting. Everyone was asked, "Do you fully trust everyone in this room?" After a pause they were then instructed, "If the answer is 'yes', stand up". About 25-30% stood. There was an uncomfortable silence and several had second thoughts and sat down. In short, robust intra-team trust was not present. Work was necessary, therefore, to produce a strong team. Four immediate and short term problems were:
- To get people to accept that there was a problem;
- To agree a way forward;
- To build a guiding coalition to carry the process;
- To create the right team climate and the right personal skills to make this possible.

These were addressed as urgent priorities.

The Story

This section picks out highlight events, many concentrated in the period 2000-2002, that created the SLT as a functioning social entity. The process began in late 1999 at this time the senior author, with a background in social change and working with the ADF, was asked to join the effort.

Creating the SLT

Early in 2000 it was decided focus on developing a Senior Leadership Team (SLT), including *all* star ranked 'blue suiters', irrespective of placement in the ADO. The inclusion principle was designed to overcome 'disenfranchisement' of those in (e.g.) tri-service locations.

The SLT would meet several times a year (it has since settled at quarterly meetings) and the focus would be informal discussions and team and culture building. The meetings would not have an agenda, the 'here and now' would be de-emphasised and no decisions would be sought about on-going matters. Instead, the ambition was to create a collective, collegial and cooperative climate to underpin on-going conversations about Air Force interests and identity.

This model was initially controversial for people used to focused, action oriented activity and some said that it was a waste of time since it didn't "do" anything. Over time, however, the character of the meetings became accepted and is now "taken for granted". An important theme was the 'casual' nature of the meetings, exemplified by dress, speech and so on. This exemplifies "method as model": i.e., every method we used needed to 'model' the type of culture aimed for. Given an aim to move away from hierarchy, formality, command and control towards a culture that was collective, collegial and cooperative this was 'modelled' by as many methods as possible: dress code being a visible and effective tool in the kitbag.

Confrontation

From the start, accepted realities were challenged and confronted in order to break down complacency. The underlying model was a J curve, shown in figure 2, below: follow the J 'down' – provoking conflict and getting things "out on the table" – in the belief that this would later lead to rapid improvement.

Figure 2: J Curve Model of Confrontation

The approach of steady growth that eschewed conflict (the red line) was rejected as pleasant but unrealistic. Many devices were used. For example, familiar seating arrangements were changed and instead of bland, low value discussions each meeting had "dead cat" session, symbolised by placing a statue of a dead cat, with a visible tyre mark across it, on the table. The most important early challenge, however, was to get the SLT to explore how good a team they really were. An early workshop led to a nine criterion model, arguing that the team members:

- Were innovative and flexible;
- Showed good intra-group communication;
- Showed good inter-group communication (rest of RAAF);
- Had a common purpose;
- 'Walked the talk';
- Had good team skills;
- Were willing to listen and learn;
- Were professional, with the right composition;
- Had passion, drive and commitment.

Each SLT member then rated where they believed the team stood, ratings were collected and results calculated. The same 9 criteria were then faxed to all available Wg Cdrs and Sqn Ldrs who were asked to assess the senior officers on the same criteria. Responses (155) were collected and collated. Mean scores were computed and compared and showed large differences between the two groups. The SLT ranked themselves (on average) more highly; and the higher the score the SLT gave themselves the bigger the gap.

These findings fitted with survey results (mentioned above) showing lack of faith in senior leaders and really created debate about what needed to be done. Each star rank officer also interviewed people from LAC to SQN LDR about their views of the Air Force. Emphasis was placed on listening and not talking and tape recordings of interviews were collected (partly to ensure that they had not delegated the task to staff).

The interviews were valuable because the senior officers were directly confronted by the world in which their juniors lived. They learned how things looked to others, and were gratified by the positive response they received.

These challenging activities slowly built openness and trust and as this occurred, further challenges were created. For example, everyone was asked to write notes on behaviours that frustrated them in others and on things they did themselves which they knew were counterproductive. Looking firstly at counterproductive behaviour, common answers were:
- jump ahead of others' thought processes and do not allow them to fully present their position.

- ... interrupt someone else's 'story' to express an opinion, before having thought about it – and disrupting them.
- ... not listen to others with my full attention and try to really understand what their meaning is.
- ... determining I know the answer/solution and not allowing others to fully express their views/opinions.

The typical answers to what they found frustrating was:
- "...people don't listen to what I want to say or presume they know what I am going to say, and interrupt to answer/counter me."
- The juxtaposition – showing that their counter productive acts corresponded to what frustrated them when they received it – led to a very open discussion and the view steadily emerged that there was a problem and that members of the SLT did need to develop new habits.
- Cognitive-behavioural workshops.
- It steadily became clear that progress was needed on two, closely interconnected fronts:
- actively improve some working relationships; and
- increase the 'soft' skills and emotional intelligence of senior officers.

Tony Grant, head of Coaching Psychology at the University of Sydney, a successful executive coach and academic, was asked to create a workshop series designed to:

> Enhance self knowledge and capacities and hence develop greater leadership skills and teamwork which are needed to help develop and prepare RAAF for the 2000's and beyond.

The underlying model was cognitive-behavioural psychology, a highly effective basis for positive change in adult life. The 1½ day workshop provided a space where everyone was "at risk of learning" – about themselves and others. Partly by design, partly by luck the first group included the entire top echelon of the RAAF over the 5 years 2001-2005 inclusive.

The CBW was a considerable success. Despite some scepticism among those invited (mainly from an aircrew background and thus not always keen to embrace 'tree hugging'!) the process was powerful and involving. It increased skills and also built a camaraderie and commitment that carried the group forward through the challenges that lay ahead. The success motivated CAF and others to recommend strongly that all the team attend CBWs – which they did – and to cascade this to the GP CAPT level.

Values Teams

Other initiatives were being trialled in parallel. One was the creation of 'values teams' at most major bases. These were created for several reasons, and two stand out:
- To create a cross rank, open discussion forum where cultural and change issues could be explored;
- An opportunity to involve star rank officers directly in grass roots contacts by convening these informal meetings.

A central question was "what kind of Air Force do you want to work in? Ideas generated were explored in day long, intensive workshops by a wide range of personnel and common themes emerged. These were melded into a draft 'values statement' and returned to the groups for comment. A revised version was then presented to the SLT which suggested a few, minor amendments and the amended version was agreed to by all groups. This was endorsed by the SLT as a new values statement for the Air Force (see Appendix 1).

Development of a 'Behavioural Compact'

Following directly from the Values Teams, the question was posed, "If this is the kind of Air Force our people want to work in, what do YOU have to do as a senior leader to exemplify the values and 'walk the talk'?" This topic was extensively work-shopped by the star rank officers, who developed a series of behavioural guidelines. Once these guidelines were clarified, agreed and endorsed, the next step was to turn them into a statement, which it was agreed would be called the 'behavioural compact' (see Appendix 2.) Compliance with the terms of the compact was then assessed by 360 feedback (although this is now less emphasised.) A recent illustration of the extent to which new norms have become internalised arose at an SLT meeting in late 2004.

The 'cultural' issue is regularly revisited and many methods have been used. On this occasion, the group was asked various 'cage rattling questions' which were mind mapped by small, interchanging groups at work tables. Questions posed included:
- Pretend the SLT is an organised religion: What are the '7 deadly sins'?
- Pretend the SLT is an organised religion: What are the '10 commandments'?

The answers were revealing and indicate a clear adoption of the new value system.

7 Deadly Sins

- Destructive criticism.
- Passive attendance.

- No commitment to the SLT (i.e., no attendance).
- Being too serious – smiling is good, not smiling is not good.
- Waving your own flag (self promotion).
- Intolerance.
- Pulling rank/position.

10 Commandments

- Be thyself (see 9).
- Listening: speaking ratio of approx. 10:1.
- Be honest, sincere and frank.
- Leave rank at the door.
- Contribute.
- Show intellectual and moral courage.
- Enjoy yourself.
- Have passion.
- Be humble.
- Don't BS.

Despite the light hearted process that produced them, these two lists indicate the adoption of a deeply held set of values of a team that has become – as intended – collective, collegial and cooperative.

SLT at Bases

Another, telling innovation was the habit of regularly holding SLT meetings away from AFHQ on serving, active bases. Routinely, the first afternoon is devoted to small teams of star rank officers going out to meet people across the base to ask them about the issues that are of concern to them.

Possibly more than any other single thing, this willingness to travel, mingle, listen learn and take the feedback seriously began to convince the majority of Air Force that their leaders *did* care about them. Even when the troops weren't sure *why* their base was awash with star rank officers, the fact that it was and that these officers were listening was really a powerful emblem that "something is happening".

The Outcomes

This is a complex story and many other things were going on, but our contention is that the change has been successful – Air Force has learned to "do something different", exemplified by the different way that the senior leadership operates and its success in spreading important messages about values based leadership.

So what? That is, does all this make a difference? This is hard to measure exactly, but the following facts all point the same way. Both Navy and

Army were faced with similar challenges, but neither service took the radical steps that Air Force took. As of mid 2005:
- Air Force has significantly *higher morale* than Navy or Army, as measured in the official surveys;
- Air Force has significantly *lower wastage* than Navy or Army, as measured in the official discharge figures;
- Air Force has been *able to meet its recruiting targets* which Navy and Army have not been able to achieve;
- AM Houston reported to his SLT that he was convinced that these differences were a result of the successful response to the pressures identified in 1999 and steadily dealt with since.

In short, Air Force has successfully met the challenge of downsizing, developing a culture appropriate to military operations in this period. The key was to actively build an adaptive culture and to invest in making this visible through change at the top, based on and exemplifying positive, purposeful leadership.

The Lessons

Many lessons emerge from this experience. First: faced with a new problem it is imperative to find new ways to operate, because if you do what you have always done, you will get what you have always got.

Downsizing leads to dislocations and dysfunction. In turn, this undermines trust and when trust falls, transaction costs rise. Active and purposeful work needs to be undertaken to maintain or rebuild trust if the organisation is to move forward effectively.

It is easy to misdiagnose the problem and, following from this, prescribe the wrong treatment. Calls for more command, more obedience and more discipline are common – and wrong.

"... it ain't over 'till the fat lady sings." There are numerous people, especially in the 'middle' of the organisation, who are quite happy with the old ways. It is crucial to balance workforce, structures, systems and strategy as suggested by Joyce (see above). Without balance, the old systems offer high inertia (at best) or opportunities for resistance to change (at worst).

Change of type we have talked about creates a legacy. The most obvious legacy for the RAAF is the functional team (the SLT) and growth in the individuals concerned. This impact spreads through the organisation, directly and indirectly.

The final lesson, for others learning from the RAAF experience, concerns transferability to other contexts. The trick lies not in following the details but in grasping the underlying principles and applying them to the unique situation in which one finds oneself. The key principles are:
- Build a guiding coalition of senior leaders willing to experiment and accept innovation;

- Create space for change at the top – even if this means side-lining some senior players who are too wedded to the old ways;
- Recognise that in conditions of complexity, detailed 'command and control' fails, dislocation is not managed and unintended consequences rampage. Instead aim for flexibility and an adaptive culture;
- Search for a balanced response to external crises/pressures (see the Joyce pyramid model);
- Consider the impact of change on trust and the 'psychological contract' – it is easier to lose trust than build it, and loss of trust is costly;
- Don't consider 'soft skills' dispensable – they aren't and the price of losing them is also high;
- New models of warfare – such as 'mission command' or 'network centric warfare' – are highly congruent with, and indeed call for the sort of changes we describe above, so making changes does not undermine your military capacity, instead it may well enhance it.

Appendix 1: The RAAF Values Statement

The RAAF stands for:

Delivery of effective, precision aerospace power;
Defence of Australia's people, security and interests;

The RAAF aims to:

- Be a professional, highly motivated and dedicated team;
- Develop and support its people;
- Be a safe and equitable place to work.

The RAAF expects that its people will:

- Display honest commitment to the RAAF Values.
- Strive for excellence as both leaders and followers.
- Be fair to and respect the rights of others.
- Encourage diversity in all its forms.
- Balance work and personal commitments, including family and relationships, for themselves and those they work with.
- Work together as a team.
- Communicate in an open and honest manner.
- Be capability focussed and operationally ready.
- Be professional and innovative.
- Be recognised for their loyalty, integrity and determination.
- Serve with pride and dedication.

The RAAF values its people.

Appendix 2: The Behavioural Compact

SENIOR LEADERSHIP TEAM
BEHAVIOURAL COMPACT

To live our shared values, I commit myself to:	
• set the example • value my people • build a cohesive team, and • improve my effectiveness and that of our Air Force	*Therefore I will* • provide a high standard of personal leadership and accountability • use my authority and influence in an ethical manner • act to strengthen the team environment at all levels • respect and support the needs of our people and their families • seek to learn and develop my skills and capabilities to remain relevant to the evolving Air Force *Through this we will* • cultivate (foster) an enduring Air Force culture which supports and develops our people and encourages innovation.

I will be measured by the Executive and Senior Officer Appraisal and Development Report on a 360 degree basis.

Signature Block

BEHAVIOURAL ACTIONS / DEFINITIONS

Provide a high standard of personal leadership & accountability.
This means that I will....
- provide support to my subordinates, peers and superiors
- provide an example to the individual & the team, & display a passionate enthusiasm for our profession
- coach and mentor
- provide direction (vision)
- encourage accountability & ownership with appropriate delegation
- set and achieve realistic goals for myself and my team
- delegate properly & effectively
- value and share knowledge
- foster innovation & bi-directional learning
- create time to think
- provide balanced feedback
- have the courage to provide difficult feedback – "bite the bullet"
- make the tough calls
- not tolerate poor performance

Act in an ethical manner.
This means that I will....
- use my authority for the benefit of the Air Force
- act with humility & maintain perspective
- act with integrity to meet Air Force goals

Strengthen the team environment at all levels.
This means that I will....
- align my team
- create & sustain team cohesion
- coach my team & peers
- encourage and reward individuals, appropriately and meaningfully, for their contributions to the team
- recognise the contribution of those with whom I deal
- enable and empower individuals by seeking and encouraging contributions to the team effort
- manage upwards in a constructive manner

Respect & support the needs of our people and their families.
This means that I will....
- identify and address the needs of individuals and families, teams, peers & the community
- establish a balance between work and family for my people
- successfully manage the impact on my people of work stress and change

Seek to learn and develop my skills and capabilities.
This means that I will....
- take time for self-reflection to identify my strengths and weaknesses
- seek and share new knowledge
- seek to grow professionally and personally

CHAPTER THREE

LEADERSHIP IN ADVERSITY

LEADING CHANGE:
THE DEFENCE AVIATION REPAIR AGENCY

Air Vice-Marshal Peter Dye

Introduction

For 2 years I was directly involved as a Board member, Deputy Chief Executive and Senior Air Force Officer in a major change programme – the creation of the Defence Aviation Repair Agency (DARA) from the extant, but separate, RN and RAF aircraft repair organisations and the subsequent transition to trading fund status. I cannot say that the experience was pleasant, in fact, it was the most difficult 2 years I have faced in my career – for reasons that will become apparent.

Scale of The Change Programme

None of the above is to diminish the scale of the challenge faced by the DARA. Two separate organisations spread across 4 individual sites ranging from the very large (St Athan – 1,000 acres and 3,000 personnel) to the small (Almondbank – 18 acres and some 400 personnel) had to be brought together into a single coherent entity. The move to trading fund status demanded new processes, new organisational arrangements, new attitudes and different working practices. The scale of the exercise is indicated by the fact that by my reckoning there were at least 12 major change initiatives underway at any one time – ignoring external or centrally-driven changes.

Leadership under these circumstances was testing. We had to create, virtually overnight, a new collective sense of identity on the basis of a shared vision of the future while actively working to unravel every element on which the existing organisations had been constructed – and incidentally while still delivering significant quantities of aircraft and components safely and efficiently to the frontline. The tensions, contradictions and ambiguities that arose are probably common to all major change programmes, but the DARA faced additional problems.

Legacy Issues

The decision to create a joint aircraft repair organisation was not without its critics and it would be fair to say that neither Service was exactly enthusiastic. To add to the legacy of mistrust that this created, there was a real sense that the larger sites and the larger Service (the RAF) would prevail in any rationalisation that might emerge. Beyond this, Fleetlands had recently undergone a fairly emotional restructuring exercise – that had soured management/union relations – while St Athan had been subject to a long-running market-testing programme that had eventually been abandoned.

Other significant 'soft' issues arose from the presence at St Athan and Sealand of substantial numbers of Servicemen, whereas, both Almondbank and Fleetlands were, and always had been, exclusively civilian manned. Finally, the geographic dispersion of the sites between England, Scotland and Wales added further spice to what was already a very exotic cultural cocktail.

Leadership

Leadership in a large organisation cannot be exclusive to the Chief Executive or his senior executives. A great many individuals, all the way down to the shop floor have a part to play, yet the immaturity of the DARA and the scale of the prospective changes meant that the leadership focus fell heavily on the 12 individuals comprising the DARA Board. The sheer size of the Agency and geographic spread meant there was an inevitable limit to the contact time possible between Board members and the 5,000-strong workforce, but a sustained programme of mass and team briefings, communications lunches and personal visits was initiated to address the problem; as far as was practicably possible. I have to commend the Chief Executive in particular for his personal example – at times his energy seemed quite daunting. On the debit side, however, was that the Chief Executive was also the focus for deep suspicion if not active mistrust on the part of some of the workforce, notably at Fleetlands where the unions felt betrayed and immensely bitter about recent job losses. This prejudice found a ready audience both at St Athan and Sealand.

Board Dynamics

While the Chief Executive will always have a central role to play, leading change in a modern organisation is a collective activity. The skill sets and functional responsibilities are beyond the capabilities of a single individual. This is as true of an Agency as it is of the Services as a whole.

The dynamics of any Board are complex, variable and difficult to analyse. My experience with the DARA demonstrated the importance of leadership, and, just as importantly, of followership in providing the strong, coherent and persuasive vision that underpins any successful change programme.

Unfortunately it also provided a case study in how personality types interact or, more precisely, fail to interact.

Some of this was excusable, if not inevitable. The majority, but not all, Board members were imported from the precursor organisations (including the Chief Executive and myself). We certainly brought a personal legacy in terms of history, prejudices, loyalties, etc that could not be readily exorcised and undoubtedly provided an obstacle to building an effective top level team. However, there was a sustained effort to develop a strong and binding ethos through workshops, away days, coaching, facilitation and so on.

It was clear early on that the Board was inclined towards a preference for action and intuitive decision making rather than a more reflective, consensus-based approach. As time went by, it seemed to me that the extrovert, energetic, action-orientated personality came to dominate – in some academic circles this is known as the 'Field Marshal' type. This arose not so much through a deliberate policy, but in the form of attrition as postings, sackings, resignations and illnesses provided the opportunity to recruit like-minded individuals.

Least this seem a somewhat subjective view, the team-building work that the Board undertook – while certainly providing invaluable insights and greater self-awareness – confirmed the dominance of the 'Field Marshal' personality. To be fair, the characteristics of such individuals are not unsuited to managing a change programme. Indeed, their energetic, decisive and clear-sighted nature often brings them leadership roles. Unfortunately, the directness of their personal style can sometimes cause problems for them with others.

Shock

The impact of a major change programme on an organisation can be likened to stepping out of one's living room straight into a tropical jungle. The certainties and safety of the known disappear to be replaced by a world where nothing is secure, where the language can be daunting, if not incomprehensible, and where a proud tradition (and/or personal beliefs) can suddenly be regarded as an obstacle to change. Under these circumstances, even apparently simple and straightforward initiatives, such as DARA's desire to call stations 'sites', wings 'business streams' and squadrons 'facilities', can be sufficient to cause considerable anger. The extensive employment of consultants can only add to the general feeling of alienation.

Stress

It is my personal view that the level of stress created by a major change programme cannot properly be understood unless it has been experienced. The issue is not simply about job security; it is about self-esteem, the depression that arises from a sense of helplessness and the corrosive effect of cynicism and mistrust. These problems can so grip an organisation that normal behaviour breaks down. At DARA this included work stoppage (not quite a strike), persistent leaks to the Press, lobbying of MPs, possible sabotage and a significant increase in stress-related illness. This echoes the linkage established in the Whitehall Health and Stress study between stress (in the form of an individual's lack of control and a poor effort/reward balance) and ill health.

Although, it might be presumed that Servicemen would be less vulnerable than their civilian colleagues to such pressures, the following quote from the CASWO in December 1999, following a visit to St Athan, indicates otherwise:

> "I have rarely experienced the depth of emotion and conviction expressed ... the friction between Service and civilian elements of the workforce has always been part of life at St Athan, however, the formation of the Agency has provided an ideal target for those who dwell on the negative aspects"

This also serves to highlight another aspect of change, the way in which it can create or exacerbate differences between organisational sub-groups. This is not an emotional luxury confined to the Service/Civilian divide. In the DARA it was also present to varying degrees between the Services, between unions (industrial and non-industrial) and between sites.

I put a great deal of effort into reassuring the RAF cadre, in the form of open briefings, regular personal visits and engagement with managers at all levels. Nevertheless, I have to wonder whether the fundamental problem was actually soluble. Indeed, the subsequent Air Force Board Liaison Team report observed that:

> "There remained a feeling of being cast adrift from the RAF mainstream with a sense of erosion of traditional Service discipline and command chains"

A further issue that caused increasing difficulties was the confused organisational arrangements we had been gifted at St Athan. In a misguided endeavour to 'protect' the Service cadre, command and disciplinary authority fell to the station commander while 'control' fell to the Chief Executive and myself. The result was that everyone was confused as to who was really in charge and the relationship between the Agency and the station went from bad to worse.

The decision to remove all Service personnel from the DARA by 2003 was, therefore, neither entirely unexpected nor unwelcome. It was also not unconnected with the question of whether one can hope to retain military ethos in a commercial, or at least a commercially focussed, organisation.

Personal Impact

Change programmes place leaders under an immense personal burden. Effective leadership demands concern for those to be led. In a close-knit organisation there may be a high degree of empathy between leaders and followers, built around a common culture and a binding ethos. How then can leaders find the strength to take an organisation forward knowing the impact that change will have on the very people they care for?

This can be a diffuse concern or extremely personal. Over a period of less than a year, 2 of my senior staff (a civil servant Grade 7 and a wing commander) asked to be relieved of their duties because of stress. Another 2 (including a group captain) fell prey to stress-related illness. Even some of our union representatives fell victim to stress. Could I have done more for them, should I have done more?

Change at the DARA was inevitable and necessary, but I disagreed with the way it was being introduced and I could literally see the casualties. The pain that this caused was exaggerated by the sense of isolation that we all felt to a greater or lesser degree. It seemed at times as if the teacher had left the room and we were at the mercy of the school bully. This may seem a rather emotional way of describing the situation but it sums up the prevalent mood.

I recall one morning at home, just before my daughters went to school when we found ourselves all in tears over a minor family argument. This was not, by my repressed standards, normal behaviour. The cause, however, was the strain and pressure I was facing at work.

There was also another, more corrosive problem, the increasing difficulty I had in my followership role. I was constantly irritated, and sometimes appalled at the approach taken towards people and the simplistic response to complex issues. You might say that, in terms of temperament, we were not entirely compatible.

Perhaps this would not really have mattered if there had been a better balance in the make-up of the Board, but there wasn't. Moreover, it appeared that the 'common-sensical, intuitive, action-man' leader personified, at least to some external eyes, the qualities needed to bring about essential change. In other words, if a few eggs had to be broken, so be it ....

Impact On The Organisation

With apologies to any cosmologists, I suggest that all organisations, even in a steady state, encompass ambiguity. Change is a permanent state of affairs and, as a result, there are gaps (interstellar space) between aspiration and reality, between policy and process and between assertion and belief. Change programmes widen these differences and as the 'galaxies' that represent the current and future states start to recede from each other, so out of the cosmic dust emerge concern, fear, uncertainty and insecurity. These effects are inevitable but not necessarily destructive, moreover, they can be mitigated – if not largely avoided – by strong leadership, building on trust, confidence, a feeling of belonging and conscious involvement.

My personal view is that the DARA Board focussed too much on the hard aspects of change, utilising a checklist approach, rather than emphasising the people dimension. Tangible deliverables were preferred to the more complex questions about individual attitudes or team ethos. In essence, managing change was given greater prominence than leading change. The irony was that 'real' change – in the form of effective and sustainable change – only occurred when behaviours changed.

The impact of all of this on the DARA was more difficult to quantify. In my personal opinion an organisation had been created that lacked any spirit or soul. The lack of a binding ethos and widespread cynicism actually weakened the chances of DARA's long term survival. Not surprisingly, perhaps, a recent anonymous employee opinion survey found severe problems with trust and values.

Lessons

What lessons do I draw? In as much as what I have had to say is a personal view; perhaps I should merely conclude with some observations.

- Leadership in a modern organisation is a collective activity. The role of the Chief Executive is central but it is vital there is a senior team that shares, and is seen to share, a common ethos, values and vision.
- Change is never easy and can be extremely stressful for all involved: leaders and followers; Service and civilian; management and unions.
- The temptation to avoid aligning command, control and disciplinary chains must be resisted if change is to be effectively implemented and unit cohesion maintained.
- Change exacerbates internal divisions and can lead to a breakdown of normal behaviour through fear and uncertainty.
- Tension and ambiguity are the natural partners of change but they are not insurmountable obstacles when confronted by effective leadership.
- There is a tendency in major change programmes to concentrate on the 'hard' aspects of change rather than the people element.
- In fact, organisations can only change when behaviour changes.
- Individual and team training are essential tools in assisting an organisation to cope with change.
- Leaders need to be prepared (and trained) for their role in leading and managing change.

THE AIR SURVEILLANCE AND CONTROL SYSTEM[1]: CHANGING MINDSETS TO REALIZE EFFECT

Malcolm Crayford [1] & Brian Howieson

"Personnel are neither frightened nor opposed to change, provided that it is change that makes sense to them. They see the flaws in the way we operate at present as clearly if not more clearly than anyone." [2]

Introduction [3]

The Editors of this book invited us to write this Paper so that we may offer our views on the significant leadership challenges which have faced the Air Surveillance and Control System organisation since the end of the Cold War and importantly, following the events of 11 September 2001. It may seem odd to the reader that this paper was presented under the theme of 'Leadership in Adversity' at the RAF Leadership Centre Conference, *Beyond Command* in July 2005; however, we hope to demonstrate that the organisation has had to negotiate significant leadership challenges particularly in the last 4 years and will continue to do so in the immediate future in the most demanding of circumstances, both internal to the Air Surveillance and Control System organisation and external within the bounds of the Service itself.

This Paper has three principal sections:
- The development of an Air Surveillance and Control System Vision and effects of Transformation.
- Operations Support Branch Coherence?
- Overcoming institutional resistance to the evolution of an expert cadre of Air Battle Management[2] specialists.

---

[1] Air Surveillance and Control System (ASACS) is the network of fixed, mobile and airborne radars, associated communications, and facilities that provide for the detection, recognition, reporting and control of interception and engagement of airborne vehicles within the detection range. For the purposes of this Paper, ASACS personnel encompass the Operations Support Branch (Fighter Control) Sub-specialisation and the Aerospace Systems Operators/ Managers of Trade Group 12.

[2] ABM functions at the tactical level include Surveillance and Recognised Air Picture (RAP) Production, Data Link Operation and Management, Sensor Operation and Management, Airspace Management and Control, Optimising Information from Space assets, Weapons Direction and Control.

Throughout the Paper, we are reminded that the Effects Based Approach, facilitated by a Network Enabled Capability[3], will shape the future conduct of air and space operations. Effects Based Operations, either wholly or in part, will drive the core aspects of force development, from individual training through to equipment. Critically, we will argue that if the Effects Based Approach, facilitated by Networked Enabled Capability, really has the potential to deliver on its promises, underlying elements of our extant culture and doctrine must be re-examined. Current paradigms must be challenged, as cultural and doctrinal changes are likely to be just as important to the development of the Effects Based Approach as Network Enabled Capability itself. Therefore, in order to realise fully the potential of an Effects Based Approach, we argue that leaders of tomorrow must think differently about the ways in which our current culture and doctrine governs and guides the employment of our future 'Warfighters'.

The Development Of An Air Surveillance And Control System Vision And The Effects Of Transformation

To many people, the perception of the Air Surveillance and Control System is a Cold War focused organisation with diminishing relevance to modern expeditionary operations. Who could argue? Following the Cold War, the UK's Air Command and Control structure[4] remained focused on meeting individual force needs and was exercised largely from fixed sites, utilizing legacy systems that were designed for the Soviet threat. Although, the infrastructure was reduced during the 1990s, its structure, complete with hardened underground bunkers, perpetuated the 'Citadel UK' or 'ivory bunker' perception. The Air Surveillance and Control System organisation struggled to adapt to the change of emphasis to the Joint nature of operations and the emerging concept of the Joint Rapid Reaction Force. The only concession to this posture was the highly successful integration of Air Surveillance and Control System personnel as Mission crew on the E-3D Airborne Warning and Control System aircraft and the establishment of No 1 Air Control Centre[5] at RAF Boulmer in 1995.

But why was there such turmoil within the organisation? The answer was relatively straightforward although difficult to resolve. In the mid 1990s, following the rustication to Strike Command of many Ministry of Defence tasks, there had been a lack of strategic vision, high-level policy guidance and

---

[3] In simple terms, NEC is an information superiority-enabled concept of operations that generates increased combat power by networking sensors, decision makers, and shooters to achieve shared awareness, increased speed of command, higher tempo of operations, greater lethality, increased survivability, and a degree of self-synchronization so that information can be translated into synchronized and overwhelming military effect at optimum tempo.

[4] **U**nited **K**ingdom **A**ir **D**efence **G**round **E**nvironment.

[5] 1ACC is now an Air Combat Support Unit declared to the JRRF; however, in 1995, it was established primarily to relearn the lessons of mobility and was provided with an austere capability to fulfil the tactical picture compilation and weapons employment tasks.

direction of Air Command and Control[6] within both the Service and wider joint arena. The lack of Air Command and Control harmonisation within Strike Command was compounded by the then Group structure, which was functional and focused towards traditional capability-based platforms. The introduction of the Strategic Defence Review in 1998 and the development of the Joint Rapid Reaction Force proved the catalyst for change. The focus on expeditionary operations required the UK to field an independent command and control capability that could stand-alone or be integrated into bilateral or coalition operations. The development of the UK Joint Force Air Component Headquarters[7] and the procurement of a subordinate Tactical Air Control Centre with supporting T101 long-range mobile radars for No 1 Air Control Centre, sought to fill the urgent need for a deployable ground based system to support Air Command and Control operations.

The tragic events of 11 September 2001 also proved a decisive point for the organisation. With much of the Service focused firmly on expeditionary operations, the renegade attacks on the US reinforced, once again, the importance of NATO's Integrated Air Defence System and the pivotal role of the Air Surveillance and Control System and Quick Reaction Alert Force for UK Homeland Defence. A revised UK Airspace Security Task[8] was adopted and robust procedures developed to deal with the potential renegade aircraft threat; this also involved the military and political leadership at the highest levels. The asymmetric attacks in the US provided a renewed focus for the static elements of the system that, until then, had been in a parlous state of decline. There was also an acceptance that the organisation needed to optimise its Cold War estate for operational synergy: estate rationalisation and a move from the bunker environment would also attract significant financial savings. The relocation of elements of the system to areas that would facilitate greater integration with our aircrew would provide an environment in which to develop the Air Battle Management experience of Air Surveillance and Control System personnel across the broad spectrum of air operations similar to the benefits accrued by those personnel exposed to E-3D operations since the early 1990s. This would enable the Air Surveillance and Control System community to contribute more to expeditionary operations and would allow the specialisation to move towards greater involvement in Air Battle Management and Air Command and Control which, in turn, would increase recruitment and retention. In short, to stay relevant, the organisation needed to transform the ground based elements and quickly.

---

[6] AirC2 – operations, which ensure the efficient planning and execution of air power.
[7] The UK JFACHQ was officially formed in March 2000; an Initial Operating Capability was declared in October 2000 and a Full Operational Capability in October 2001.
[8] The UK Airspace Security task objective is 'to provide a continuous RAP and an air policing capability, providing for the interception and possible destruction of rogue and hostile aircraft, to maintain the integrity of the UK's airspace'.

The development of a Vision[4] that detailed a concept for the evolution of the specialisation to support evolving tactical Air Battle Management needs and Air Command and Control operations was endorsed in 2002 and was key to the transformation process. This vision served 3 important roles: first, by clarifying the direction of change it simplified thousands of more detailed decisions; second, it motivated our personnel to take action in the right direction, even if the initial steps were personally painful; and third, it helped coordinate the actions of our personnel in a remarkably fast and efficient manner. With a common understanding of the Vision, establishing a sense of urgency was also key to gaining cooperation across the organisation[9]. However, the Vision generated significant intellectual and emotional challenges across the community. What will this mean for me? My family? The Air Surveillance and Control System organisation? What alternatives are there? Do I really believe what I'm hearing? The intellectual task of developing a Vision was difficult enough but the emotional task of communicating the Vision to our personnel and implementing the transformation process was even tougher. Implementation of the Vision has required strong leadership at every level; a sense of urgency and effective communication has engendered trust, which, in turn, has kept the transformation process on track.

The deployment of No 1 Air Control Centre in support of Operation TELIC in 2003 was a decisive point in the transformation of the deployable ASACS elements. However, the initial planning for the Centre's involvement in Operation TELIC was controversial. There appeared to be a lack of understanding at both Strike Command and the Permanent Joint Headquarters of the Centre's operational capabilities and a failure among some planning staffs to view the efficacy of the E-3D and the Centre as complementary assets. Despite a highly successful deployment on Exercise in Oman, a view often heard by frustrated Air Surveillance and Control System staffs at Group was that "No 1 Air Control Centre can't be deployed as they had not been deployed operationally before" (even the E-3D Force had to start somewhere!). Fortunately, the deployment was at the request of the US, who appeared well briefed on the Centre's operational capabilities; the deployment was also supported by the senior leadership in the Service. Initially deployed to reinforce the existing detachment at Mount Olympus, Cyprus in support of the deployment and fighting phases of the war, the Unit established 24/7 air surveillance of the Eastern Mediterranean and provided control to the wide bodied aircraft at RAF Akrotiri in transit to and from theatre (some 3500 movements). The Centre redeployed subsequently to Tallil Air Base in Southern Iraq from April 2003 to January 2004 in support of the next phase of operations; this facilitated the release from Operation TELIC of the UK's E-3D

---

9   The sense of urgency was driven primarily by equipment obsolescence of the UKADGE Integrated Command and Control System and the demise of the associated communications bearer and, in our view, the events of 11 September 2001.

aircraft and the recovery of a United States Marine Corps Tactical Air Operations Centre that had been in Northern Kuwait since 1996.

Under the most arduous of conditions, and operating, at times, in temperatures above 50 degrees Centigrade that exceeded the design specification of the Unit's radars and recently delivered Tactical Air Control Centre, No 1 Air Control Centre (tactical callsign 'CROWBAR') proved their ability to play a core role in the delivery of tactical Air Battle Management and Air Command and Control. Integrating successfully with the US and operating in a 360 degree battlespace in the Southern Area Defence Coordinator role, the Centre contributed effectively to the delivery of air power in pursuit of the Commander-in-Chief Strike Command's precept: *Precise campaign effects, at range, in time.* The Air Surveillance and Control System now had a cadre of individuals, in addition to those employed on the E-3D aircraft and the UK Joint Force Air Component HQ, who had been exposed to the wider aspects of Air Command and Control. No 1 Air Control Centre was now an operationally proven Force Element at readiness and a complementary asset to the E-3D Force for expeditionary Air Command and Control operations.

In the static domain, the transformation was similarly dramatic. Following implementation of Strike Command's Minor Unit Basing Study, RAF Neatishead and Buchan, complete with their Cold War underground bunkers, were closed in June and October 2004 respectively; the Air Surveillance and Control System had finally thrown off the 'Citadel-UK' cloak. The 24/7 Air Command and Control requirement to meet the UK's Airspace Security task has now been centralised at RAF Boulmer following the successful delivery and operational work up of IBM's £60M Command and Control System. Our personnel at the NATO Control and Reporting Centre now operate one of the most technologically advanced network enabled capabilities in the World. The relocation of No 1 Air Control Centre to RAF Kirton-in-Lindsey in Lincolnshire[10] in late 2004 facilitated greater integration with the complementary Intelligence Surveillance Target Acquisition and Reconnaissance assets at RAF Waddington and will enable closer coordination with the communications units earmarked for RAF Scampton. The opening of the second NATO Control and Reporting Centre at RAF Scampton in early 2006 will enable an Air Surveillance and Control System Force Command[11] to be reconfigured with a Hub at RAF Boulmer, focused on Force Element generation and management including responsibility for the Standing Home Commitment, plus a Satellite at No 1 Air Control Centre Kirton-in-Lindsey / Control and Reporting Centre Scampton focused on deployed warfighting support and operations.

---

[10] 1ACC's move to RAF Kirton-in-Lindsey is an interim step prior to the Unit's eventual move to RAF Scampton.

[11] As part of Strike Command Transformation, the ASACS Force Command will be reconfigured under the command and control of the Stn Cdr RAF Boulmer.

Optimising the estate for operational synergy has, of course, achieved significant savings but station closures and the relocation of No 1 Air Control Centre has also involved the movement of hundreds of serving and civilian personnel together with their families. Where stations have closed, this has led inevitably to civilian redundancies and while the transformation process has been extremely successful thus far it has not been achieved without pain! Indeed, there remains continued uncertainty for the 1000 personnel based at RAF Boulmer following announcement that the Station will close in 2012[12]. Nonetheless, despite this uncertainty, the organisation has evolved from its previous Cold War posture and personnel have embraced willingly the transformation process. In doing so, Air Surveillance and Control System personnel have been exposed increasingly to expeditionary operations either as part of the E-3D Force, UK Joint Force Air Component HQ or No 1 Air Control Centre. The operational Air Command and Control capability at RAF Boulmer has enhanced the UK's ability to address the potential renegade threat and the reconfigured Air Surveillance and Control System Force Command structure, with a Hub and Satellite construct will serve to keep the organisation relevant to the enduring Air Command and Control Core Air and Space Power Role[13].

Operations Support Branch Coherence?

Given the progress of the transformation and the broader operational exposure in recent years, we would argue that Air Surveillance and Control System personnel have developed considerable expertise in the exploitation of tactical Air Battle Management skills and are familiar with the challenge of Network Enabled Capability. Experience with the E-3D, UK Joint Force Air Component HQ, No 1 Air Control Centre and other environment Air Battle Management entities has also prepared personnel for the tactical command[14] level of Air Command and Control, particularly in the strategy to task arena from the development of Air Operations Directives to the production and dissemination of Air Tasking and Airspace Control Orders. Personnel also have a wealth of experience in the Missile Warning and Space Surveillance tasks as part of the Ballistic Missile Early Warning System at RAF Fylingdales. Exposure to Space Command and Control has also increased in recent years with Air Surveillance and Control System personnel assigned to the US Space Based Infra Red System in Colorado. Focus must now be placed on developing these nascent skills to enable personnel to provide decision support within the

---

[12] The uncertainty is caused primarily by funding difficulties to relocate the School of Fighter Control and NATO CRC.
[13] The FASOC vision of agile air power encapsulates 6 enduring core air and space power roles: AirC2, Counter-Air-Operations, Air Operations for Strategic Effect, Integrated Air Operations, Rapid Global Mobility and ISTAR.
[14] The authority delegated to a commander to assign tasks to forces under command for the accomplishment of the mission assigned by higher authority. .

Knowledge[15] and Decision Superiority[16] environment. Adoption of the Decision Superiority construct provides the foundation upon which to shape our Battlespace Management capability for the future. The Air Surveillance and Control System community has evolved to an organisation that is well placed to provide Decision Support; however, we would contend that an obstacle in the path of progress is the current structure of the Operations Support Branch, which increasingly lacks relevance against today's Effects Based Operations driven context.

The Operations Support Branch[17] offered the opportunity to form a single cohesive branch with the sole purpose of supporting aerospace operations and the overall Air Command and Control process. Unfortunately, this opportunity has not been exploited fully and we retain a disparate organisation of 6 specialisations, each with limited scope, lacking unity of purpose, collective identity and a personnel strategy for future development. Individuals across the Operations Support Branch readily identify with the critical ethos and warfighting support aspects of their respective specialisations but they seldom, if ever, refer to themselves as Operations Support Branch. If the Branch is to undertake a significant role in the future of the Service, it must develop its corporate identity as a branch, with a clear idea of its collective function to support the core air and space power roles. Presently, despite the creation of a collective branch, its officers are developed generally on specialist lines to prepare them for senior appointments within their own specialist areas. Employment in wider aerospace operations or in the Air Command and Control process at higher levels has not been common and senior officers, with an Operations Support Branch background, have not generally been supported with the appropriate level of training (e.g. attendance on the Higher Command and Staff Course) to fill higher command and staff appointments. This shortfall may have been acceptable in the past but will be unsustainable if the Branch is to be relevant to the future Agile Air Force Concept[5].

We argue that the Branch needs to be restructured to support the Effects Based Operations construct. The Main Operating Base/Deployed Operating Base requirement demands Force Protection and the enabling role of Air Traffic Control and Flight Operations staff to support aircraft operations. However, there is also a second entity that draws on the synergy between the Air Surveillance and Control System (Joint Operations, J3) and Intelligence (J2) staffs to deliver Air Battle Management and decision support to the warfighter. Essential to this process is the need to integrate Communication and Information

---

[15] The gaining, disseminating and maintaining of a greater level and quality of useful knowledge than that held by an adversary.

[16] Individuals who mentally manoeuvre at best speed – relative to their adversary – through the OODA cycle.

[17] The OSB was formed on 1 April 1997 from the integration of 5 specializations: Fighter Control, Air Traffic Control, RAF Regiment, Flight Operations and Intelligence. Provost/Security was added on 23 June 2003.

Systems (J6) specialists to provide the agile communications systems that will facilitate Network Enabled Capability. As the skills and experience of individuals grow, they will become increasingly engaged in the Decision Superiority construct providing decision support at various levels, from the tactical to the operational, to assist the decision-making warfighters. Evolution through and training in the Decision Superiority construct will enable Decision Supporters to develop the Phronesis18 necessary to become decision-making warfighters in their own right. Implementing a more coherent approach will not be easy but, once stovepiped perceptions have been removed, the new structure would be populated by a more effective, better educated workforce focused on the delivery of the Core Air and Space Power Roles. While the structure of the Operations Support Branch can be made more coherent and an expert cadre of non-flying Branch Air Battle Management specialists developed to support the Effects Based Operations construct, we argue that the final obstacle to achieving this aspiration is cultural.

Overcoming Institutional Resistance To The Evolution Of An Expert Cadre Of Air Battle Management Specialists

Fortunately, we have progressed to the point where most people recognize that the sharing of information is essential to make sense of the increasingly complex battlespace. While the pursuit of the Effects Based Approach and Network Enabled Capability requires technological innovations to occur, Transformation is more than just acquiring new equipment and embracing new technology: it is rather the all-encompassing process of thinking creatively, recognizing and integrating those personnel who have the relevant skill-sets, and leveraging new operational concepts in order to create an advantage against current and potential future adversaries[19]. If we are to realise the full potential of the Effects Based Approach we would argue that we must transform our overall culture[20]; — a culture that is developed through leadership, education and increased emphasis on concept development and experimentation. Interestingly, we note that the word culture only appears *once* in 'Network Enabled Capability', (Joint Service Publication 777 Edition 1 (2005))[6]. We need to encourage a culture of risk taking, new thinking, and intellectual courage. The pursuit of the Effects Based Approach has important intellectual, conceptual, and cultural components, which turn technological advances into military effect. As Air Chief Marshal, Sir Brian Burridge says:

---

[18] See p85 and pp134-138 to John Adair, *Effective Strategic Leadership: An Essential Path to Success Guided by the World's Great Leaders*, (2002). London: Macmillan Publishing. Phronesis is the Greek term for practical wisdom "*a blend of intelligence and experience served by character*" that enables individuals to function as an effective leader.

[19] In the debate (and associated literature), 'integration' is often overlooked. Integration is crucial: it is about developing old capability in new ways.

[20] Culture is defined as: "*The arts and other manifestations of human intellectual achievement regarded collectively*". Source: Oxford English Dictionary (2005).

"We now need flexible platforms and agile people whereas in the past we needed agile platforms and flexible people. We really need agile people and the only way we can have the agility is for you to take it upon yourself to educate yourselves and think deeply and conceptually about the issues we face." [7]

Turning pieces of information into shared situational awareness and developing a cadre of Air Battle Management specialists in support of the Agile Air Force Concept will require the expertise and experience of more than just the 'flying cadre' of the Service. The term Air Battle Management is not well understood and there is resistance to change in ideas suggested by non-flying personnel. As Machiavelli wrote: "Men often oppose a thing merely because they have no agency in planning it.....or because it may have been planned by whom they dislike." [8] We would contend that there exists a particular mindset issue which we have termed the 'aircrew focused' Moral Component. This is the view that you have to be operational aircrew before you can send crews into battle. As Dr Alan Stephens pointed out in the Air Power Leadership Conference in 2002, "given the historic domination of our Service by fighter pilots, there are those who regard command, authority and responsibility as a given right rather than as privileges that should be earned". Dr Stephens went on to say that "being a pilot will not necessarily be a prerequisite for aerospace command; nor, indeed, might it even provide the most suitable apprenticeship". Aircrew, particularly fighter pilots, tend to only respect their own peer group; is there a culture of institutional arrogance prevalent across our Service?

Changing an *Airman's Perspective* is on the critical path to exploiting the potential of the Effects Based Approach and the Agile Air Force Concept; education alone will not be sufficient. The 'way we do our business' will need to change in order to establish new cultural and institutional norms (for example, desirable attitudes and behaviours about sharing information, collaboration, and relationships within the Service). To implement fundamental change in our culture, leaders must step forward willingly to institute this paradigm shift. The Service (via its leadership) must engender a climate where cultural barriers diminish. Indeed, the emergence of systems operators and those flying and non-flying Air Surveillance and Control System specialists involved in Air Battle Management and Air Command and Control will serve to challenge the traditional Airman's Perspective and institutional mindset. Indeed, Air Surveillance and Control System personnel do not see themselves simply as passive collectors and distributors of information; the operational development and wide range of competencies and skills held by these personnel culminates in a Tactical Control[21] and/or Tactical Command qualification which draws on warfighter skills, without which the warfighting task would be impossible.

---

[21] The detailed and usually local direction and control of movement and manoeuvre necessary to accomplish missions or task assigned.

Conclusion

The Air Surveillance and Control System organisation is not well understood across the Royal Air Force; however, we would argue that the Branch has had to negotiate significant leadership challenges since the Strategic Defence Review and in particular following the renegade attacks of 11 September 2001. The development and endorsement of the Air Surveillance and Control System Vision defined what the future should look like and leadership aligned those personnel behind the vision, inspiring them to make it happen despite the many obstacles. The closure and relocation of Air Surveillance and Control System elements in 2004 has allowed the organisation to optimise its estate for operational synergy. The operational deployment of No 1 Air Control Centre to Iraq was without doubt leadership conducted in adversity and greater integration with our aircrew, particularly in the E-3D Force and UK Joint Force Air Component HQ, has provided an environment for Air Surveillance and Control System personnel to develop Air Battle Management experience across the broad spectrum of air operations. The organisation's expertise expands beyond the commonly held perception of defensive counter air (Quick Reaction Alert) operations. Whether operating on the E-3D aircraft, UK Joint Force Air Component HQ, No 1 Air Control Centre, NATO Control and Reporting Centre, Ballistic Missile Early Warning System or other Air Battle Management environment entities, Air Surveillance and Control System personnel have demonstrated core strengths that enable them to support Air Battle Management and the wider Air Command and Control process. This operational experience offers the potential to develop a core cadre of Air Battle Management specialists to support the delivery of Air Command and Control in the future Effects Based Operations construct.

To meet this aspiration, however, there is a need to bring more coherence to the Operations Support Branch; further integration of disparate specialisations without considering the evolving operational need would not bring greater cohesion. This can be achieved by seeking natural synergies that focus on the Force Protection and operations aspects to support the Main Operating Base/Deployed Operating Base and the delivery of tactical Air Battle Management and Air Command and Control in support of the 'warfighter'. Air Battle Management specialists will be increasingly engaged in the Decision Superiority construct providing Decision Support at various levels, from the tactical to the operational. With the right leadership and direction, a cadre of Air Battle Management specialists, within the Operations Support Branch, can be developed and with the right training, some will develop the Phronesis necessary to become decision making warfighters in their own right22.

---

[22] This issue is expanded upon by Group Captain Mark Ashwell in his paper: Operations Support Branch – Some Thoughts: 18 December 2004.

The final obstacle to achieving this aspiration is cultural; this will require a fundamental change and a redefinition of the relationship between various Branches within the Service. The Service's commitment to Transformation is an explicit recognition that something needs to change sooner rather than later; existing command and control concepts and processes are no longer adequate to accommodate current and emerging threats. Changing mindsets is inextricably linked to changing long-held precepts about the way we do things. People are central to the Effects Based Approach, for it is people that turn concepts into realities within the battlespace. Doctrine will need to be developed and/or modified to emphasise the principles inherent in the Effects Based Approach, the new roles that battlespace entities will play, who is best suited to provide this knowledge and the nature of their interactions. To exploit the potential of the Effects Based Approach fully will involve significant, if not fundamental changes in how the Service is organised and Strike Command's Transformation is part of this process. Individuals will need to adopt new attitudes, accept more responsibility, learn new skills, master new approaches, and learn to work with (and accept) specialists without pre-conceived opinions or prejudices. In short, we must leave outdated paradigms and mindsets behind. The *status quo* is not an option; transformation that includes addressing our culture is just as essential if we are to remain relevant as a Service.

Endnotes

1. Principal Author: Group Captain 'Ginge' Crayford is currently the Station Commander at RAF Boulmer.
2. The authors would like to acknowledge the help of Group Captain Mark Ashwell for his comments and advice with earlier drafts of this paper.
3. Secretary of State for defence in a speech outlining the Strategic Defence Review at the Royal Institute for International Affairs on 12 March 1998.
4. 'A Future Vision for ASACS' – A paper by Deputy Commander in Chief Strike Command for the Air Force Board Standing Committee dated October 2002.
5. Project Trenchard – Agile Air Force Concept. A paper by Commander in Chief Strike Command dated 31 March 2005.
6. Network Enabled Capability, JSP 777 Edn 1, (2005). Produced by DCIC Design Graphic on behalf of D CBM/J6 and Published by Ministry of Defence UK© 01/05 C100.
7. See 'Iraq 2003 – Air Power Pointers for the Future' by Air Chief Marshal Sir Brian Burridge in *Air Power Review*, Volume 7, Number 3, Autumn 2004.
8. See p81 to Kaplan, R.D. (2001) Warrior Politics: Why leadership demands a pagan ethos'. Random House. US

PUBLIC VALUE AND ADAPTIVE LEADERSHIP

Professor John Benington

In this brief presentation I am going to discuss the testing and application of two key concepts – public value and adaptive leadership – in the policing of the Drumcree demonstrations in Northern Ireland.

I had 20 years experience as a manager in the public and voluntary service in the UK, before retreating to become an academic 20 years ago. In that time I have found very few academic theories of leadership and public management which do justice to the complexity of decision-making at the front line of public service. Two frameworks which we have found helpful are those of Public Value (Mark Moore, Harvard University Press 1995), and Adaptive Leadership (Ron Heifetz, Harvard University Press 2001).

I was taken by surprise when, whilst outlining these two concepts to a class of 50 senior public managers on our Warwick MPA course (a public sector MBA) in October 2001, I was challenged by a chief superintendent in the Police Service of Northern Ireland (PSNI) who was sitting in the back row of the class, to apply and test out the usefulness of these theories in the policing of the Drumcree demonstrations in Northern Ireland, in which Protestant and Catholic groups clash each summer.

So over the past three years I have had the privilege of shadowing (now) Assistant Chief Constable Irwin Turbitt and his colleagues in the police and the British Army, as they developed a highly innovative approach to the policing of Drumcree, based partly upon the theories of public value and adaptive leadership. I will briefly summarise the main dimensions of those theories, and then Irwin will describe the testing of those theories in practice at Drumcree, over the two years when he was silver commander for the operation.

Mark Moore's book *Creating Public Value*, based on his work at the Kennedy School of Government at Harvard in the USA, has sparked off a lot of further thinking and work by colleagues at Warwick University in the UK, to see if it is possible to develop as strong a concept of public value, as of private value in the private sector. I define public value more broadly than Mark Moore, to include two separate aspects: first, what does the public value? Second, what adds value to the public sphere ?

The first of these questions (what does the public value?) is concerned with the value which different sections of the public place upon different services. This goes well beyond the notion of individual consumer satisfaction, and involves discovering the relative values which different sections of the public place upon the satisfaction of various needs and desires, and their evaluation of the quality of specific public services.

The second question (what adds value to the public sphere?) is more complex, but if anything more important. This focuses on those actions and activities which add benefit to the community or to the common good. This includes adding long term political, economic and social value for example through investment in education and health services, arts and culture. It also includes activities which the public may not value in the short term, but which are judged to be in the public interest – for example regulation of smoking, binge-drinking, and car emissions.

Public Value

I highlight six characteristics of public value. The first is that it's not just created by the state or the public sector. Public value can be created, or contributed to, by either the public, private, voluntary or informal community sectors, or all four working together.

Secondly, the processes of public value creation vary from service to service. The public sector is a conglomerate of very different kinds of activities. Public value creation in the field of criminal justice is very different from public value creation, for example, in the water and sewerage service, or public value creation in transport or libraries. We need to analyse the "public value chain" in some detail, to highlight how and where public value is added in specific services and activities.

A third characteristic is that public value focuses attention, not just on inputs, activities and outputs, but much more on outcomes. This leads directly to the fourth characteristic – that public value requires longer term perspectives. The outcomes from investment in public health, for example, may not become visible for up to 20 years, in terms of reductions in the incidence of diseases like cancer, cholera, malaria, and TB.

Fifth, much public value is generated not by the producers (professionals, public servants) alone, but in a process of co-creation between the producers and their users, at the front-line. So public value in education is co-created through the interactive relationships and exchanges between teachers and pupils, in which each have their own responsibilities for the learning process. Public value in the hospital service is created largely in the inter-actions between patients, their families and carers, nurses, doctors, ward orderlies and so on. Public value creation at Drumcree depended upon a radical restructuring of some subtle relationships between the police and a wide range of different stake holders in that area of Northern Ireland.

Finally public value is often created right at the front line. While it involves strategy its actual creation takes place in that point of interface between the professional and the people who are using their services. Now we can take weeks to unpack this concept, but I'm just going to leave it there as a snapshot and hope that it will be brought to life by Irwin as he talks.

Adaptive Leadership

The second concept is that of adaptive leadership; developed by Ron Heifetz, also from the Kennedy School of Government at Harvard, and there are six principles for leading adaptive work which you'll see are brought to life when Irwin gives the case study, see figure 1 below.

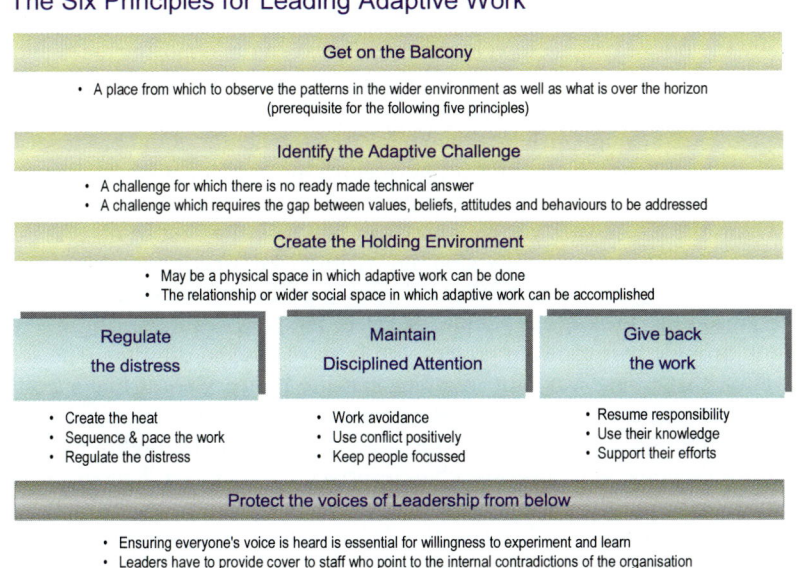

Figure 1: Six Principles for Leading Adaptive Work

The first is the need to observe the situation from what Heifetz calls the balcony – a place from which to watch the patterns in the wider environment as well as what is over the horizon. This observing the battlefield, on which the practitioner will engage, from the balcony is a prerequisite for the following five principles. From the balcony then it is necessary first to make a distinction between technical problems and adaptive challenges. Technical problems are problems to which there is a known solution and the challenge is really just to do it, 'JFDI' as someone said to me recently. Adaptive challenges arise from problems like those associated with 'Drumcree'; complex problems to which actually we do not know the solutions and the critical thing is that we ask the right questions as we work towards those solutions. Addressing adaptive challenges also requires the gap between values, beliefs, attitudes and behaviours to be addressed. Let's be clear by the way that adaptive doesn't mean that you adapt, it means that there will have to be changes and adaptations in thinking and behaviour. Adaptive problems require fundamental changes, in thinking and behaviour to resolve them. So having distinguished between technical problems and adaptive challenges it is necessary to identify the adaptive challenge on the battlefield below the balcony. It seems to me that watching Irwin and the policing of Drumcree, he identified that one of the adaptive challenges was that too many people were exercising their rights, e.g. to demonstrate, but not accepting the responsibility to do that within the framework of the law. A pattern of behaviour had developed over the years whereby the police had, as it were, refereed between the opposing sides and had stood in the middle while rocks, Molotov cocktails, bombs and so on were thrown at them. The police had sustained high levels of injury and, as they attempted to reduce this risk they had increased the height of the barricades that separated them from the public. By identifying the adaptive challenge that people, Loyalists and Nationalists, have a right to demonstrate but have to do that within the framework of the law, Irwin had to insist first of all that people should take that responsibility and he symbolized that by arguing for the dramatic lowering of the barricades. A very significant and visible pushing of the responsibility back on to people, in effect the police were saying we're not going to provide barricades to protect you from that responsibility. The second innovation that I saw was him insisting that the police were actually going to successfully enforce the law and take serious criminal charges against people who broke the law at Drumcree. This involved prosecuting highly respectable people who'd come out, gone to a church service but then had demonstrated and broken the law and the enforcement of the law, the application of the law, was itself a very radical action because this has not been done successfully before. Technical attempts had been made but the focus now was on getting the right outcome.

Creating a safe but challenging holding environment is the next principle of leading adaptive work. This is the notion that if you set in motion a process of challenging peoples thinking and behaviours; you have a responsibility to stick with them and to help to manage that process. It doesn't mean that you just project responsibility back on to them and let it all happen, that's the conditions for civil war. The creating of the safe but challenging holding environment says that you're going to be in there leading the change process, orchestrating the challenges but taking responsibilities for the boundaries within which it takes place and within which the giving of the work back to the people, another principle, takes place.

We all would prefer to have leaders who solve our problems for us and to dump and project our problems on to other people who we erect as God like figures or as devils. None of us like having the responsibility for solving our problems pushed back on to us, we will resist it, we will feel uncomfortable and a great deal of feeling will be unleashed. Some of the case studies we've had this afternoon demonstrated that very, very honestly and very well.

Regulating the distress, another principle of leading adaptive work, is the notion that once you've created the framework in which this challenging adaptive thinking and adaptive behaviour has got to go on, you have a responsibility to keep the temperature at the correct level. High enough for the thing still to simmer, but low enough that it doesn't boil over. One of the things that I saw Irwin do very professionally and very cleverly in Northern Ireland was keep the temperature up enough for people to be pushed out of their comfort zones but not to allow the bubbling pot to boil over. It's like a pressure cooker, if you turn the temperature up too high the thing explodes, so you regulate that distress keeping the temperature going so that the change process is simmering but not letting it go to a point where it boils over and the changes are lost.

Paying disciplined attention to the issues, another principle, is the notion that in these uncomfortable change processes where we're challenged to change our thinking and our behaviours, we will all want to displace attention onto something else and there'll be all kinds of pressures on us to divert to other issues and the maintaining of disciplined attention goes right back to the identification of the adaptive challenge. If we spent a great deal of time identifying what is the critical change in thinking and behaviour that is necessary, then we need to be able to keep attention on that issue and keep coming back to it.

Finally protecting the voices of leadership without authority is the notion that in managing or leading, if you like, this very complex volatile change process with many different stake holders, it's very important not just to listen to the dominant voices, the voices that claim your attention from the main stake holders. And in Drumcree one of the main lessons I learned over the 3 years of having a chance to not only observe the police and the Army at work but also to speak to people in the Orange Order and the Garvaghy Road Residence Coalition is the very different sources of authority that are at stake there. For the Orange Order their flag shows where their source of authority is. Their authority comes directly from the Queen and God and the Bible, their authority is from above and nothing will shift them until they feel that they have authorization from above, there will be no resolution unless they feel it's consistent with those sources of authority. For the nationalist community involved in the Garvaghy Road Residents Coalition, however, they take their authority from below, it's the voice of the people on the street and they're constantly checking that with their membership on the street. So you have two quite different sources of authority and subtlety different ways of having to listen to them in the many, many meetings which Irwin and his colleagues held to keep listening to the voices of the people that they were working with.

And then the final point, with which I'm going to conclude, is a critical one and a great challenge for those of us in business schools and perhaps in the Armed Services. It is the notion that effective leadership of these kinds of change processes involves constantly oscillating between the balcony position, in which you have a strategic overview, and the battle field position in which you are right there with them among in the bullets at the front line. Now traditionally we teach that in the private sector you have to make a clear separation between strategy and operations and their different kinds of activity carried out by different levels of people. That's true in many public services as well, with the operational responsibility very often lying in the middle of the organization. I've heard in some of your case studies today that you're talking about situations which require your strategists to have an absolutely embedded knowledge of what's happening at the front line, but equally your front line people need to be strategising as well.

Now Irwin, because he's a very unusual and extremely dangerous policeman and because he thinks innovatively, decided that the distance between the strategic command headquarters, where he could look at what was happening over the Drumcree front line with CCTV cameras, was too far away from the battleground.

In 2002 there was serious disorder and injuries at the front line and the headquarters where we were was over a mile away so it took three or four minutes to get out there. This may not seem long but in the complex volatile situation that is Drumcree it is too long.

So in 2003 he told me he had a surprise and he had actually got the Army Engineers to build a physical balcony in the field above the Drumcree bridge so that he could move between the balcony and the battlefield literally within seconds and could constantly be moving between the strategic overview of the whole battlefield, if you like, and the front line.

So two bits of theory; public value and adaptive leadership and a case study now of how that's been tested over a 3 year period in Drumcree.

© Irwin Turbitt, Institute of Governance and Public Management, Warwick Business School 2005

PUBLIC VALUE AND ADAPTIVE LEADERSHIP IN THE POLICING OF 'DRUMCREE' IN NORTHERN IRELAND

Assistant Chief Constable Irwin Turbitt

I am Irwin Turbitt and, as John Benington has said, I am a police officer from Northern Ireland. About 30 years ago I joined what was then the Royal Ulster Constabulary (RUC). I am now a member of the Police Service of Northern Ireland. In my previous post I was the District Commander of a place called Craigavon only widely known, unfortunately, because it contains the parish church of Drumcree. For two years I was the Silver Commander for the security operation at Drumcree. Let me explain what that means in command terms. We work on a gold, silver and bronze system. Gold is the strategic level of command and the Gold Commander, my boss, sets the strategic aims for the operation. The Silver Commander takes these aims, creates a plan then implements and commands it. This was my job. The Silver Commander has a number of Bronze Commanders below them who may be responsible for an area of ground, such as the area around the Drumcree Bridge, or who may have a particular function, such as the collection of CCTV evidence. In terms of manpower I had around 3000 people allocated to me for Drumcree; that is, 1000 police officers and 2000 soldiers (4 battalions). Legally, I was in command of all personnel. In addition to this we were given access to Royal Engineer resources and also to air assets through the Army Air Corps.

Now, whenever we talk about any situation in Ireland we cannot avoid including some history. However, in a country where history is used "as a quarry from which each side hews boulders to throw at the other" (Stewart 1997) there is no such thing as history but rather our history or their history. So, clearly my description of history will be entirely partisan and is intended only to support my case!

The annual Drumcree parade began almost 200 years ago in 1807 and although it is sometimes said that it only became problematic in recent years the following two examples show this is not so.

In July 1873, 100 Police with fixed bayonets confronted an Orange mob in 'The Tunnel' area and during the disturbance several people were injured and one killed by Police bayonets (Ryder & Kearney 2001, P 36).

In 1905 a Catholic watching the Parade pass through Obins Street was murdered when a Protestant in the parade produced a revolver and shot him dead. Prolonged rioting between the Police and several hundred Orangemen followed and that evening the Police blocked the mouth of Obins Street to prevent another Orange Parade going through The Tunnel area (Ryder & Kearney 2001, P 37).

From my personal professional perspective I first became aware of the situation in 1985, when the parade was re-routed by the then RUC. This started a series of difficult annual policing operations which fizzled out in the early 1990s. A map showing the various routes taken by the parades can be seen below in figure 1.

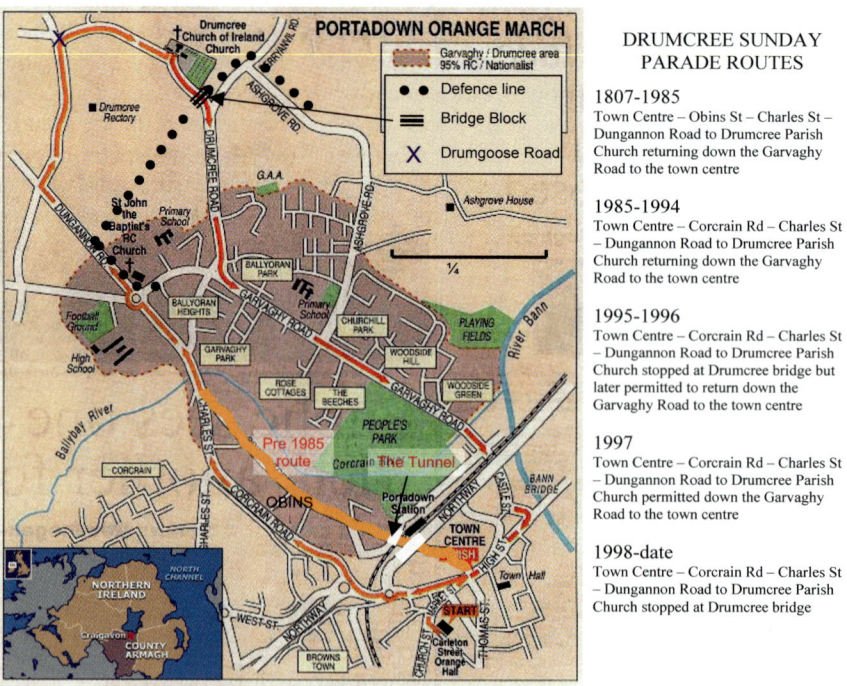

Figure 1: Drumcree Sunday Parade Routes

Where you stand depends on how you describe Drumcree. Ryder and Kearney in their Book 'Drumcree' offer the following reasonably balanced description:

> "At issue is an annual Church Parade by some 1200 members of the all Protestant Orange Order and two bands who insist on what they see as their inalienable civil right to march along the Garvaghy Road in Portadown [following a church service at Drumcree parish church] despite the fact that the Catholic community who live there are overwhelmingly opposed to the passage of the march and believe it is their right not to have to endure it (Ryder & Kearney 2001 p XVI).

To the outside world the parade is an annual event, happening on the Sunday before 12th July each year. Whilst it is certainly larger on this day than any other, since 1998 the parade has occurred every Sunday throughout the year and so, as the District Commander it becomes a weekly operation.

Following the difficulties of the late 1980s when it was the outward route that caused most contention, the inward route along the Garvaghy Road became increasingly controversial and in 1995 the RUC decided that the parade should be prevented from progressing down the Garvaghy Road at all. It was decided to stop the event at Drumcree Bridge and this lead to a stand off and frantic negotiations before the parade was allowed to proceed with agreement two days later.

This event is now known as Drumcree 1 and the nature of the negotiations, the subsequent agreement and resulting march remain controversial and contested. The following year, in 1996, the situation was even more problematic. The conflict continued for 5 days, during which there were over 100 incidents of intimidation, 758 attacks on the police and 662 plastic baton rounds fired by police.

On the morning of Thursday, 11 July, the Chief Constable reversed his original decision to re-route the parade. The RUC moved quickly onto the Garvaghy Road, supported by large numbers of military, and cleared the Nationalist residents from the road, pushed them back into the estates on either side of the road and allowed approximately 1200 Portadown Orangemen to march down the Garvaghy Road.

The decision sparked off major discussions about who governs Northern Ireland, the role of policing and the impartiality of the police force. The Roman Catholic Archbishop of Ireland, Cardinal Daly spoke for many when he said:

> "I don't think there is any way in which the decision could have been favourably received but the way in which it was executed made it still more unfavourably received. It had a devastating effect on the relationship between the RUC and the Catholic community. I have no doubt about that." (Ryder & Kearney 2001, P 170)

The mishandling of 'Drumcree II' in 1996 imposed a terrible legacy on the RUC, and, at a single stroke, destroyed 25 years of painful and increasingly tangible progress in transforming the relationship between the RUC and the Catholic minority community (Ryder & Kearney 2001, P 177). The RUC appeared either unprepared, or unable to stand up to intimidation from the Orange Order (Jarman et al 1998).

In 1997 the new Chief Constable, Ronnie Flanagan, decided that the lesser of two evils was to force the parade quickly down the Garvaghy Road rather than force the parade to stop. Despite being over a lot quicker, the incident was particularly unpleasant. 1998 saw the first year that the parade was stopped successfully and, although it has been attempted every single Sunday from then until now, I can tell you that there has not been a parade beyond the bridge at Drumcree since July 1997.

When I turned up in 2002 as the Craigavon District police commander, there seemed to be an opportunity to rethink our operational approach to policing Drumcree. 'If you always do what you've always done, you'll always get what you've always got'. What had so far been happening at Drumcree was that we had always been doing the same thing, but had been expecting to get something different. We therefore needed to first change our thinking. That was our adaptive challenge. A few examples will help illustrate this.

One element of our challenge was to be more successful in prosecuting those people breaking the law at Drumcree. Not a difficult task you may say; however, policing in the normal way involves the constable collecting evidence in his/her notebook, compiling a report and then appearing in court. That system becomes impossible during periods of conflict such as those at Drumcree as evidence is very difficult to collect in the heat of the moment by officers being physically attacked. Historically we had addressed this technical problem by using passive closed circuit television (CCTV) with the assistance of the Army. By recording everything that was happening we collected huge amounts of surveillance coverage which was then passed over, post event, to a large team of detectives who went through the hours of video tape collecting evidence. Clearly this was a very slow process and the prosecutions were taking about a year to administer which was obviously neither efficient nor effective.

To improve the prosecution lead times we started using our CCTV proactively. In live time we were then able to identify targets and follow them, collecting evidence as situations developed. This not only allowed us to process the cases very quickly, but also meant that we had stronger cases overall. In the past, the classic defence was that of a respectable person, who had never been in trouble before, getting carried away in the heat of the moment and perhaps throwing a single stone. The proactively targeted CCTV cameras could prove the deliberate involvement of an individual over a longer period of time.

The second key adaptive challenge was that of the barrier at Drumcree Bridge. A key part of our operation was to separate and contain the two opposing communities and the Royal Engineers produced a great number of physical obstacles to help do this; barbed wire, huge barricades and such like. The key one was the barrier at Drumcree Bridge. This consisted of 2 large shipping containers with steel welded onto the sides to form a large barrier which we called a crowd control obstacle (CCO). It weighed 30 tonnes and the bridge itself had to be strengthened in order to facilitate it. In addition to this CCO we ploughed the field adjacent to the bridge on the Orangemen's side to make it difficult to walk across to reach the river. If the river was crossed we had a coil of barbed wire and some large criss-cross barbed wire obstacles as well. This scale of defence had developed over a number of years as a response to extreme violence and the threat of extreme violence directed at the security forces by elements within, and associated with, the Orange Order, who were enraged by having their parade stopped at Drumcree Bridge. The down side to all this was that the obstacles worked just as effectively at keeping us away from them as they did at keeping them away from us. Over the years the attacks across the barricades varied from being shot at with golf balls, as if on a driving range, up to incidents with machine guns and blast bombs. Nobody was ever held to account for these attacks and we knew that, as with children, if an offender is not sanctioned at a reasonable level then next time the boundaries will be pushed and the scale of the offences will escalate.

We realised that the CCO had become like a totem pole at which people would come and worship by throwing stones and bottles etc and that we had no way of reaching them to apprehend them for their crimes. We could not get through the barrier to reach them. So, I decided that we needed a much smaller barrier; one which we could get through quickly.

However, this would also mean that the aggressors could get through to us and so we had to develop a good fall back defence. Police leaders work, in my opinion, with a psychological contract with the public order police, more aggressively known as the riot police. This goes something like this; we all understand this to be dangerous work and that somebody might get hurt, however when officers do get hurt it is important that those that do that, pay the price. In a democratic society the price paid is through the normal judicial processes. My promise to the public order officers was that with their help these processes would be followed through and people who attacked them would pay a proper price.

One further change I wanted to make was how we mentally described the situation. We had become mentally shaped by the topography of the ground in the area of Drumcree Bridge. We were the good guys on one side of the river whilst the Orange Order were the enemy on the other side. It seemed to me that this was wrong as the Orange Order were also citizens, not enemy forces, many of them were law abiding and never engaged in trouble. So although we were physically separated I wanted to start to think about how the good guys on both sides of the river could cooperate to deal with the bad guys as a way of co-producing public value at Drumcree.

We agreed to hold regular meetings with the Orange Order, with the Garvaghy Road residents (GRRC) and with various political parties. It was important to keep in touch with the various sources of leadership in the Drumcree conflict. Historically we had only met when there was a crisis happening but in 2002 we agreed to meet every day during the 10 day operation irrespective of whether there was a crisis or not. I decided to employ a no surprises policy. This appalled the military because obviously you can't tell 'the enemy' what your plans are. However, as I pointed out, we were not informing the enemy of our plans, we were telling the citizens and tax payers how we were going to jointly police the proceedings. So, we showed the various groups photographs of the new barricades and talked them through each of our ideas. Of course, when I outlined to the Orange Order that if anyone broke the law they would be prosecuted they were in full agreement because they really did believe that they were running a lawful, peaceful protest and that any trouble caused was not their responsibility.

During the 2002 July parade, when our new strategies were first tested we saw disorder despite our compromises, resulting in the injury of 31 officers. The news reports outlined the hard work put in by the authorities to scale down the security operation and the fact that the police felt let down and the disappointment felt in that failure. These reports were based on information given to the press by ourselves. We had changed our media strategy so that it was fully integrated with, and greatly added to the operational effort. Our reasoning was taken from the old adage that sometimes to win the war you have to lose the battle or as Sir Robert Mark (former Metropolitan Police Commissioner) put it; "in public order policing for the police to win they have to be seen to lose". This is part of the process by which the public decide what is acceptable and unacceptable. I think this is also applicable to modern military operations where the success of an operation, as opposed to an incident, is often decided more in the media that on the battlefield.

Now, the immediate outcome of 2002 may not look like a great success to you and to be honest it didn't feel like a great success to me at the time. I had made promises to people who had subsequently been injured. Fortunately, the second part of the operation worked well and within 3 hours of the disorder happening the first arrests had been made, as a result of evidence taken by video cameras. Air assets were used to track the offenders down and arrest teams were sent to pick them up. The following morning the news headlines weren't "Officers injured at Drumcree." Instead they started with "5 people will appear in court this morning charged with riot offences." The price paid by the Orange Order was much more severe than ever before. Having friends and colleagues in prison, some of whom spent a long time on remand, brought the adaptive challenge home to them very sharply because they realised that they weren't running the lawful, peaceful protest that they had told themselves they were.

In terms of holding the Orange Order's attention, to the challenge of running a lawful peaceful parade, the fact that the criminal justice system worked very slowly helped. Even though we had completed our investigation very quickly and all 29 charged were convicted, this did not happen until December 2003. However while people continued to be held on remand awaiting trial, the Orange Order leadership was very keen to work with us in order to prevent a repeat of the disorder of July 2002 in July 2003. This meant that to a surprising extent Drumcree 2003 was co-produced by the Police Service of Northern Ireland and Loyal Orange Lodge No1, following a radical restructuring of relationships, and it worked. So for the first time in more than 20 years, in 2003 on Drumcree Sunday, nothing happened at Drumcree. The public value created was nothing, no disorder, no damage, no injuries and no arrests. So, you can see that sometimes we employ a vast amount of resource in order to produce nothing. In such circumstances of course nothing is of great public value.

I moved on at the start of 2004 but John Benington and I went back that July to watch as visitors. My most immediate observation was that some of the things that we had really struggled to get agreement on the previous year were now accepted as if they had been happening forever. One example of this was the joint police / Church of Ireland check point. We used this to stop and search everyone going into the church because that gave us complete control of the area. However, in order for this to be seen as acceptable we had to organise it as a co-production with the church and it had been difficult to get agreement for this. The following year however the church initiated the contact and asked the police what time they should meet to help with the check point. The check point was treated as if it had been there for years.

So, I have taken you, very briefly and skimming over a great deal of important detail, through my story of Drumcree. I have taken you back to its beginnings in the 1800s up to the present day. I have shown you the changes that have taken place in the last 4 years and the results that have been achieved. I hope you see all this as a useful case study for the creation of public value using adaptive leadership.

Bibliography

Heifetz, R. A. *Leadership Without Easy Answers*. Cambridge, Massachusetts: Belknap Press, 1994.

Heifetz, R. A. and Laurie D. L. *'The Work of Leadership'* in Harvard Business Review on Leadership, Cambridge, Massachusetts: Harvard University Press, 1997.

Heifetz, R. A. and Linsky M. *Leadership on the Line Staying Alive through the Dangers of Leading*. Cambridge, Massachusetts: Harvard Business School Press, 2002.

Jarman, N, Bryan, D, Caleyron, N. and De Rosa, C. *POLITICS IN PUBLIC: Freedom of Assembly and the Right to Protest. A Comparative Analysis*. Belfast: Democratic Dialogue, 1998.

Mark, R. *In the Office of Constable*. London: Collins, 1978.

Moore, M. H. *Creating Public Value – strategic management in government*. Cambridge Massachusetts: Harvard University Press, 1995.

Ryder, C. and Kearney, V. *Drumcree the Orange Orders Last Stand*. London: Methuen Publishing Ltd, 2001.

Stewart, A. T. Q. *The narrow ground: aspects of Ulster, 1609-1969*. Belfast: The Blackstaff Press Ltd, 1997.

CHAPTER FOUR

LEADERSHIP
IN THE AIR

THE ART OF LEADERSHIP IN THE AIR

Group Captain John Jupp

The Army would say that we in the RAF set ourselves a considerable leadership challenge. The Air Marshal's place is not in the fighting but well behind the lines.[1] He directs air operations from the Command Air Operations Centre (CAOC). We then compress several layers of command within the CAOC and expect our squadron commanders to fight in the very thick of the battle, unlike their Army Lieutenant Colonel counterparts who are a discrete distance from it, able to direct all their troops. I want to address not why this is the case but how it is that aircrew do lead in the air. I suggest that it is the deep and enduring trust both up and down the leadership chain, which allows leaders in the air to give away their power to vastly increase the effectiveness of the team. This success, bred from professionalism, then feeds right back into the trust which is fundamental to making it all work. In 1912 one CJ Burke wrote a list of 29 maxims for flying. Some quite obviously included his thoughts about leadership in the air, my favourite being:

> *"When training pilots, no machine should go without knowing what it is to do, do it and it alone, then land."*

The same could be said of operational missions. Burke clearly thought though, that the machine had a much better idea of what was about to happen when a student pilot took to the air than the pilot had himself. He may have been right; some might think he still is! The reality though, is that machines do not lead, the people in them do that; leadership is fundamentally an activity dealing with people. Even Unmanned Air Vehicles need human activity behind them to get airborne and do their task.

First let us look at the period at the beginning of military aviation to which CJ Burke, the commander of II(AC) Squadron, belonged. It was the first test of the new way of fighting wars, the First World War. Consider Captain Albert Ball. It has been said of him that he was no-one's pupil: at the time he joined the RFC past experience in air fighting was so small as to afford no guidance; yet, although by no means a finished pilot, this youth worked out a system, which it is no exaggeration to say, made him the terror of the airmen exposed to him.[2] Ball though, was a loner. From the first, he wanted to fly single-seat fighters but was posted to an Army Cooperation Squadron. Luckily for him, 2 single-seat fighters were then allocated to the squadrons and he was allowed to use them most of the time. He quickly showed this to be his forte. It was also said of him that he was always thinking out the tactics of fighting in the air and was never happy till he had tried out his theories in practice. Air Marshal Sir J F A Higgins, at one time his commanding officer, said that:

> *"the encouragement given to the whole Force by Ball's startling series of successes cannot, in my opinion, be overestimated [3]."*

Air Marshal Higgins was writing about the poor morale of the Royal Flying Corps at the beginning of the War, when British losses in the air considerably exceeded those of the Germans. Ball's example clearly played a leadership role in all that the RFC achieved at that time. Inspiring trust in the pilots that they could win, he was showing the way. Cecil Lewis, a fighter pilot of the time, recounts the fear that could hold the pilots:

> *"You sat down to dinner faced by the empty chairs of the men you had laughed and joked with at lunch. They were gone. The next day new men would laugh and joke from those chairs. Some might be lucky and stick it for a bit, some chairs would be empty again very soon [4]."*

He also goes on to describe some of the flying antics that experienced pilots, that is those who survived the enemy, got up to relieve the strain. The thrill of just not killing yourself, of having some semblance of control over the event, contrasted pleasantly against being shot down by the aircraft you did not see, the anti-aircraft fire or just passing artillery shells or random rifle fire from either side. Lewis's own trick was to fly a turn inside the crater on the Messines ridge (created by the explosion of the huge mine used to take the ridge by the British) below the level of the rim. In this atmosphere the example of Ball and his great success in trying to level the odds is clear. Lewis says: *"He never boasted or criticised, but his example was tremendous[3]."* Pilots trusted him and what he did.

    Though Ball was evidently showing the way, it could be said that he did not actually lead in the air. He was a loner, so much so that he chafed at the restraint imposed upon him by the presence of a passenger[2] – his word for the observer in the back of the 2-seat aircraft he occasionally had to fly. When he flew in the single-seaters he most often flew as a singleton. His tactics were not subtle; he would single out the one he was going to shoot down and attack headlong.[4] He did not look for tactical advantage but went straight in, surprise and ferocity seeming to carry him through. He often came back with his machine shot to pieces. One account stated that onlookers were surprised to see him come in for an awkward, floating landing – he was not a superb pilot but safe and accurate. It turned out that his controls had been completely shot away and he had landed on the trim. His engine had been shot up as well and he was covered in oil. Nevertheless, so angry was he at being shot up in this way that he wiped the oil off his face and took out his second aircraft, a Nieuport, and within 2 hours was back with yet another Hun to his credit.[4] A dedicated air fighter and fearless man, and a huge example to all in the RFC at the time, Ball's professionalism and success inspired the trust in other pilots that is necessary for leadership to work. He did, perhaps, do more than any other man to turn around the technical superiority the Germans had at that time of the war. If he had survived though, it is not clear whether he would have made a good leader in the air in the more traditional sense of being at the head of a formation, but he was not called upon to do that.

Ball's Squadron Commander, a Major Bloomfield, led his squadron in other ways. He did have enormous drive and determination attending to every detail, *"activity and organisation personified"*, as Cecil Lewis puts it.[3] He chose the best pilots to ensure that his squadron was a success – headed by Captain Ball, and did all in his power to raise morale – acquiring musicians to make a squadron band from wherever he could find them. He even had all his pilots out for a run before breakfast, kept them busy all day (when they were not flying) and turned them loose on the town at night. Leading in the air does not seem to have been Bloomfield's thing though; that was left to others, particularly Albert Ball. Bloomfield was giving away his power to those who could make best use of it to enhance the combat effectiveness of his squadron. It does indicate that what is done on the ground is important in establishing some elements of the trust necessary to lead in the air.

Manfred Von Richthofen on the other hand loved to be at the head of a formation, the bigger the better. He was cool and calculating and entirely ruthless in the air [he] sought an advantageous position and then struck unflinchingly and with precision. He never hesitated to break off a fight at the exact moment when he judged that the tactical advantage had passed to his opponents.[2] There were no radios or other means of communication at the time, just visual signals from the cockpit, which worked to greater or lesser effect. Pilots followed Richthofen because he had great success; he brought professionalism to his job. If pilots stayed with him they were likely to survive and shoot down some of their enemy, at least as a formation. Here it is easy to see the start of the hero tactics that the Luftwaffe used in the Battle of Britain some years later. For the British, Edward (Mick) Mannock had similar qualities to Richthofen and began formation leadership in the air. He too depended on reputation and the belief that if you stayed with him you were more likely to be successful and survive. Then, as now, success was a very definite factor in leadership in the air. Both Mannock and Richthofen inspired trust from their professionalism and success and allowed their followers to get on with the job.

By so doing, they led their squadrons in a more normal sense as a formation in the air.

If leadership is about people, as I asserted at the beginning, then communication is vital to enable it. Communication between aircraft was very limited indeed in this period, placing great emphasis on what leaders did on the ground. Even by the time of the Amiens campaign, which started the Allied offensive that eventually brought the First World War to a close, many elaborate forms of communication were being used from aircraft to ground and ground to aircraft and even aircraft to aircraft. Though primitive radios were available and trialled none was found to be useful. All the signals were physical ones, white patches on soldier's kit, flares and other visual signals, dropping of messages and so forth. It was only in the Second World War that voice communication was used in combat.

In the Second World War, large, multi-crew bombers were used for the first time and leadership in the air had a more human element within a tight-knit team in the air. Any examination of this subject cannot ignore Leonard Cheshire's contribution to leadership of bombers and bomber squadrons in the air. George Roberts, his navigator in the early days, said of him and the absolute faith he inspired:

> "I flew with other captains, but it was only with him that I felt I was doing my job with real confidence; tackling a trip not just as another one, but with a direct interest in its result and success. It was such a temptation to drop the bombs as quickly as you could and get the hell out of the area. We felt we owed it to him to do our best, knowing that he would do the same for us (apart from the dreadful thought of those eyebrows meeting in a frown). With others, I felt it was a question of 'will we get back?', not the right spirit I agree [5]."

Why did he inspire such faith? His rear gunner Richard Rivas:

> "I began to feel rather lonely and cut off from the others, and wondered what was happening at the other end of the aeroplane ... Almost as if he had been reading my thoughts Leonard said ... 'How are you Revs?' ... Those four words bucked me up no end. I felt again that I was not the only person in the aeroplane, and once more felt part of the crew [3]."

The first of these extracts shows the effect of good leadership on output. Cheshire's leadership of his crew in the air was inspiring enough for them to put aside real concerns about their own safety and work to the benefit of the team and the task. To improve their output for the benefit of the cause, not just to survive. But success and survival were bound together where Cheshire was concerned, as his efforts to get a crippled bomber back showed. During this period Cheshire's Whitley was hit on his bombing run up to Cologne. The shell set fire to a flare in the aircraft, blowing out a hole over 3 metres long in the fuselage, another had gone through the front turret. Although Cheshire apparently lost his composure for a while, he still dropped his bombs, got the crew to put the fire out and decided that he would fly home despite losing most of the maps in the gale blowing through the aircraft and wondering how long before the aircraft might fall apart. He not only got back to England but also to the right airfield! His coolness under pressure and his **genuine** concern for his crew were evident to them all – he had called his rear gunner, Rivas, forward during the crisis to ensure he was not trapped in the rear turret. Clearly luck also played a part in his recovery to England in that night fighters and further flak did not interrupt them, but then, as Virgil said, *"fortune favours the bold."*

The example that Cheshire set leading his crew, and later as the Commanding Officer of 76 Squadron, was an enormous inspiration to all his men. He never asked any crew to do what he would not himself do. Yet he was not a brilliant flyer like Micky Martin of 617 Squadron, rather, similar to Albert Ball, he was accurate and safe with a determination to master his task. To be familiar with his machine so that he could give his whole attention to the bombing or the enemy rather than having to give his attention to staying in the air. Also like Ball, he was known for studying the techniques of bombing with intense perception and intelligence. The 76 Squadron joke being that as soon as Cheshire walked into the bar, you could see him starting to work out how much explosive it would need to knock it down.[6] This knowledge, professionalism, determination and success were blended in Cheshire to an extraordinary degree with an empathy for people. He understood what it was that they wanted, how to approach them and get them to believe in him. For example:

> *"A young wireless operator, who had arrived at Linton the previous day, was climbing into the truck for dispersals when he felt Cheshire's arm round his shoulder. "Good luck, Wilson." All the way to the aircraft, the W/Op pondered… "How the hell did the CO know my name?"*[5]

> Or: *""Hello Read." I did not know he knew my name. "Hear you had a few problems tonight … Would you like to come and have a chat about it?" My first meeting with the nicest and most considerate squadron commander I ever met. It mattered not one iota that I was not in his squadron or his responsibility. I needed help and advice and he was ready to give it."*[3]

These are the stories that those who served under Cheshire remember and are clearly the things that inspired them at the time to perform for him in the air. They faced huge odds and challenges to their lives, yet they did not just plough on in form only, under Cheshire they really tried to do their best to achieve the optimum results. The blend of success, professionalism, intelligent approach to the problems of the task and what we would now call an emotionally intelligent approach to his people achieved wonders for Cheshire, and it is not just the sympathy he exuded, remember George Roberts fear of his frown.

What is also very clear from this brief study of Cheshire is that his leadership in the air depended to a very great extent on what he did on the ground. The trust and understanding that he built up by his efforts for his personnel on the ground was paid back to him in the loyalty and effort they gave back in the air. When things happened in the air, then as now, they happened quickly. Little time was available for consultation or eliciting views, decisions had to be made and acted upon, the trust built up on the ground and his understanding of the individuals being vital to making the team work in the air. The contrast with Cheshire's successor at 76 Squadron is stark. A substantial number of Lack of Moral Fibre cases arose after his departure and the 'Early Return' rate went up dramatically. So much so that Sir Arthur Harris felt it incumbent upon him to make an almost unprecedented visit to the Squadron 6 months after Cheshire's departure to remind the crews in the most forceful terms of their duty.[6] Cheshire's successor was not experienced in Europe, having flown out of Aden for the first part of his war. He was dogged by poor luck, having engine failures and leaks and, on one occasion, flew a reciprocal course after take off towards the Atlantic by mistake – a heinous error. When he discovered it, he had insufficient fuel to complete the mission. The crews made no allowances; they were neither sufficiently afraid of his anger nor interested in his good opinion to complete an operation if they felt disinclined to do so. Nor does Harris' visit to the Squadron seem to have had much effect; it took a new CO with some drastic measures and much greater example in the air to turn the squadron around.

Interestingly, Cheshire was himself not well liked when he joined 617 Squadron some time later. Partly because of the bond that had built up amongst the 617 crews as they worked towards and then flew on the Dams Raid and partly because of the inspiration that Gibson had given them in forming the Squadron. However, Cheshire was also not trusted because of the book he had written on life in Bomber Command, *Bomber Pilot*. The book had given a rather over glamorised, syrupy, picture of the job that most in the business had not taken well to. This is an interesting side of Cheshire; he was no stranger to self-publicity. After he got his first medal, there is a story of him and his crew going into a club, sitting at a table when the singer announced over the sound system that all present should feel privileged as Leonard Cheshire DSO was with them. Cheshire rose reluctantly to his feet as the lights were turned on him and his crewmember next to him asked who had let them know. Cheshire replied in a side whisper, *"I did, you fool."*[5] This sort of thing was not to the taste of the hard nuts on 617, but Cheshire's example in the air, his dedication to the task, knowledge of the technology that enabled 617's achievements, his all round professionalism coupled with his emotionally intelligent approach to his people won them over. One pilot remarked as he watched Cheshire fly in at low level in a Mosquito to mark the e-boat pens at Brest that he was damned glad it was not him, because of the ferocity of the ground fire. But he followed him in a few minutes later; such was the trust that Cheshire inspired. But Cheshire also trusted his men, empowering them to get on with the job – he was there while he could be in his Mosquito, but the Lancasters continued the job long after he had gone.

What of smaller aircraft and their more remote forms of leadership in the air? In the Battle of Britain, the pilots were on their own. They had radio and could talk to each other but there was no physical contact in the air as there could be in a bomber. As over half of the communication between people is not by voice but by body language, much of the usual communication between people is not available. There are no stories of how a leader really was in the air, only how he seemed on the radio. There are stories of efforts on the radio to get wounded men to bail out of crippled aircraft, unsuccessfully, and so having to watch as a fellow pilot flew into the ground.[7] Some would say that once the fighting was joined, the pilots fought alone. Sometimes this was true, but it was not the intention or necessarily the outcome all, or even most, of the time. Both sides had tactics to concentrate firepower. At the beginning of the Battle the German tactics were superior to ours with more flexible formations and roving briefs for the fighters. However, perhaps harking back to the Von Richthofen days, the idea was for the lesser pilots to follow the 'ace' and protect him while he collected more kills.[3] The RAF concentrated, by and large, with enabling all pilots to get kills. Leaders of squadrons, such as 'Sailor' Malan, constantly looked for ways to improve tactics and help his pilots. Whether one regards his methods as misguided or not, Bader was doing the same with the 'Big Wing'. Malan eventually produced his guidelines for fighter pilots – 'Ten rules of Air Fighting'. Equally, his success in the air, his calculated use of the elements to gain tactical advantage whenever time permitted and his personal bravery set the example that others could follow. The theme emerges again that the trust built up on the ground, the empathy for people and the success and example in the air are necessary for leadership. Empathy is not all 'cuddly stuff', I always remember coming across a painting in an Army mess entitled "Wellington Comforteth his Troops". It was of a man strapped to a gun wheel being flogged in front of the whole army.

The counter point is also interesting here. Some stories of opinion of leaders of the time, those that did not pull their weight on the ground and who were not trusted in the air, are fascinating but quite unprintable they are so libellous! Less controversial are the ones of squadron commanders who were not so capable in the air, did not understand the business and led attacks from a position of tactical disadvantage. They were followed only so far as personal survival allowed, at least by those who understood the dangers. The results were all too often terminal. Clearly not as effective as the strong, professionally skilled leadership of the likes of Malan. The theme is strengthened, then; deep, perceptive and adaptable understanding of the environment in which you work that breeds the success needed to set the example in the air coupled with an understanding of the people and the gaining of their trust, and trusting them, is how leadership in the air was done. The hard work on the ground enables not only the quick decision making necessary because of the time compression of the air environment, but also the strong followership necessary for success.

Does this remain true today? Certainly the speeds of modern flight are faster than those of the 1940s. The time pressures that aircrew work under have not lessened at all. In the air, the most ubiquitous form of communication is the radio. Granted the quality of transmission is rather better than the 1940s (mostly!) but aircrew are denied any communication with body language in the fighter and bomber world, and body language is known to comprise over half of normal communication. There are no-longer big bombers but there are many large aircraft types that the RAF operates, including multi-crew helicopters. To take the E-3D Sentry as an example, the crew is made up of smaller teams all reporting ultimately to the captain who shares power with the tactical director who runs the 'fighting' part of the aircraft. This hierarchy is one of specialist skill, not one of rank. The tactical director may well be out ranked by anyone else on the crew, or indeed most of them, but he still holds the power acknowledged by all. The same may be true within the smaller teams. In the air, any member of the crew will hold 'pole position' if it is their expertise that is needed to solve the issue that has arisen. The higher up the hierarchy of skill the more they know they have to listen to the expert of the moment. Crew Resource Management can be seen to be working very well. Indeed, the tactical director gains power by giving it away. Having set the intent, or strategy, or mission goals, the overall effectiveness of the platform is enhanced by the **lack** of control, the degree of freedom, that the tactical director and the aircraft captain allow the teams. This unleashes the skills of the team rather than constraining them. This is what Mission Command is supposed to be.

The degree of freedom allowed is, clearly, governed by the degree of trust that the directors have in their team members. Trust that can only be generated by their knowledge of those people's skills, strengths and weaknesses. Baselines are set by the common standards of passing courses or being appointed to higher positions within the hierarchy of skills, but enhanced performance is gained by personal knowledge of the people involved, regardless of rank.

This effect can also be observed within the smaller aircraft fleets, most particularly within the combined air operation scenario (COMAO). Our training system is set up so that the most able can lead, not those of the highest rank. Within formations control can be passed to those who have the most knowledge even if they do not have the greatest skill; indeed, if the overall leader of a formation does not hand over this power, the effectiveness and even survival of the formation can be very badly affected. In the COMAO, a fleet of possibly 60 or more aircraft set out in a coordinated fashion to create effects in the battle space. Each aircraft type and each formation will have their own specific goals, the whole COMAO relying on each other to achieve an enhanced effect. Without the reliance on others, the trust in them to do their part in a professional way, the COMAO will be less effective; at its extreme, will not work. The more power those who control the COMAO can give away the more effective it can be. How is it that this trust is generated to allow this giving up of power? Over the years the collective training events undertaken, such as Tactical Leadership Training and the Combined Qualified Weapons Instructor courses, where every type briefs together, flies together and debriefs together, have allowed the understanding of skill and professionalism of each aircraft type by the others. Again, it is what happens on the ground, the brief and the de-brief, that is vital to building up the trust which is so necessary for the COMAO to work. Some of the individuals also become, by reputation, almost trusted agents within one force for the personnel of other forces. Those forces whose talk is louder than their actions, and vice versa, become known and accounted for. The same effect can be seen between nations in coalitions. It is what has been happening between the USAF and the RAF over the years of exercises such as Red Flag and in the operations over Iraq since the early 90s.

This then is the essence of leadership in the air. Trust, deep and enduring, allows leaders to give away their power just as fast and as greatly as they can. Not abrogating their responsibility, but enhancing the effectiveness of the formation or aircraft. The trust is built up from the training over the years and the subsequent knowledge of individual's expertise, strengths and weaknesses. Also by the professionalism in general of those who fly other types. This disaggregated leadership, the empowering of those who can seize the moment, greatly enhances the effect of the aircraft, formation or COMAO. Proper collective training is vital to engender this spirit. However expensive and difficult the training may be it must be done as, to use Trenchard's words, *"...it makes just this difference, that between victory or failure."* To give away power is not new, Nelson knew this and it made him the world's greatest naval captain:

> *"Driven by Nelson's simple ideas, unleashed by his transfer of responsibility to individuals,[the Battle of the Nile] was a brilliant combination of individual talent and team effort."*[8]

Hugh Dowding and Keith Park did it just as well to achieve the RAF's greatest victory, the Battle of Britain.[9] All the people I have talked about have been very different, but they have been working to similar ends to provide excellent leadership. In summary, individuals can make a significant difference but these individuals can be significantly different.

Endnotes

1. *Leadership*, Air Vice-Marshal J R Walker. Air Clues, October 1987.
2. *Captain Albert Ball, A Historical Record*, R H Kiernan, from the foreword by Air Marshal Sir J F A Higgins, Penguin Books 1940.
3. Ibid.
4. *Sagittarius Rising*, Cecil Lewis, Peter Davis, London 1936.
5. *The Biography of Leonard Cheshire VC*, OM, Richard Morris. Penguin Books 2000.
6. *Bomber Command*, Sir Max Hastings. Penguin books 1979.
7. *The Most Dangerous Enemy – A History of the Battle of Britain*, Stephen Bungay. Arum Press, 2000.
8. *Nelson and Mission Command*, Edgar Vincent, 2004.
9. *Command or Control, Leadership in the Battle of Britain*, Stephen Bungay.

LEADERSHIP FROM TODAY'S COCKPIT

Squadron Leader Harvey Smyth

Aircrews operating in today's cockpits are subjected to a dynamic, technologically demanding and physically challenging environment from which they must lead whilst often making decisions, the outcome of which could have strategic effect. The RAF's increasing role in expeditionary operations has allowed more aircrew to experience more operations around the globe on a more regular basis. It is not uncommon for first tourist aircrew to have experienced several different operational environments. Moreover, leadership from the cockpit has evolved over the last 10 to 15 years, moving from the more ordered and structured approach of Combined Air Operations (COMAO) to dynamic scenarios such as those experienced whilst conducting Close Air Support (CAS) or Time Sensitive Targeting. Additionally, continual advances in technology, such as datalink and digital communications, have allowed the battlespace to effectively operate in real time, where decisions are being made at the 'coal face' of the battle in order to reduce timescales and allow us to remain well inside the adversary's OODA loop (Observe, Orientate, Decide, Act). This paper will begin by looking at the most recent thinking with regards to the theoretical attributes required of a good of a leader, as detailed by the RAF Leadership Centre. It will then move on to discuss how leadership from the fast jet cockpit has evolved over the last 15 years before finally investigating how advances in technology have affected cockpit leadership.

The Theory

The most recent leadership attributes detailed by the RAF Leadership Centre are: warfighter, courageous, emotionally intelligent, flexible, willing to take risks, mentally agile, physically robust, able to handle ambiguity, politically and globally astute, technologically competent and able to lead tomorrow's recruit. This list of qualities can be placed under one heading that encapsulates the cockpit leader of today: a flexible, modern-day decision maker. Additionally, a good cockpit leader must be an effective communicator; this skill will be looked at in more detail later. So, according to the most recent theory, today's cockpit leader must be flexible in thought and deed, must know when to take a risk (and perhaps more importantly know the difference between a calculated risk and a gamble), must be worldly wise and finally must be physically and mentally able to cope with modern technology (possessing the ability to operate a 9G capable aircraft/weapons platform whilst deciphering a complicated coded data link message). These qualities effectively describe every front line cockpit leader who has participated in recent operations such as those seen in Iraq and Afghanistan. Executing Time Sensitive Targeting or conducting 'danger close' CAS, where weapons are employed within one kilometre from friendly troops who are in close contact with the enemy, epitomize Clauswitz's 'fog of war'. Today's cockpit leaders must have the flexibility of thought and robustness of character described above to succeed in today's ever-changing operational environment.

The Evolution of Cockpit Leadership

Demands on the cockpit leader have evolved dramatically over the last 15 years. During the Cold War, every fledgling airman aspired to ably lead a COMAO mission into 'badlands'. Acting as the Mission Commander of 60 or 70 aircraft, all of varying capability, was considered the most demanding job a cockpit leader could conduct, especially if sat in a single seat fighter. The ultimate training environment was at Nellis Air Force Base whilst supporting Exercise RED FLAG. Leaders would gather their team, brainstorm, plan and face-to-face brief COMAO missions against a known enemy and static target set. A leader who could produce a credible performance in this role was considered 'at the top his game'. These were the days when operations were of a more pre-planned nature, the majority of the target sets were identified well in advance and assets were allocated according to best capability against specific Desired Mean Points of Impact on the Air Tasking Order.

Operation GRANBY in 1991 was perhaps the last time the RAF experienced true COMAO business. We now find ourselves in a more dynamic world, with the evolution of digital technology allowing the battlespace to be more fluid and less pre-planned. Operation ALLIED FORCE in 1999 was a turning point for cockpit leadership. Pre-planned COMAOs still occurred, attacking static targets such as bridges and airfields, but there were equally as many non-planned targets serviced through the combined use of airborne Forward Air Controllers and CAS aircraft. Aircrews were forced to make targeting decisions in the cockpit instead of in a planning room, a concept that was alien to many. Additionally, many formations were dislocated from one another, positioned mainly at a variety of airfields throughout Italy. The historical gathering of like minds around a planning table was non existent. Aircrews got airborne with a map of their intended area vice a specific target plan and attacks, including the decisions associated with them, would be completed in real time, overhead the target area; a much different environment to that of an air-conditioned planning room, especially if at night. Whilst ALLIED FORCE was limited in its jointery, since there were very few friendly ground troops to integrate with or deconflict from, it was a step in the direction towards the time sensitive targeting and dynamic cockpit leadership experienced during Operation TELIC in 2003.

During Op TELIC, those involved with the Counter Scud Campaign experienced one of the best examples of the evolution of cockpit leadership. Their mission was to operate jointly with a land element (consisting mainly of coalition Special Forces) to deny the Iraqi regime the ability to launch Scud missiles from the Western Desert. The Air Tasking Order simply tasked aircrew for 'Non-Traditional Information, Surveillance and Reconnaissance missions, or what became more commonly known to those involved, Scud Hunting. Extensive use of air-to-air refuelling assets allowed a standard sortie to last up to 9 hours. Minimal pre-planning or decision pre-emption could be achieved since the location of the target set was unknown. Cockpit leaders would react to events as they happened in real time: self-assessment from the cockpit determining positive identification of potential targets, in-cockpit application of the laws of armed conflict, evaluation of collateral damage and continuous self-assessment of Rules of Engagement were the entire norm. All these decisions happened in the cockpit (sometimes at night) whilst integrating with ground manoeuvring Special Forces, deconflicting from organic fires such as mortars or artillery and all the while avoiding the threat. Op TELIC proved that cockpit leaders are now operating in a world where reducing the kill chain, or sensor to shooter time, could have strategic effect. To do this they were making more and more decisions in-cockpit, sometimes with a degree of calculated risk because of the ambiguity of the fog of war; decisions that in previous years, may have been made in a Combined Air Operations Centre or some C2 building located away from the controlled chaos of the battle space.

Current ops in the Middle East are very different to the 'good old days' where you could get around a table with your team, plan in advance, pre-empt difficult decisions and lead from the front by injecting enthusiasm and personality. However, the task for cockpit leaders has not fundamentally changed, even though we have progressed to a more dynamic tactical environment. The main difference is that we now ask our aviators to be able to start the leadership process from the cockpit, as opposed to in a planning room. This paper suggests that today's cockpit leader still needs to be able to lead COMAOs. However, unlike 15 years ago, where this would have been considered the pinnacle of ability, this has now become the baseline from where the modern tactical cockpit leader must build his leadership abilities.

Effect of Technology on Cockpit Leadership

Arguably, the first phrase every RAF Officer learns during initial training is 'flexibility is the key to air power'. This phrase holds as true today as ever. Advances in technology, especially in the area of digital equipment, have allowed us to take flexibility to a completely new level. Exploitation of this newfound flexibility is essential in order to get inside our adversary's OODA loop – a loop that has tightened considerably since the increase of asymmetric threats such as suicide bombers and fundamentalist terrorists. Phrases such as time sensitive targeting, dynamic targets, emerging targets, reduced sensor to shooter times and completing the kill chain have all become common place on the shop floor of front line squadrons.

However, for the modern cockpit leader to excel, a final essential leadership attribute must be mastered: communication. Not only must a leader be able to communicate in all the 'normal' ways such as voice, enthusiasm, persuasion and personality but the skills of communicating with information technology (IT) are also a necessity. Communication no longer stops at the spoken word. It has transcended into the art of getting your leadership point across via IT, be it on e-mail, as part of a data linked message or during a video tele-conference. Moreover, with the advent of networked enabled capability (NEC), cockpit leaders are now able to communicate laterally and vertically throughout the battle space. Therefore, they must also be au fait with cross component and cross coalition terminology. Cockpit leaders must be able to 'talk the talk' of the common soldier operating on the ground, communicate with their controlling authority about Law Of Armed Conflict or Rules Of Engagement issues, understand a coalition ally whilst appreciating cultural differences and then know and understand the correct 'lines to take' when confronted by the media. Every modern day cockpit leader must be an effective communicator in all these areas and as technology advances apace, so too must the leader's communication skills.

Additionally, advances in technology have forced cockpit leaders to do in the cockpit what they used to do around a planning table with their whole team. Cockpit leaders seldom get the chance anymore to lead a formation or package in the old COMAO style, where there is an opportunity to impress upon the team the most basic of leadership skills: personality, enthusiasm, persuasion or 'the human element'. Field Marshal Slim, undeniably a great military leader, had this to say about leadership:

> "...leadership is that combination of example, persuasion and compulsion that makes men do what they want to do; in effect it is the extension of personality. Leadership is the most personal thing in the world, for the simplest reason that leadership is just plain you..."

The basis of this statement concentrates on the human element of leadership, or *transformational* leadership. The ability to influence people to do things they may otherwise not want to do, by use of personality, including the most basic form of communication, voice. This type of human element approach, or transformational style, is what we experience when a mission commander rallies his team to produce a solid COMAO plan and then face-to-face briefs everyone on the 'whys and wherefores' of their upcoming mission; firing up the team and generating the 'one team one fight' spirit. The power of voice and physical presence as communication tools is incredible. Emotion can be conveyed in a way that technology is yet to replicate. Receiving a radio message in the cockpit tells the aircrew much more than just the message itself. Emotion can be sensed easily and establishment of trust (or mistrust) can be achieved simply through the emotional nature of the message (confident, panicked, breathless, under fire?). Technology denies us this emotional element. As technology develops, we lose some of the personal element of cockpit leadership. You cannot tell from a data linked message the originator's emotional status. In an NEC cockpit, the leader simply receives commands; clinical, precise and via technology. These commands are obeyed, not because the originator is considered a great leader but simply because military people follow orders. This transactional form of leadership is becoming more the norm in the data linked / NEC cockpit environment.

To that end, as technology develops, it is extremely important for today's cockpit leaders to be able to combine transformational and transactional leadership styles and to appreciate when and how to exploit these differing skills. For transactional leadership to work, cross component and cross coalition *trust* must be established. This trust is formed during realistic, collective training. Trust must be established before entering operations, if transactional styles of leadership, in the form of data linked messages to and from cockpits, are to be successful.

Additionally, it is no longer good enough to be an expert in solely your field of expertise. Cockpit leaders must have a solid working knowledge of all those components in the battle space with whom they may be linked and have influence upon. Breadth and depth of knowledge, bolstered with development of trust with *all* players on the network, will allow NEC leaders to flourish. Nevertheless, the art of transformational leadership is not dead. In fact, it is very much alive and as important as ever. Cockpit leaders must remain adept at the human element of leadership because it is this style that will allow essential trust to develop.

Trust established in training, through joint and combined exercises such as those experienced at Ex RED FLAG, is essential if we are to have successful transactional leadership from the NEC cockpit during operations. As we enter the NEC world, our cockpit leaders must be proficient at both transformational and transactional leadership. The former mainly for leading in the ground environment; during planning, briefing and training to enable a solid establishment of trust to form with all those you may eventually have transactional exchanges with via the network when airborne.

Summary

Cockpit leaders today no longer find themselves solely in the pre-planned world of static target sets and COMAO plans. Operational environments have become more dynamic and unpredictable. To that end, cockpit leadership has evolved to a point where leading a COMAO is now the base line standard of aircrew capability as opposed to the pinnacle.

In today's dynamic world of Time Sensitive Targeting and decreased sensor to shooter times, cockpit leaders must become 'modern day decision makers' – willing and able to take calculated risks (not gambles) whilst remaining flexible and ready for ambiguity. Moreover, today's cockpit leader must be a communicator, possessing the ability to communicate in a common language across the components and the coalition. Advances in technology, especially in the areas of digital equipment and datalink, allow the cockpit leader to apply influence across the battle space. Therefore, aircrew must have a greater breadth and depth of professional knowledge in order to appreciate the effects of their leadership decisions upon others. This can be achieved by increased exposure through realistic joint and combined training. By conducting regular and realistic training an engrained trust will be established which will allow cockpit leaders to succeed in transactional leadership as well as the more traditional transformational leadership methods. Today's aircrew must be skilled at both these methods of cockpit leadership if they are to be successful in the fast moving battlespace we now experience.

Finally, it is important to end with the fact that our cockpit leaders are rising to these new challenges on a daily basis. Current expeditionary operations, no matter where located, continue to present our aircrew with complex situations, the majority of which are dealt with in the cockpit. As long as our training continues to evolve realistically with the changing face of dynamic operations, we will continue to maintain credible and capable leaders in our cockpits.

© Sebastian Cox 2005

CHAPTER FIVE

HISTORICAL ADDRESS

SWORDS INTO PLOWSHARES? A HISTORICAL PERSPECTIVE ON AIR FORCE LEADERSHIP IN THE AFTERMATH OF THE FIRST AND SECOND WORLD WARS

Sebastian Cox

The leadership of the Royal Air Force in the immediate aftermath of both the First and Second World Wars faced difficult and challenging problems which are certainly not without resonance in our own era. The respective Chiefs of the Air Staff (CAS), in 1918 initially Sir Frederick Sykes, rapidly replaced by Sir Hugh Trenchard, and in 1945 Sir Arthur Tedder, found themselves leading a military service into a period of peace after a major and debilitating war which had strained the resources of the nation to breaking point. They were tasked with making very large scale reductions in squadron strength and manpower whilst at the same time maintaining sufficient military effectiveness to ensure that the RAF could perform its basic military role. In both instances, however, they faced a deeper challenge.

In Sykes' and Trenchard's case this was the very fundamental one of attempting to ensure the RAF's continued independent existence beyond its first birthday on 1 April 1919, in the face of attempts to strangle the infant service on the part of his unremittingly hostile fellow chiefs. In addition there was a paramount need to establish and develop a wider and deeper understanding of the potential, indeed potentially revolutionary role of air power in war. At the time however, the situation was hardly propitious. The Government, led by the Treasury, understandably and quite rightly were pressing the urgent need for massive reductions in defence spending and wholesale demobilisation of manpower. This in turn made the RAF very vulnerable to suggestions from the other Services that large scale savings could be implemented by the simple expedient of abolishing a separate RAF and dividing its constituent parts between the Royal Navy and the Army. The RAF also needed to maintain the technical skill base that had been so painstakingly built up during the War and which rapid demobilisation now threatened, and to provide some long term assurance of the Service's future. This, it should be remembered, at a time when the shock and scale of the recent sacrifice were such that it was being spoken of as the War to end all Wars, a view which in and of itself made strategic planning difficult, as we shall see.

In Tedder's case, he too was faced with a situation in which Britain's severe economic difficulties necessitated wholesale reductions in frontline strength and manpower. Whilst the independence of the RAF was not per se directly threatened, and the large and increasingly unfriendly Soviet presence clearly represented a threat, the situation was greatly complicated by the recent appearance of atomic weapons and jet aircraft. This alone introduced great strategic uncertainty, not the least because the attitude of the only nuclear power, the United States, was also problematic, as the Congress's passing of the McMahon Act forbidding the sharing of nuclear information with her erstwhile ally and nuclear partner made clear. In addition, the introduction of jet aircraft effectively made much of the RAF's existing conventional force obsolete or obsolescent, even if it was accepted that nuclear weapons did not actually make them strategically irrelevant. If the country, and indeed Europe was to rely on a US nuclear umbrella – and don't forget that the McMahon Act had effectively sealed a US nuclear monopoly for some time to come, though the Soviets broke it more rapidly than anticipated – but if the UK was going to shelter under that umbrella what necessity was there at a time of severe economic difficulty for large conventional forces, including air forces? And what point was there in maintaining and indeed renewing such forces at great expense if nuclear weapons effectively made them redundant in a bipolar world.

In this paper we will look at how Sykes, Trenchard and Tedder faced these challenges, and the extent to which they were successful in leading their Service through these difficult times and establishing in each case the foundations for a strong post-war Air Force. I shall follow the story chronologically starting with Sykes and Trenchard after World War One and moving on to Tedder in 1945. The first point to make with regard to Frederick Sykes is that he faced one particular difficulty at the time of the Armistice in November 1918. Namely, it was in fact just that; an Armistice and not yet fully-fledged peace. In theory, the warring powers could decide that they were unable to reach agreement at the Versailles Peace Conference and start the war again. In practice this was never likely given the defeats Germany had suffered in the field and the occupation of large parts of her western territories, including cities such as Cologne by the Allies. It was nevertheless an unwelcome complication. Sykes, as CAS was responsible for three major strands of policy: providing expert advice to the Government on the aviation terms to be negotiated in the Peace Treaty, he also had to direct the demobilisation of the wartime RAF, and simultaneously retain a sufficiently effective force both to police the Armistice and to establish the long term prospects of a Service which was regarded by many as a novel and not entirely wise wartime experiment which could now safely be discarded.

Sykes, in concert with his fellow Air Council members, nevertheless produced a memorandum on the post-war functions of the Air Ministry and Royal Air Force. He produced a set of assumptions for future Air Force policy amongst which were that the peace would prove enduring and that the "suspended state of war" existing in the form of the Armistice would not relapse into conflict. That there would be no war between the major powers for twenty years, and that pressure for disarmament would grow and pressure for rearmament be largely absent except possibly in Japan. All of which were reasonable and reasonably accurate assumptions. From this Sykes proceeded to lay down the need to first establish the future strength and constitution of Air Force, because at the time all its officers were either on loan from the other services or holding only temporary commissions in the RAF, and of the NCOs and airmen only 1 per cent were enlisted for anything other than the war's duration. Furthermore, without a definite postwar establishment, demobilisation could not be properly conducted. There was also a need to settle the ownership of RAF aerodromes since many had been requisitioned under the Defence of the Realm Act and would need to be purchased or returned to private ownership, yet obviously without a settled frontline strength no such decisions could be made. Leaving aside civil aviation, which was also to come under the Air Ministry, Sykes therefore laid down that the RAF would need specialised units for naval and army co-operation together with what he referred to as an Air Fleet consisting of home air defence units to protect the UK, and a striking force, i.e. a force capable of independent air operations. In all, Sykes recommended a post-war RAF of 154 Squadrons of which 82 were to be full strength squadrons and 72 cadre squadrons. Subsequently, in January 1919 he reduced this requirement to 62 full strength squadrons and 30 cadre squadrons, the latter to form the basis of the UK training organisation. Yet, when placing this revised estimate before the Air Council, including his Secretary of State, one Winston Churchill, Sykes commented that this was only an interim scheme until the Peace Settlement was in place and *"He hoped that the consideration of the after the war scheme [in other words the settled peace time air force] would not be prejudiced by the fact that the reduced numbers were being asked for in the interim period"*.[1] In other words he was suggesting to his political master, who was attending his first Air Council meeting, that the 62 Squadrons were a minimum and that, implicitly, the peacetime RAF should be larger still. This at a time when the Treasury was demanding cuts in expenditure to a level 20 per cent less in real terms than the equivalent expenditure in 1914, when the Royal Flying Corps had mobilised four squadrons for war and had a total personnel strength of 2073.

    The traditional view is thus that the visionary Sykes unwisely failed to take due account of the prevailing political and economic circumstances in which he was operating and that this led Churchill to replace him with Trenchard. According to Trenchard's biographer, Churchill had been advised by the previous Secretary of State, Lord Weir, that he needed a CAS with the resilience and character to stand up a peacetime Air Force in the face of hostility, retrenchment and precipitate demobilization. Weir recommended Trenchard to Churchill with the words *"Trenchard's your best man for that. He can make do with little and won't have to be carried"*.² The implication being that Sykes would be extravagant. According to this view of RAF history the wily and more politically astute Trenchard is summoned to see the Secretary of State at the War Office at the end of the first week in February 1919 and is invited by Churchill to submit his outline scheme for an Air Ministry and RAF, which he duly does. Trenchard's estimate is so much more realistic than Sykes's that Churchill manoeuvres the latter sideways into the job of Controller of Civil Aviation and replaces him with Trenchard, thus ensuring that a politically astute officer, one able to cut the RAF's coat to suit its cloth, is in post for the difficult battles ahead.

There is only one problem with all this, namely that it doesn't actually fit the facts that we know. Firstly, we know Trenchard attended his first Air Council meeting on Thursday 13th February; we also know that he then became very ill with the particularly virulent influenza that killed millions of Europeans that year.³ As a result Trenchard appears to have been absent from Air Council meetings from February to mid-May, and it was exactly during this period that the Air Council met to consider and agree the Air Estimates to be put to the Treasury. These estimates were based on the RAF's strength falling to a peacetime establishment of 6000 officers, 53500 NCOs and airmen and a WRAF strength of 6500. Sykes' January 1919 scheme had postulated a 62 Squadron RAF with **fewer** officers, though slightly more men.⁴ Trenchard's memorandum of 5 February, written in response to Churchill's request, postulated an 82 Squadron RAF. On 17th February, before he fell ill, Trenchard had written to a fellow officer that he was working on a peacetime strength of **about** 50000.⁵ There was therefore little significant difference between Trenchard and Sykes. What is more the Air Council, meeting in February and March under Churchill, looked at squadron strengths ranging from 80, at the low end of the scale, 100 squadrons in the middle and on up to 133 at the high end. The Council, again remember with Churchill in the chair and no CAS present, agreed that, quote, *"bearing in mind the uncertainties as to the number of squadrons which will ultimately be required as a peace establishment"* and the relatively small cost differential between the 80 and 100 squadrons schemes [actually the later was 8 per cent more expensive for a 25 per cent greater size], they agreed on an establishment of 102 squadrons.⁶ Thus with Trenchard already CAS, though *hors de combat*, the Air Council under Churchill had plumped for an RAF bigger than that suggested by the man who had been moved sideways because his scheme was too ambitious. Life at the top can be strange at times!

So, if Trenchard did not enter office with a ready-made programme of greater modesty than his predecessor's, what are we to make of their relative leadership in the immediate post-war period? Was Sykes simply the victim of the undoubted animosity of Trenchard and since the latter remained CAS for the next ten years did he simply use his position to ensure that his rival's contribution was obscured or reduced in subsequent years, whilst carrying on his policy? The answer to these questions is a complex one and it shows that both men made major contributions to ensuring the survival of the RAF as a separate and effective military force whilst at the same time revealing that Trenchard was almost certainly better suited both to the vicious bureaucratic fight which ensued, and to providing inspirational leadership to the RAF in its early years.

Whilst Trenchard did not enter the lists as CAS with a radically different programme from Sykes, and certainly did not influence the Air Council to greater "realism" than his predecessor when he first arrived, he was nevertheless better equipped for fight ahead. The historians who criticise Sykes for his visionary but unrealistic programme are half right. His initial programmes were certainly unrealistic, one postulated an RAF of 350 squadrons, that is larger than its wartime peak, yet he modified them to such an extent that they were little different from Trenchard's own proposals. Sykes' problem however, was twofold; firstly, by the time he revised his plans he had already established himself in the eyes of his political masters as someone whose wilder ambitions would need reining in. Hence when Lord Weir praised Trenchard to Churchill as a man who would make do with little he was implicitly criticising Sykes, the man in post, as being the opposite. The second factor in the equation which convinced the powers that be, most importantly Churchill, that Sykes was not the right man, was Sykes' own character. Trenchard wrote of Sykes *"I fear none of the RFC thought much of this officer as he was too secretive and narrow-minded to the last degree."* Though hardly a disinterested witness, Trenchard was not alone in thinking this.

The most recent biographical study of Sykes by Eric Ash, a serving USAF officer incidentally, offers us a number of insights in this regard:

> *"...his true character did not reveal itself to those who suspected a devious nature. A short, thin man who stood erect but exhibited the effects of battle on his small frame and the strain of command on his face, Sykes was not physically impressive compared with Goliaths such as Trenchard....One fellow airman mentioned that Sykes had a first class brain, but a personality which strangely engendered mistrust in those with whom he served. Sykes was clever, but not witty; to him most military humour was of too low an intellectual level – not funny, just vulgar."*[7]

His lack of humour, indeed lack of the human touch with all but those very close to him, combined with a ferocious intellect to give the erroneous appearance of a scheming somewhat Machiavellian personality. He was also intensely hard-working, but the military of the day liked to pretend that hard work was somewhat infra-dig. His hard work would have been an advantage if combined with a less serious demeanour – work hard play hard would have made him friends, where work hard alone made him enemies.

Sykes, in essence, only had part of the make-up of a truly great leader. Whilst he had intellect, vision and foresight in abundance, he lacked the drive to carry through his ideas and, as Eric Ash points out *"the warmth to win affection from his peers and subordinates – he was too calculating to be an inspirational leader."*[8] His own private secretary believed that though Sykes could be heroic and inspiring to some, he was a dour and defiant intellectual to those who misunderstood him.[9] Not many dour and defiant intellectuals stand out in history as great leaders, with the possible exception of Karl Marx, and even he required the assistance of the undoubtedly inspirational firebrands Lenin and Trotsky before his intellectualising had much real impact.

So, leaving aside the fact that they led to Sykes' removal from office, would these disadvantageous traits in his character and personality have mattered in 1919 had he remained CAS? He had, after all warts and all, reached the top, so had he stayed, would he have achieved any less than Trenchard?

To answer that question we need to consider what Trenchard achieved and as importantly the way he achieved it. As we have seen, Trenchard owed his appointment in part to Churchill's perception, prompted by Weir, that he would make do with less and would not need to be carried. Both judgements were undoubtedly right. Trenchard had already proved, when in command of the so-called Independent Force of strategic bombers in 1918 that he could make much of very little, perhaps too much in the eyes of some critics. But, as we have seen, Sykes may not have been so very different in this regard. Where Trenchard differed from Sykes was in his capacity to inspire, and not just those in his immediate circle. That said, the irony is that Trenchard was to prove adept at exactly the sort of calculating, not to say scheming politicking that drew such criticism down on Sykes. There is much evidence to suggest that Trenchard was actually much more deserving of such epithets, but, and it is a big but, he combined it with an inspirational leadership style. What is more, most though not quite all his manoeuvres were aimed at the enemy, which in the post-war era were in descending order, the Navy, the Army, the Treasury, and lastly the French. Some might say not much change there then.

I cannot resist telling a well-known story to illustrate Trenchard's style: Whilst commanding the RFC in France Trenchard had approved the posting of a particularly aggressive and effective officer called Louis Strange back to the UK for a rest from operations. The postings system was, you will be surprised to learn, just as efficient then as it is now, and promptly posted Strange as a flight commander to 12 squadron, which, whilst it was in the UK at that time, was actually scheduled to depart for France and so, much to his delight, Strange rapidly found himself back at the hub of the RFC in France at St Omer. There the squadron was inspected by Trenchard who asked Strange what he was doing there and reminded him he was supposed to be in England. Trenchard turned to his faithful ADC Maurice Baring and told him to make a note that Strange was to go back to England. Strange waited events rather hoping that the matter would be forgotten. A few days later however, Trenchard was at the airfield once more and his eyes lighted on Strange who was preparing to fly a new fighter. Trenchard turned to Baring and said "I thought I told you Baring to remind me to send Strange home?". He then turned to Strange and boomed at him *"Go home, at once, Strange."* *"Yes Sir"* says Strange saluting smartly, but Trenchard knew his man and knew very well that Strange might still somehow contrive to ignore the order. So Trenchard repeated the order *"Go home, at once, Strange"* and, pointing at a nearby aircraft, added *"In that machine, NOW!"* Of course this was in the days before the engineers had thought up the Form 700. The machine was a dilapidated Maurice Farman, famous for having a top speed of 40 mph, and a stalling speed of 30 mph. In Strange's words *"All the same I could do nothing but salute again and take him at his word..."*.[10]

The story illustrates not only Trenchard's unique leadership style but also how, as commanding general he made it very much his business to know his squadrons and personnel. He made regular visits to all his squadrons. Now there is, of course, a difference between commanding in the frontline and fighting in Whitehall, but when he became CAS for the second time in 1919 Trenchard had a clear understanding that his principal problems were, firstly the preservation of a separate Air Force, and secondly retaining a cadre of experienced and effective personnel. Remember that he is now in charge of a Service which only has officers retained on wartime service none of whom yet hold permanent commissions in the Air Force, for the simple reason that there are no permanent commissions in the Force and that was for the simple reason that no-one is actually certain that the Air Force itself **is** certain to survive as a separate entity. Most of his men are also on wartime enlistments and will leave shortly if they are not offered some permanency and even then many will go. Self-evidently he needed to persuade the Government to grant commissions, which he did in August 1919, but with typical Trenchard foresight he also proposed and had adopted the idea of short service commissions, an innovation which the other two services regarded as ludicrous, but which both would subsequently adopt.

In addition Trenchard, as I have said, was no mean player in the Whitehall game. He bombarded his minister with memoranda on the new service. Specifically he began to challenge head on the suggestion that the RAF should once more be absorbed into the Army and the Navy. He pointed out that if the RAF was to be capable of conducting independent air operations and supporting the other services it would actually be more and not less economical to have a separate service. Using an analogy which captured Churchill's imagination he argued that if the only operations which were envisaged were the conveyance of munitions or the taking of photos directly on behalf of the other services then the air service would be mere chauffeurs and could be subsumed in the existing services, whereas if they were in addition to undertake air operations which were not only led but commanded and planned by airmen then clearly a separate and distinct entity was essential. It is interesting to note that Trenchard stated that he did not think there would be any necessity for the RAF to conduct such independent operations in Europe for at least twenty years – a rather prescient forecast in 1919. He also gave it as his opinion that the RAF should be made responsible for its own supply services and not, as some proposed, rely on one or other of the other services, as it had in fact for most of the First World War. Again in an uncanny forecast of the future he said he saw no difficulty if an entirely separate organisation was set up to supply ALL the three services as a whole but that he could not countenance the RAF being reliant on one or other of the existing services, predicting, not unreasonably, that such a scheme could not work.[11]

For most of the early months Trenchard was still beset by severe financial problems, not the least of which was that the original air estimates voted by Parliament in March 1919 essentially voted moneys to run down the RAF, but because the future of the service was not settled voted little or nothing for its continuing existence. Trenchard proposed to the Chancellor through Churchill that he be told of an interim ceiling within which he could spend essential money to maintain at least some existing framework until such time as the future of the service was definitely settled. In replying to Churchill the Chancellor accurately summed up the problem. *"We seem to be moving in a vicious circle. Trenchard wants to know what money he may spend: we want to know what forces he has thought necessary to maintain, and what is involved in individual items of proposed expenditure, and so we each put questions to the other to which neither can give an answer."*[12]

Matters came to a head in the autumn of 1919 when the Government, not before time from the increasingly hard pressed RAF's viewpoint, began to consider future peacetime expenditure. The result was the famous policy statement that no major European war should be assumed for the next ten years and no provision should be made for forces to undertake one. Trenchard correctly anticipated that it would hit the new service hard, and would increase inter-service rivalry, which in the circumstances of the time was not good news for the fledgling RAF.

Faced with severe financial retrenchment Trenchard made some ruthless decisions. He knew very well that the human dimension was the foundation of the service. He therefore resisted immediate Army and Navy pressure to permit the other services to train RAF officers. He later wrote

> *"I was continually being pressed by the high-ups that the army and navy should train my people to be "officers and gentlemen". I could then take them over for flying training in the squadrons and form the RAF that way. I could also use their medical, dental, engineering, clerical scientific and spiritual*

> *facilities. It would save untold money. After a little cogitation I came to the conclusion that if I formed squadrons, and built my own bases, schools and technical institutions as well, there would be a howl for more economies. Equally I knew that if I decided to have a few fighting squadrons and to use all the maintenance and other branches of the older services, I should be guilty of misusing a force that would grow more and more necessary for national defence on its own account. I therefore decided – and gradually convinced my Secretary of State that we ought to defy the other services and risk unpopularity by building foundations with nothing much else to show – but foundations that it would be hard to destroy. I wanted very few squadrons – just enough to gain experience and carry out domestic roles in our overseas territories."[13]*

At the end of November 1919 Trenchard presented his Secretary of State with an eight page memorandum in which he set out his ideas on the future organisation of the Air Force, a document which so impressed Churchill that he had it published in what became known as Trenchard's White Paper. It was an admirably concise vision of the future Air Force, and the human dimension formed its core. In it he stated, quite correctly I think, in a paragraph entitled, with typical Trenchardian forthrightness, EXTREME IMPORTANCE OF TRAINING, that:

> To make an Air Force worthy of the name, we must create an Air Force spirit, or rather foster this spirit which undoubtedly existed in a high degree during the war, by every means in our power. Suggestions have been made that we should rely on the older Services to train our cadets and Staff officers. To do so would be to make the creation of an Air Force spirit an impossibility.[14]

In terms of actual squadrons, Trenchard initially settled for just twenty four and a half squadrons. But within a short time he established Cranwell, the RAF staff College and the Apprentice School at Halton. In a sense the former two were essential but hardly innovative, but it is little realised today just how remarkable Halton was. When it had been established many children in this country did not continue their education much beyond fourteen – if they did then the local state education authorities could charge them, though the extent to which this happened varied. But, leaving aside the cost, on the other side of the equation many working class families regarded the additional income generated from sending boys to work at fourteen as very welcome.

By offering effectively free additional extended education to boys and one which gave them a valuable trade which could then lead both to settled employment in the RAF and afterwards, Trenchard instituted his own minor social revolution which tapped into a vast under-exploited human resource which was to prove of inestimable worth to the RAF. What is more, he offered the top three apprentices scholarships to the RAF College at Cranwell, thus further breaking down the social barriers to progress for talented individuals.

Most writing about Trenchard concentrates on his theories of air warfare, but in my view his greatest legacy was his understanding that the RAF needed strong human foundations, that these could only be built on firmly rooted training institutions, and that all else flowed from that. You have only to look at the imposing edifice of College Hall at Cranwell to see that Trenchard meant what he said and literally put the very little money he had into creating concrete institutional foundations for the Service. He correctly anticipated that the human product of these institutions, imbued with an Air Force spirit and ethos would provide the seedcorn on which squadron strength could be built up later. In that regard he subsequently outmanoeuvred his Army and Navy opposite numbers in the Whitehall jungle, not the least, it has to be said, by resorting to telling them one thing and subsequently doing another, something for which Sykes has gained an undeserved reputation – such are the rich ironies of history. I think it unlikely that Sykes, for all his undoubted vision regarding air power, would have proved either so adept at politics, or have had the broader vision and leadership skills to attend to the human side in quite the way that Trenchard did.

Trenchard was single-minded, focussed, determined, and shrewdly realistic and ruthless in determining what he could and could not do. Simultaneously, both by his actions, his words and his own character he inspired his subordinates throughout the Service and gave the lead to the RAF in establishing its traditions – traditions which served it well in the subsequent world-wide conflict a generation later.

Which brings us to 1946 and Sir Arthur, later Lord, Tedder. Tedder had already proved himself a successful joint and coalition commander, notably as Eisenhower's Deputy Supreme Commander during Operation Overlord. In many ways he was the antithesis of Trenchard: physically small in stature, undemonstrative not to say quiet (his most recent biographer titled his book "Quietly in Command"), intellectual (he was a Cambridge graduate who had published a serious historical study on the Royal Navy). He too was faced with downsizing an Air Force which at its peak strength in 1944 had numbered 1.2 million men and women. Its aircraft were largely obsolescent piston-engined types, and, as we have mentioned there was the additional complication of nuclear weapons. As with Trenchard, manpower was to prove a consistent bugbear to Tedder during his tenure as CAS. Although the demobilisation of personnel was handled very much better than it had been at the end of the First World War it was never going to be easy. One problem, tame perhaps rather than wicked, was that the RAF was heavily involved in the demobilisation of Army units in the Far East, flying large numbers home via well established transport routes. The RAF stations on the routes, however, had to be manned, and this unsurprisingly caused discontent amongst the RAF personnel who saw the flow or Army personnel heading homewards. This led to some strikes and discontent in 1946.[15] Nevertheless, by and large, demobilisation went smoothly, but it brought headaches in its wake as Tedder sought to maintain sufficient strength to man the frontline squadrons and the RAF's worldwide commitments. Tedder sought to make the service attractive to new recruits, building on its wartime achievements and reputation, he found increasingly difficult to do so. In 1948 Tedder warned that the question of manning was in danger of dictating the order of battle of the post war RAF. He went out on something of limb in a speech at Halton urging the necessity of further recruiting; well knowing that it would be reported in the press and would not be well received by his political masters.[16]

Tedder sought to ameliorate these problems by introducing several new officer branches, and a new trade structure. Tedder also presided over the issuing of new specifications for the new generation of jet aircraft, notably the V-bombers and the Canberra, which, although they did not enter service until after he had gone, were to provide the backbone of the RAF at the height of the Cold War. Like Trenchard before him Tedder both sought to maintain the human foundations of the service and give it an intellectual lead. He delivered a series of lectures, known as the Lees-Knowles lectures, at Cambridge in which he laid out his own vision of air power. Subsequently published as a booklet which was widely distributed within the RAF, Air Power in War, remains one of the most concise and sensible expositions on air power in joint warfare that has ever been written and I commend you to read it.[17] Tedder also ran a command exercise, Exercise Thunderbolt, whose express purpose was to examine the direction of the Second World War strategic air campaign.[18]

In practical terms Tedder also presided over one of air power's most notable triumphs in the Berlin Airlift, an entirely bloodless and therefore too little appreciated political victory with very far reaching consequences. He also maintained and fostered his strong wartime ties with the USAF, itself now an independent service from 1947. In the increasingly fraught political atmosphere of the early Cold War it was Tedder and his USAF opposite number Carl Spaatz who agreed that the UK should provide basing for USAF nuclear bombers in Europe. Remarkably Tedder seems to have undertaken most of the negotiating for this initiative entirely of his own accord, without really consulting the Government of the day. Equally remarkably he pulled it off without being fired. When he relinquished the post of CAS he was promptly despatched to Washington as Chairman of the UK's Joint Mission and also as the UK Representative on the Standing Group of the new North Atlantic Treaty Organisation.

If Tedder had one failing as CAS it was his inability to find a way to curb the excesses of his army opposite number, Bernard Law Montgomery, but in that, of course, he was not alone. Nevertheless, Tedder's gifts as a diplomat, even though they proved inadequate when dealing with Monty, did allow him to establish the close peacetime relationship with the USAF which has proved so mutually beneficial in the last fifty years. His quiet leadership skills resonated with those of Labour postwar Prime Minister Clement Attlee in much the same way that Trenchard's combative streak had found a ready echo in Winston Churchill. Though one doubts that Tedder really enjoyed his time as CAS, like his illustrious predecessor he too provided a remarkably effective leader in a problematic period for the RAF.

All three CAS's contributed in their very different ways to the development of their Service and the intellectual and physical foundations on which it rests today. Their differing approaches all had merit and all in turn merit further study – they all have something to teach us in today's straitened circumstances.

Endnotes

1. Air Historical Branch [hereafter AHB], Air Council, Minutes of the 73rd Meeting, 20 January 1919.
2. Andrew Boyle *Trenchard*, p.328.
3. AHB, Air Council, Minutes of 77th Meeting, 13 February 1919. Boyle, pp.333-5
4. The National Archive [hereafter TNA] AIR6/19. Air Council Précis 346, Memorandum, Demobilization and formation of Air Forces to co-operate with Grand Fleet and Armies of Occupation, 18 January 1919.
5. Boyle, p.333.
6. AHB Air Council Minutes of 79th and 80th Meetings, 24 February and 4 March 1919.
7. Eric Ash, Sir Frederick Sykes and the Air Revolution, p.202.
8. Ash, p.192.
9. Ash, p.201
10. Peter Hearn, *Flying Rebel – the story of Louis Strange*, pp.50-51.
11. Note by CAS 11 September 1919, quoted in Boyle pp.342-3. See also Trenchard's *Memorandum on the Status of the Royal Air Force*, 14 August 1919 in TNA AIR9/5.
12. Quoted in Boyle, pp.340-341. Original in Trenchard Papers, RAF Museum Hendon, MFC76/1/34.
13. Quoted in Boyle p.341.
14. AHB, *Command Paper 467.* "An outline of the Scheme for the Permanent Organisation of the Royal Air Force". 25 November 1919.
15. On this aspect see Sir David Lee *Eastward – a history of the Royal Air Force in the Far East 1945-1972,* pp.8-11.
16. Henry Probert, *High Commanders of the Royal Air Force,* p.39.

17. Lord Tedder, *Air Power in War,* Air Ministry Pamphlet 235, 1947.
18. AHB, Air Ministry *Exercise Thunderbolt,* 2 Vols, 1947.

CHAPTER SIX

OPERATIONAL LEADERSHIP

LEADERSHIP: FORCE DEVELOPMENT PROCESSES FOR THE COMMAND AND CONTROL OF AIRPOWER

Major General Stephen M. Goldfein

Thank you very much for the opportunity to be in the company of fellow warriors and for giving me the chance to discuss the ways in which we grow leaders to execute the command and control of air and space power. I bring the regards of our Chief of Staff, General Jumper, and the respect of all the airmen of our United States Air Force. Having fought together in the past, and knowing that we will fight together in the future, reinforces the importance of this type of dialogue for both of our Forces. The purpose of my talk is to present thoughts on the United States Air Force model of developing operational level leadership for the application of air and space power. My presentation will focus on the importance of training our leaders to take strategic objectives and convert them into operational directives that allow for the tactical application of air and space power on today's battlefield. Here's how I propose to go about this.

First I would like to discuss what a leader needs to be able to do in a Combined Air Operations Center (CAOC). To do this I have consolidated various notes, classes and briefings into a "checklist" of ten fundamental rules for Air Operation Center success. These ten fundamental rules have been developed with inputs from past and current Joint Force Air Component Commanders.

Next, I will discuss Force Development, which is a term being applied to the methodical process by which we strive to prepare our United States Air Force officers to be leaders. The essence of this approach is to define the necessary character traits and skills in our officers to allow them to lead forces in a combined or joint air operation; and then develop these officers through training and experience to be ready when called upon. There are several character traits which we are trying to develop and the list is fairly large. I will narrow the focus down to some of the traits I feel really "jump out" as applicable to leading forces in combined or joint air and space operations.

After I present the checklist and a summary of leadership characteristics I will conclude with challenges that we will face that will most likely impact the rules and conduct of the command and control of our forces in the future. These challenges include, command and control of our airspace with relation to constraints imposed by national borders; the challenges created by new technology like networking and stand-off weapons and Unmanned Aerial Vehicles, the small unit distribution of ground troops in an ever expanding battlespace; the need to evolve the kill chain into a process that takes minutes versus hours, and working to integrate coalition forces who bring various levels of technology, experience, and competence to the fight.

Module 1

I believe there are ten fundamental rules for senior command and warfighting at the operational level. Rule number one is to master your processes. My new boss, General Ron Keys, calls this knowing your business and managing your time. One of the early lessons we learned in standing up the Joint Force Air Component Commander, or JFACC, is that warfighting with a functional component is all about weaving together processes. As a result, our Air Operations Centers have evolved over the years into the most capable process-designed organizations in the Department of Defense. We have identified over fifty major processes and hundreds of sub-processes that are central to the conduct of major air operations. The Joint Air Tasking cycle, the combat operations "crisis" or F2T2EA (Find, Fix, Track, Target, Engage and Assess) template, the targeting cycle and the assessment cycle are four examples of these processes. These major activities are highly interrelated and interdependent. The Air Tasking Order cycle is generally pre-eminent, and you'll find just about everybody in the Air Operations Center supports it in some way or another.

Rule number 2 is to know your organization. As I mentioned, the Air Operations Center (AOC) is a process-centric organization. Although you'll find aviators, communicators, intelligence personnel, and even operations researchers in the AOC, they're all cross-matrixed into divisions and teams that leverage their combined experience, expertise, and intellectual talents. The nominal AOC is comprised of five major divisions, and can expand to a thousand plus people today which we hope to reduce in the future to somewhere between five-hundred to seven-hundred depending on the size of the conflict. As with any enterprise it's large and complex and it's important for the commander to have a rigorous understanding of its fundamental organization in order to optimize its value.

Once you know your processes and your organization the next logical step is to familiarize yourself with your people. Rule number three is to know your key people. As in any large and complex organization, good commanders develop a "short list" of their "go-to" people, based on the critical process activities, process seams, and major deliverables. The commander gets involved across the whole organization and not just on the combat operations floor where the big-screen displays are located. It's important for the JFACC to develop a solid relationship with his deputy commander. In fact, some JFACCs will have more than one, especially when they're able to bring in a flag officer who is dedicated to major mission areas, such as an Army Air and Missile Defense Commander to assist with the Area Air Defense Commander's job.

Other key senior advisors include the Director of Mobility Forces (DirMobFor), and the Director of Space Forces (DirSpaceFor). Successful JFACCs make sure that each of these officers know their expectations and ensure they understand the limits of their authorities to make decisions on the commander's behalf.

Additionally, since the Joint Functional Air Component is comprised of people and capabilities sourced from across the entire joint force, it's important for the JFACC to work closely with senior component liaisons sent to the AOC. These include people such as the United States Army's Battlefield Coordination Detachment Commander and the Special Operations Liaison Element Chief. Although they don't report to the JFACC, but to their respective component commanders, they're all key stakeholders in how the air component approaches joint warfighting.

Most successful JFACCs have learned early to leave the "day-to-day" routine, business practices, and running of the AOC to the JAOC director. Oftentimes the air component's success depends on this individual's organizational skill, commitment to team-building, and leadership. In American slang we call this "having great playground skills". I'll discuss the importance of these traits later when we cover leadership traits and characteristics. The JAOC director is normally the JFACC's "go to" person for any and all AOC issues, and a solid relationship with this officer is imperative.

In any job, the most important person to know is your boss. This is rule number four. Just like any successful military organization, the Joint Force is dependent on trust, confidence, and alignment – where all of the stakeholders are on the same sheet of music. Where the Joint Force Commander's job is to communicate his mission, guidance, and intent to the subordinate components, every good JFACC is eager to develop a solid relationship with the JFC and fully understand what the boss is saying. It's essential that the JFACC understand when, where, and how to best communicate with the JFC.

One key technique for gaining understanding and developing trust and confidence is the briefback process. In the briefback, each subordinate component commander tells the JFC what they heard as guidance and offers their unique interpretation and perspective. For example, if JFC guidance is to achieve air superiority, the JFACC will normally offer a definition of air superiority, scope of the effort, and timetable for completion.

Having an understanding of your boss and his needs is critical, but it is equally important to know what is critical to yourself. Rule number five is: know what's critical to you and be prepared to make the call when you need to.

In a joint force built on commanders' trust and confidence, it's not good enough for component commanders to simply know the JFC's guidance, mission and intent. The onus is on the JFACC to clearly demonstrate to the boss that he "gets it"; then communicate what he wants to the AOC staff. Again, a comprehensive briefback is the technique that allows this to happen. Of course history suggests that the JFC will be a ground commander. Building rapport and trust involve transparency in apportionment, allocation, and targeting all toward the benefit of integrated strategies.

We've also observed over the past several years that the character and effectiveness of the AOC as an organization is heavily influenced by where the JFACC focuses his effort and attention. Results here have been both positive and negative. Every JFACC came up through the ranks perfecting skills at the tactical level. All were successful in doing these things; otherwise they'd never have made it to the JFACC level of command. But, the necessary skills and dispositions required for warfighting command at the operational level are distinctly different. Nobody gets to the JFACC level with a birthright that automatically entitles them to success in operational-level warfighting. Referring to General Keys again, he reminds us that ultimately the whole effort comes down to personalities and wills.

Rule number six is to know whether you are winning or losing. This is one of the areas where we've really got some work to do in the AOC is this whole business of operational assessment. We've always been pretty good at figuring out if we're "doing things right," as in delivering the right ordnance on the bridge span to interdict enemy movements along a key highway. We routinely collect pilot mission reports, analyze imagery, and determine our mission effectiveness.

But, as we continue to develop our effects-based approaches to warfighting, the larger question we now find ourselves asking is "are we doing the right things." By dropping the bridge span, have we degraded the adversary's ability to deploy second-echelon forces to the battlefield? These types of questions are more intellectually challenging, require greater joint integration, and can consume quite a bit of intelligence surveillance and reconnaissance capability to answer. Although we're not quite to the point of having an optimized architecture to get all relevant information to every decision-maker as quickly as we'd like, our emphasis on the issue is helping us rapidly improve the process. Remember, assessment information is only pertinent if it supports the commander's decision making, and warfighting decisions are made twenty-four hours a day, seven days a week, not when a staff schedules them.

Assessment doesn't have to be all bells, whistles, and elegant PowerPoint. General Tommy Franks used a simple and intuitive slide to derive his assessment during operation Iraqi Freedom. It portrayed levels of effectiveness toward achieving his desired end states across four domains. These domains assessed the enemy's capabilities in the areas of leadership, security apparatus, military and population. Each day, in consultation with his staff, General Franks measured the campaign's progress across these four domains based on the stability of the Iraqi regime. Victory was of course measured by a total collapse of the four domains. The Combined Force Air Component Commander thoughts that help guide this are: clarity of mission, unity of command, robust Rules Of Engagement, making sure resources meet required needs, knowing the political will of the players, and focus on an exit strategy.

One of General Moseley's responsibilities as JFACC during Operation Iraqi Freedom was to ensure victory. Rule number seven is to know your key responsibilities. Every Joint Force Commander will tailor the Joint Force organization to assign key responsibilities to the JFC staff or subordinate component commanders. Normally, the JFACC will also take on air defense and airspace management jobs in addition to running the Air Component. These are not trivial responsibilities. They bring requirements to develop comprehensive plans, such as the air defense plan and airspace control plan. Similarly, in these roles, the JFACC publishes daily air defense and airspace guidance in the Tactical Operations Data and Airspace Control Order, respectively. These are big jobs, but they are only the tip of the iceberg. The purpose of the commander is to win…not to explain defeat.

I'm sure we've all heard George Bernard Shaw's famous quote about our two nations being separated by a common language. Frankly, this separation is not unique to just our two nations, but to joint warfighting as well. This is the root of rule number eight: master the terminology. Oftentimes, we've observed that airmen from different nations will tend to understand each other just fine. On the other hand, watching United States Army officers and United States Air Force officers trying to get their points across can at times be quite "entertaining", but joint warfighting is a "team sport". These communication challenges underscore the importance of using deliberate, precise and well-defined terms to communicate guidance, intent, and desired effects.

Terminology is important, particularly as it applies to the understanding of doctrine. Know your doctrine is rule number nine. While Joint and Service doctrine gives the Joint Force Commander a credible and historically proven starting point for tailoring his operations to the mission at hand, it is not a comprehensive recipe book for success. Different situations and conflicts require different approaches, arrangements, and practices. However, without a solid foundation in doctrine, what we eventually find is people "making things up" and potentially doing far more harm than good.

Just like in any military organization, one of the commander's key jobs is to represent and advocate the Air Component's interests to the various external customers. Rule number ten is only the JFACC can be what I call "Mr. Outside". Certainly, staff-to-staff peer relationships are important, but the keys to making things happen are oftentimes the personal commander-to-commander relationships. Another important area here is the role of the commander in "telling the Air Component story" to the various distinguished visitors and media personnel who may come and visit the AOC. There is only one viable opportunity to create a favourable first impression. Good commanders capitalize on this opportunity.

The bottom line for the ten rules is this. Professional competence doesn't come easily at the operational level. Nobody gets there without hard work to learn fresh skills. Trust and confidence are the "glue" that holds a joint warfighting organization together. But, if it's not adequately nurtured by honesty, integrity, and clear communications, it can imperil the whole joint organization in a heartbeat.

Module 2

Now, that we've examined our ten rules based on the past experiences of our JFACCs let's take a look at this topic from a bit more scientific perspective. The United States Air Force research laboratory began their study of JFACC mission essential competencies about two years ago. Their preliminary results identified capabilities needed for success in the highly integrated JFACC team environment. They include a solid understanding of resources, capabilities, limitations, centers of gravity, and vulnerabilities from the joint and coalition perspective as well as the adversary perspective.

The commander's personal contribution implies taking a proactive approach towards future strategy and planning, anticipating, articulating, and responding to the changing nature of the campaign as it unfolds. In this context, situational awareness and understanding refers to broad horizontal and vertical knowledge needed to put individual tasks in context for supporting the mission. The JFACC also needs to be adept at using both formal and informal approaches in dealing with stakeholder organizations, agencies, and hierarchies to achieve mission objectives. The joint and coalition team creates an environment that facilitates team building through open horizontal and vertical communication, feedback, education, and innovation. Finally, the JFACC's personal and organizational battle rhythm establishes consistent expectations and milestones for effective communications and decision-making in the context of the JFC's battle rhythm to ensure a coordinated campaign.

In addition to the top-level mission essential competencies, the research indicates that successful JFACCs also exhibit high levels of proficiency in a series of sub-competencies. These supporting competencies include: trust, confidence, balance, decisiveness, adaptability, interpersonal communication, projection, multi-tasking, concentration, negotiation, courage, acceptance of risk, and objectivity. There are probably no surprises here, these attributes are at the core of effective team building, decision-making, and joint and coalition warfighting. They ultimately ensure the respect necessary for the CFACC to be successful.

Our United States Air Force is taking an active approach to developing leaders with these key qualities in our new approach to Force Development. In this process, called the Air Force Senior Leader Performance and Development Management System (P&DMS), we seek to deliberately create Air Force leaders by methodically developing in them enduring leadership competencies. By deliberately exposing people to a broader range of experiences, this will ensure each airman's developmental experience is both valuable and meaningful, and by cultivating the enduring leadership competencies, the Air Force creates leaders who are more flexible and adaptable in a force that has an even greater sense of belonging and importance. There are eleven enduring competencies being evaluated in our Air Force senior leaders. I will focus my discussion on a few of them as they apply best to our ten rules, mission essential competencies and supporting competencies.

The first enduring competency is the ability for a leader to shape institutional strategy and direction. What our United States Air Force seeks to grow is a leader with the ability to establish critical long-range success factors and goals designed to achieve mission and organizational advantage. He must be able to use his understanding of key economic, social and political trends both domestically and globally to assess strengths, weaknesses, opportunities and threats to develop strategy. He has to energize the organization through a compelling picture of the future opportunities the United States Air Force has to offer.

Second, our future operational leaders must embrace and lead change. These leaders must lead efforts to streamline processes and adopt best practices. They must learn to create an environment that supports innovation, continuous improvement, and appropriate risk taking.

Third, a key enduring competency to any operational leader is the ability to command organizational and mission success through enterprise integration and resource stewardship. In a large, technologically advanced organization like the Air Operations Center, leaders must effectively prioritize, manage, and integrate diverse mission elements across varying environments. They must address the situational requirements associated with the required response; access to resources; deployment of people, equipment, supplies, technology; and funding essential to organization and mission success.

Fourth, in a large and diverse organization like the AOC the JFACC must foster effective communication. This is a critical enduring competency that when mastered ensures a free flow of information and communication up, down, across, and within an organization by actively listening and encouraging the open expression of ideas and opinions. A JFACC must be adept at expressing ideas clearly, concisely, and with impact.

Fifth, another enduring competency ensures operational leaders influence through win/win solutions. A JFACC must be able to promote ideas, proposals, and positions persuasively through compelling rationale and arguments. He must be skilled at considering underlying consequences for key stakeholders while seeking and negotiating the optimal solutions.

The AOC is a large beast, with all the component parts working towards a common goal. Because of this, leaders must promote collaboration and teamwork. This is our sixth enduring competency. It is the JFACC's responsibility to facilitate and encourage cooperation among team members. He must recognize and share credit for success. It is essential that he work as needed with peers and subordinates to establish a group identity through mutual goals, common team practices, and structure.

Our seventh enduring competency is the ability to partner to maximize results. Leaders must work proactively to cultivate an active network of relationships inside and outside the AOC. To do this the JFACC must accommodate a variety of interpersonal styles and perspectives to achieve his objectives and remove barriers. The ability to leverage cross-disciplinary knowledge to provide integrated solutions is integral to his success.

Our eighth enduring competency is an important tool in the development of interpersonal relationships – self assessment. This allows the Combined Force Air Component Commander to understand how personal leadership style and skill impact decisions and relationships with others. With self assessment the JFACC can create a personal leadership development plan using insight gained from assessing values, personal strengths and weaknesses along with performance preferences and learning style. This aids him to apply insight and learning to improve his own leadership performance.

Finally, all leaders must inspire trust. Our ninth enduring competency mandates operational leaders maintain high standards of integrity. They must establish open, candid, and trusting relationships, and treat all individuals fairly and with respect. Personal gain is subordinate to the mission's success and demonstrated loyalty to the unit and the chain of command is paramount to organizational success.

Module 3

Armed with our ten rules and the forged character to lead an AOC the only thing left for a leader is to tackle the challenges of the future. We cannot allow ourselves to become static. Air dominance is a benefit we share, yet it is not automatic and it will not always be guaranteed. We must continue to adapt and evolve as an air and space power, it is a foregone conclusion that our enemies have and will continue to do so.

Among the issues that we will surely face I begin with command and control of airspace. There are numerous factors that play into this equation, the first being the unique geometry of the battlespace. National borders create impassable barriers that we may choose not to breach in the pursuit of air dominance. We are all seeing today a widely dispersed army demanding a theater-wide airspace command and control plan.

Stand-off weapons are becoming more prolific and their range and accuracy continue to evolve. As this occurs they become more problematic in our attempts to integrate them into our air operations plans. As an example the small diameter bomb will be released as far as sixty nautical miles from its intended target, which may be moving. This creates tremendous airspace deconfliction problems that have to be solved.

Deconflicting weapons is a hard enough job. Yet on today's battlefield we ask a JFACC to integrate, coordinate and deconflict hundreds of unmanned aerial vehicles of several types. Some of these unmanned aerial vehicles are small enough to be carried in a rucksack while others like the Global Hawk are enormous. Each one of these aircraft has their own system to control their actions and none of them are currently well integrated. As their value on the modern battlefield rises the problem becomes more and more complicated.

Space is vast and as we grow capability in this frontier we need to ensure the capabilities are fully integrated in the warfighting efforts. The stovepipes that exist must be broken down as these emerging capabilities grow and mature.

Time sensitive targeting must evolve. This process is valuable to our overall warfighting effort. I mention it as one of the fifty critical processes that need to be mastered in an AOC. The individual you place in charge of the time sensitive targeting cell will become one of your most trusted agents. This process has the capability to bring paralyzing effects to the enemy, and we must reduce it from a process that takes hours to one which occurs in minutes.

In summary I have offered ten fundamental rules every JFACC should know. These rules are sage words of advice from men who have led in battle. These fundamental rules, by themselves, are useless unless the JFACC has the character and skills to lead his organization. We are working to ensure these character traits through the development of our enduring competencies. These identified character traits allow us to grow leaders to fill our most important operational leadership positions. Armed with this knowledge our operational leaders can aggressively attack our enemies and the challenges of commanding an AOC in future combat.

I'm extremely honoured to be here. I'm privileged to be representing the wonderful airman of the United States Air Force. We have fought together and continue to fight together in our present operations. What we learn here will go a long way to ensuring we fight well together in the future.

COMMAND OR CONTROL?
LEADERSHIP IN THE BATTLE OF BRITAIN

Dr Stephen Bungay

In many ways, the protagonists in what we know as the Battle of Britain were quite alike. The two sides had similar numbers of single-engined fighters of comparable performance. There was not a lot to choose between the pilots, who were of the same age and background with similar training. On both sides, about 5% got about 40% of the kills. To explain the outcome, we must look elsewhere. The difference that made the difference was the leadership.

Hugh Caswall Tremenheere Dowding was not what one usually thinks of as a great leader. He was remote, ascetic and severe. Not for nothing was he called 'Stuffy'. Whilst his pre-war achievements as a skiing champion fitted the RAF mould, his interests in spiritualism did not, and he mystified his colleagues. Intensely private, he formalised most of his contacts with other people and had no close friends. One of those closest to him was the head of A.A. Command, General Sir Frederick Pile. Pile spent about an hour with him every day, and called him 'the outstanding airman' he met during the war. Pile also said that he was 'a difficult man, a self-opinionated man'.[1] He was an odd fish, stubborn and eccentric.

When he took on the new job of Commander-in-Chief (CinC) Fighter Command in 1936, Dowding spent four years creating the most formidable air defence system in the world. At its heart was a unique C3 system which featured the world's first large-scale intranet – using analogue technology – as well as radar. The system acted as a force-multiplier, enabling Dowding to deploy his 6-700 fighters with the effectiveness of many more. Built as a front-line position, the system had a lot of in-built redundancy and was hard to disrupt, let alone destroy. Hard core rubble for filling in bomb craters was stockpiled at each airfield, and stand-by Operations Rooms were made ready a few miles away from key Sector Stations.[2] The Germans never even understood which bits of it mattered and which did not. Even if they had, hitting the vital bits often enough to cripple rather than just impair the system would have taken more time than they had and a lot of luck.

Dowding's most important operational commander was a New Zealander, Keith Park, who as his SASO from 1938-1940 helped him to work up the system and then took over 11 Group covering the south east, which deployed about half of Fighter Command's strength. He performed with such brilliance that the Germans christened him 'the defender of London'. The Battle of Britain and the Battle of Malta are the only major air campaigns ever won by the defence. Both were won by Park.

In these two rather unlikely companions we have the builder of the defence system and its principle operator. What did they actually do to bring about the most important victory in RAF history?

The CinC: Gathering and Allocating Resources

All commanders want resources. They rarely believe that they have enough. However, by 1940, Dowding had been provided with the resources to construct the Chain Home and Chain Home Low networks, expand the Observer Corps, put in dedicated telephone lines, build operations rooms, construct metalled runways, E-pens and ground defences at his Sector Stations, and develop a large body of trained operators for his force.

All this had been done because there was a broad consensus about the importance of air defence, not just within the RAF but in the political and civilian establishments. Resourcing the system was a vast and complex undertaking in which many played a part. The introduction of Scheme K for aircraft production in 1937, which put greater emphasis on fighters, was a political decision backed by the Minister for the Coordination of Defence, Sir Thomas Inskip. The Air Ministry asked Lord Nuffield to set up the Civilian Repair Organisation (CRO) after the Munich crisis of 1938.[3] In August 1940, 35% of all Hurricanes and Spitfires reaching squadrons were from the CRO, and in September and October the proportion rose to over 40%.[4] Munich also prompted the Post Office to create the Defence Telecommunications Control organisation to deal with the plethora of urgent requests for dedicated lines and emergency circuits, and on its own initiative the Post Office suggested the construction of a new military network. This was discussed by the Chiefs of Staff and civilian engineers and became the DTN.[5] It was Wilfred Freeman, the Air Member for Development and Production, who drove the enormous increase in production volume which allowed Britain to out-produce Germany by two to one in fighters throughout the summer of 1940, though the spin-master Beaverbrook managed to take credit for it. It was Freeman too who understood the importance of 100 octane fuel and persuaded the Treasury in 1939 to construct two new refineries to supply it.[6] Dowding may have seen himself as a lone voice fighting a stupid and intransigent Air Ministry, but he had many allies working to the same ends he was pursuing. In 1940 his main resource concerns were pilots and aircraft.

In 1929, Major General E. B. Ashmore, the commander of London's air defences from 1917-18, published a book in which he stated that the adequate number of squadrons necessary to defend British air space was 52.⁷ In 1938, Dowding said he would be satisfied with 41 squadrons on whose presence he could rely. By the time the war broke out, the Air Ministry returned to Ashmore's figure of 52. In May 1940, when discussing the question of whether to send more fighters to France, Sir Archibald Sinclair told the War Cabinet in May that Home Defence needed 60 squadrons, a figure confirmed by the CAS, Sir Cyril Newall. In June he said it needed 57. Dowding stuck to 52.23

He had started sticking to it thirteen days after war broke out, when the Air Ministry decided to send four of the 34 squadrons then in existence to France, and talked about sending four more. They had thereby turned on what Dowding dubbed 'the Hurricane tap' and turning it off again was to consume much energy.⁸

At a meeting of the War Cabinet on 13th May 1940, Sinclair and Newall warned against sending any more squadrons to France in addition to the six which by then were already there. Churchill agreed. That night, a telegram arrived from the B.E.F.'s Commander in France, Lord Gort, asking for more fighters. It was followed the next morning by a telegram from the French Prime Minister, Reynaud, asking for ten squadrons. Churchill was reluctant to respond, Newall warned that once they had left Britain the squadrons would never return, and so Churchill put Reynaud off with a vague message of support. Reynaud was not put off, and called Churchill at 7 o'clock on the morning of the 15th, excitedly begging for assistance. Churchill reported this to the Chiefs of Staff meeting at 10:30, and summoned Dowding to hear his views. Dowding stressed the dangers if things were to go badly and urged that no more fighters be sent.

At the Chiefs of Staff meeting the next day, 16th May, Newall read out a message from Gamelin pleading for the ten squadrons again and saying that without them, all was lost. This time, in view of the 'new and critical situation', he agreed to send some and the other Chiefs of Staff agreed. Churchill thought it 'a very grave risk', but necessary in order to bolster the French. Four were sent, with two further squadrons held in readiness. That afternoon, Churchill left for France, where he was subjected to even more intense pleas. In the end, he wrote in his evening telegram to the War Cabinet that six extra squadrons should be sent to France in addition to the four agreed that morning. Clearly unhappy, Newall decided to fulfil the request by having three squadrons fly out to French airfields in the morning, return to England, and be relieved by another three in the afternoon.

---

[23] See Peter Flint, *Dowding and Headquarters Fighter Command*, Airlife 1996 pp. 7-11, 17, 47-8, 73, 84-5 & 89, John Ray, *The Battle of Britain – New Perspectives*, Arms & Armour Press 1994, pp. 22-4 & 52 and Vincent Orange, *Sir Keith Park*, Methuen 1984, p. 70. As a rule of thumb, most calculations were based on a fighter strength of 30% of an opponent's total air strength. Dowding was shocked after the war when Churchill wrote in *Their Finest Hour* that Dowding had told him he needed 25 squadrons. Well he might have been. Given the plethora of numbers to choose from, it is odd that Churchill picked one which was never mentioned. Unless somebody got the 52 the wrong way round...

In the meantime, Dowding had been at his desk hard at work. Deeply disturbed, he composed a ten point memorandum for the Air Ministry, and sent it to the Air Council on the 16th. Addressed to the Under Secretary of State for Air, Harold Balfour, it has become one of the most celebrated documents in RAF history.

He pointedly demanded a statement 'as to the limit on which the Air Council and the Cabinet are prepared to stake the existence of the country' and that this limit then be rigorously adhered to. He famously concluded that 'if the Home Defence force is drained away in desperate attempts to remedy the situation in France, defeat in France will involve the final, complete and irremediable defeat of this country.'

Newall wrote a note about the subject, appended Dowding's document to it and circulated it to his fellow Chiefs of Staff. They discussed it and converted it into a report of their own. It was the back-up Newall needed. The Hurricane tap was turned off. By July, Dowding had his 52 squadrons in Britain.

It is fairly clear that the fighters would have made no difference in France. The French did not need them anyway, because they had plenty of their own. After the war, the French Government looked into the question and found that large numbers of French fighters had been held in storage units. The French Air Force Commander, General Vuillemin, testified that at the end of hostilities he had more aircraft available than at the beginning.[9]

Dowding had in effect identified the main effort as the UK. There he had a prepared position and was confident that if the Luftwaffe were to attack it, he would break them, as he told his Group commanders on 3rd July.[10] He had no illusions about the capabilities of the French air defences. Nor did Newall. Once again, Dowding was giving point to a general consensus. As long as the Wehrmacht was in the West, the threat to Britain from the air was seen as paramount. It had been widely believed that the war would begin with devastating air raids which might even decide the issue. There was some surprise as well as relief when they failed to materialise. It was felt to be only a matter of time. Maintaining a strong metropolitan fighter force was a priority for the War Cabinet as well as for Dowding.

During the battle, Dowding continued to build and maintain resources. His main role as a battlefield commander was to manage their deployment between Groups, using 12 and 13 Groups as a reserve from which to reinforce 10 and 11 Groups. In August, no fewer than thirteen squadrons were moved into 11 Group, most of them in exchange for exhausted units which were transferred north. In making these deployment decisions, Dowding was pursuing a very distinct strategy.

The CinC and the AOC: Developing Strategy

In planning how to meet their enemy, Fighter Command had to choose between two basic strategic alternatives, each one of which had advocates. The first was founded on the belief that the Luftwaffe would give up if their attacks proved to be very costly, regardless of what damage they inflicted. This view was held by several officers at the Air Ministry, notably Sholto-Douglas and Stevenson, and also, with provisos, by Leigh-Mallory. Sholto-Douglas gave a very clear statement of his case in the discussions of defence strategy which took place before the war, writing in 1938:

> *"It is immaterial in the long view whether the enemy bomber is shot down before or after he has dropped his bombs on his objective. Our object is not to prevent bombers reaching their objectives, though it would be nice if we could, but to cause a high casualty rate among enemy bombers, with the result that the scale of attack will dwindle rapidly to bearable proportions."* [11]

His view did not change during the course of the battle. In a Minute written on 17th December 1940, after it was over, he states:

> *"The best, if not the only way of achieving air superiority is to shoot down a large proportion of enemy bombers every time they come over. It would be better to do this before they reach their objective if possible, but I would rather shoot down 50 of the enemy bombers after they have reached their objective than shoot down only 10 before they do so."* [24]

One might summarise this view of strategic intent as: 'Engage in large air battles in order to inflict heavy casualties.'

The other alternative was that the Germans would give up if they were convinced that they were not achieving their aim. The prime goal of the defence was therefore to remain in being and offer undiminished and constant opposition. As long as a cost was imposed for entering British airspace, how high it was mattered less than keeping one's own force in being, and being able to impose the cost again the next day. The objective would be to both minimise one's own losses in the air and damage to the defence system on the ground. It followed that it was better to break up a raid and prevent it from damaging its target by shooting down 10 raiders in the process than allowing it to bomb an airfield or radar installation, which would impair the defence's ability to meet the next raid, and shoot down 50.

---

[24] AIR 16/367. Sholto-Douglas sought to have these principles recognised and applied operationally after he took over from Dowding in November 1940. See Flint, op. cit., pp. 179-182.

The assumption behind this is that an enemy will give up if he becomes convinced that he is getting nowhere, for it is senseless to accept even moderate losses for no return.

This view was espoused by Dowding and Park. The strategic intent might be formulated as: 'Oppose all serious raids in order to deny the enemy air superiority.'

Prima facie, Sholto-Douglas had a reasonable case. However, neither he nor anybody else was able to specify how high the German losses had to be in order to be unacceptable to them. Neither side of the argument had any evidence to go on at the time because no-one had ever tried to defend a country against large-scale air attacks. Ironically, the Luftwaffe also believed it could win by engaging Fighter Command in large air battles and inflicting heavy casualties. It was a schematic rather than a strategy.

Dowding's strategy was based on more subtle insight. Bomber Command tolerated losses of 80% on raids in the first months of the war until they realised that they were doing no damage. It is the realisation that the aim is not being achieved that makes an opponent, however determined, give up. Had the Luftwaffe Commanders had good evidence that their attacks were weakening the defences and that their bombing was rendering airfields inoperable, they would have been willing to sacrifice a lot of crews and aircraft to finish the job. If they had good evidence to the contrary then any further losses incurred in trying to do so would have been a useless sacrifice.

Dowding's intent exploited the capabilities he had spent four years creating. The system, if properly resourced, was designed to stalemate any possible move an opponent could make. But only if it were run by someone who understood it and was able to translate its potential into actual operations. Having worked as Dowding's SASO for two years, Park was just such a man.

The AOC: Translating Strategy into Operations

Park translated the strategic intent into an interception policy embodied in his Instructions to Controllers. Between June and November 1940 he issued over forty of them. He modified and adapted the policy to the changing situation, constantly reviewing results and passing on lessons. However, the principles behind them remained constant and were completely aligned with Dowding's intent.

Park had to ascertain which raids were serious and guard against being caught by surprise by possible further raids designed to catch fighters re-fuelling on the ground. He had to engage the most dangerous raids early on in order to protect the ground targets. It was important to engage when in as advantageous a tactical position as possible. Speed of reaction was critical. Achieving all this would be demanding, but it was what the system was designed to do. As bombers were the only aircraft which could cause damage on the ground, they were the main target. If the Germans sent over fighter sweeps, they should be left alone. Bombers should be attacked before they bombed and if possible formations broken up by using head-on attacks. Once a raid had been repulsed, the need for force-preservation dictated that stragglers should not be pursued over the Channel. Turning a 'probable' into a 'confirmed' was not worth the added risk to his pilots.

The basic tactical unit was the squadron.25 Park decided how many to deploy against each threat and when to send them into action. In attacking any one raid, he could either use his squadrons together at the same time or individually over a period of time. Until he faced very large single raids he chose deliberately to do the latter, for several reasons.

Firstly, it was fast and simple. Each squadron detailed to attack just carried out its orders without waiting for any others. The pilots could scramble, head straight for the enemy, attack and get down again.

Secondly, it reduced the risk of suffering a major defeat. If the intercepting force were to be bounced on the climb by a gaggle of 109s, only one squadron would be lost.

Thirdly, each small formation would be harder for the escorts to detect than one large one, and would tend to confuse them, as British units would often be coming from different directions. If the escorts made the mistake of diving as a body on the first British fighters to appear, the coast would be clear for the next ones.

Fourthly, Park's fighters would be able to enter a target-rich environment, shoot at anything and get out fast, rather than exposing themselves as they queued up to attack or spending half their time avoiding collisions and shooting at each other.

Finally, raids could be subjected to almost continuous attack. German crews would learn that they could expect no let up, that the whole of the sky over southern England was a potential death-trap. This continuous pressure increased their stress and made it harder for bomber Commanders to restore order if formations got disrupted.

It may seem intuitively wrong to commit forces piecemeal. It certainly seemed wrong to Leigh-Mallory, who, espousing as he did Douglas's view of strategy, insisted on using his squadrons in a single 'Big Wing'. To many at the time, the image of a bomber fleet as a column of Redcoats and a fighter squadron as a band of Indians would have appeared aberrant.26 However,

---

[25] The best size of tactical formation had been a matter of some debate before the war. The air exercises conducted in 1939 suggested that the squadron was the largest formation which could be effectively controlled in the air. Large raids could simply be met by several squadrons acting in concert, but without wasting time forming up together into a single large formation. See Dilip Sarkar, *Bader's Duxford Fighters*, Ramrod Publications 1997, pp. 14ff.

[26] Except in the Luftwaffe. Their jargon for 'enemy aircraft', the equivalent of the R.A.F.'s 'bandit', was 'Indianer'. Whether the choice is to be ascribed to a deep understanding of air fighting or a predilection for the cowboy stories of Karl May, still a favourite with German children today, is a mystery shrouded in the mists of time.

Park's principles had nothing to do with the number of aircraft used to intercept raids, but simply the operating unit employed. If the raid were very large, two squadrons could engage it at one time. Park wanted complete flexibility, and that was very important, for he had to react to any number, sequence or size of raids. Park could say to his Squadron Leaders, as Nelson had said to his Captains at Trafalgar, that he wanted a 'pell-mell' battle and that no-one could go very far wrong if they simply closed with the enemy.

The clarity and simplicity of Park's policy aligned the organisation and freed him up from taking every decision. On most of the 'big days' he was in Uxbridge where he took personal control. On others – including September 7th – he could confidently leave things to his Chief Controller, Lord Willoughby de Broke. He could and did expect his junior commanders to use their initiative. The dangerous low-level raid on Kenley of August 18th was defeated by the Station Commander and his controller – a Wing Commander and a Squadron Leader – who took all the relevant decisions within the 18 minutes between the first detection of the raiders by the Observer Corps and their appearance over the airfield. In doing so, they ignored the normal rule that only Group could deploy squadrons, and scrambled 111 Squadron on their own initiative. Park subsequently congratulated them. Two weeks later, the Station Commander at Biggin Hill, Group Captain Grice, decided that he could put an end to raids on his airfield by blowing up the last remaining hangar himself, and did so on the evening of September 4th. He was censured but let off, for he had been proved right.

The CinC: Working on Constraints

Given that he had in Park – and in Brand, the AOC 10 Group covering Park's flank – men who understood him and whom he trusted completely, Dowding exercised very little control over them during the battle itself. He spent his time on one main thing: on removing the constraints under which his organisation had to operate, so broadening its capabilities and his commanders' freedom of action.

One of Fighter Command's constraints was pilot availability. In early 1940 Fighter Command's expansion had been limited by the supply of aircraft. By July the limiting factor was pilots. Dowding lobbied for, and got, pilots from the Fleet Air Arm, and concerned himself with training refugee pilots from central Europe, notably the Czechs and Poles to whom Dowding later paid fulsome tribute. He had more limited success with other RAF Commands. His SASO, Evill, managed to squeeze out a few Battle and Lysander pilots in August, but when he demanded thirty more in early September, Douglas at the Air Ministry told him the idea was 'very unpalatable' as the lumbering Battles would be 'extremely useful if and when an invasion occurs'.[12] The tussle culminated on September 7th when Dowding confronted Douglas directly to demand that OTU output be increased and Battle pilots re-trained. He got his way then.

A second constraint was pilot losses. Without interfering with interception policy, Dowding worked in the background to protect them. He had already insisted on his fighters being equipped with armoured windscreens and seat armour. During the Battle itself, it became apparent that Hurricanes were catching fire easily, so that even pilots who baled out quickly and survived were incapacitated by terrible burns. Dowding saw to it that Hurricanes' fuselage tanks were covered with self-sealing fabric called 'Linatex' and also had a metal bulkhead fitted in front of the pilot.27

The most serious constraint, however, on which Dowding spent most time, was the lack of night-fighting capability. The only existing method was to use Hurricanes and Spitfires on lone patrols. The aircraft were unsuitable for night flying and training was dangerous. In the first month of the Battle of Britain, 8% of Fighter Command's aircraft losses were due to night-flying accidents. Six of the pilots died. The return was meagre. A few experienced pilots like Malan and Sanders managed to catch bombers held in searchlights, but these were isolated cases. Dowding worked through many nights. He ran an experiment in the Kenley Sector using radio location apparatus known as G.L. at searchlight posts. In his view, the real answer was to fit Beaufighters with A.I. radar, a solution he presented in a paper on 21st September which Churchill described as 'masterly'. Others differed. Lindemann was unimpressed. Douglas wanted rapid results and thought Dowding was 'a little blinded' to the 'more simple hit or miss, trial and error use of single-engined fighters'.[13] A committee was formed under former CAS Sir John Salmond to examine the matter of night defence. It completed an eighteen point report in three days and Salmond sent a copy to Beaverbrook, appending a private note recommending that 'Dowding should go'.[14] Dowding marked his own copy of the report with his usual blue crayon, ticking three of the eighteen points, putting a question mark against five and a cross of disagreement against nine. Salmond meanwhile wrote to Churchill stating that his report showed that a change in leadership at Fighter Command was 'imperative'.[15] On 25th November, Salmond got his way.

The first kill made by an A.I. equipped Beaufighter was on 19th November. Fighter Command made only five other claims at night during the whole of November and December. The same pilot, John Cunningham, got another on 12th January 1941 and a third on 15th February.[16] Night fighter claims rose from 22 in March to 96 in May.[17] Dowding's solution did work in the end, but it was under the leadership of Douglas that the concept became an operational reality.

---

[27] Dowding *Despatch* Appendix F, §§ 6-7. In fact it seems more likely that the main cause of Hurricane fires were the tanks in the wing roots. See E.R. Mayhew, *The Reconstruction of Warriors*, Greenhill 2004, pp. 49-53.

The AOC: Visible Leadership

Whilst Dowding concentrated on sustaining and enhancing the capabilities of his organisation, Park concentrated on enhancing its performance, maintaining morale and defeating the enemy.

Like Dowding, Park made his intentions very clear. He communicated extensively with his controllers, Station Commanders and Squadron Leaders. He talked to all of them directly, gave them advice and encouraged debate about tactics. For example, on 20th August he issued a note to all Station Commanders about successful tactics employed by various squadrons during the heavy action of two days before, asking them to issue it to squadrons, with his own 'message of appreciation for their magnificent fighting during the past week'.[18] On 13th and 20th September, he issued sets of notes drawing lessons from the study of recent combat reports.[19] In October, he instigated a debate about fighter formations, circulating ideas from 504, 92, 66, 605 and 501 Squadrons.[20] The debate was open and challenging. Park censored nothing. He encouraged the junior officers with the most relevant recent combat experience to work out the best approach between themselves. As we might say today, he turned 11 Group into a learning organisation.

But he also knew what he wanted in terms of performance and drove the organisation by using metrics, many of them time-based. At the beginning of July he demanded an elapsed time between the order to scramble and the last plane leaving the ground of two minutes. By the end of the Battle, some squadrons were managing it in 90 seconds. He measured the interception rate, and worked constantly to ensure that a higher proportion of the units scrambled actually made contact with the enemy.

He knew that Fighter Command's greatest vulnerability was pilot exhaustion. He demanded and got more comfortable accommodation and better meals. He insisted on organising PT games at stations and even went as far as providing string bands and reintroducing guest nights for entertainment.[21] After heavy raids he visited the worst hit stations himself, taking off on most evenings in his personal Hurricane, OK 1. He went to see for himself and learn, to gather the informal information without which a commander can become blinded. He went to congratulate and encourage. He found time for individuals. He approved decorations, including Nicolson's VC. Pilot George Westlake recalls being sent to see Park when he crashed a Hurricane while attempting a dead-engine landing. Park gave him a hard time, enumerating his mistakes, then told him to go the mess and read the papers. Park turned up later, took him to lunch and told Westlake he could buy him a beer. He bought Westlake a few as well. 'From that day on,' Westlake recalls, 'I worshipped him.'[22]

The Impact of Leadership: Fighter Command 1941-42

To understand the importance of leadership and command in the context of air power, it is instructive to follow the outlines of Fighter Command's story after the Battle of Britain.

On 29th January 1941, Leigh-Mallory, now AOC 11 Group, ran an exercise reproducing the airfield raids Fighter Command had experienced in early September. His airfields were bombed while the planes were still on the ground. He remarked that he would do better next time.[23] He and Sholto-Douglas were busy with other things. Wanting to take the battle to the enemy, they adopted a policy they called 'leaning towards France'. In leaning in this direction during the summer of 1941, Fighter Command lost 194 pilots. The Luftwaffe lost 128 aircraft and recovered most of their pilots. The Germans wanted to get on with the real war in Russia, so left only about 160-200 fighters from JG2 and JG26 in France, who proceeded to do to Leigh-Mallory what Park had done to them. They did not overly care if France were bombed, so they were particularly choosy about when and how they engaged, and ambushed the huge wings of British fighters in Staffel or Schwarm strength. The confused mêlées in the air led to the sort of overclaiming characteristic of the Big Wing in 1940, so Leigh-Mallory thought he was doing rather well, and carried on. In the second half of the year, Fighter Command claimed 731 German aircraft for the loss of 411. The actual German losses were 154, only 92 of which were incurred in opposing Leigh-Mallory's 'circuses' and 'rhubarbs' over France. The Luftwaffe's kill ratio of over 4:1 was about what they would have needed to have won the Battle of Britain. Fighter Command was fortunate that the whole campaign was of little strategic significance, conducted mainly to show Stalin that Britain was trying to do something in Europe.[24] In fact, the only Luftwaffe units ever actually withdrawn from Russia were sent to the Middle East because of the RAF's activities in Malta and the Western Desert. Strengthening the RAF's fighter presence in that theatre would not only have made a major local difference but might have had an even greater impact on the Luftwaffe's strength in Russia. However, that was not on Fighter Command's agenda. As Park has acidly observed:

> *"Early in 1942 Sholto Douglas and Leigh-Mallory had 75 fighter squadrons in England, carrying out massive sweeps over France, as compared with only 52 Squadrons when the Luftwaffe was at its full strength during the Battle of Britain. When the C. in C. Middle East asked for Spitfires for Malta, Fighter Command refused...when as few as five Spitfire Squadrons could have saved Malta from the terrible blitz of spring 1942. This all arose from the mania of Sholto Douglas and Leigh Mallory for Big Fighter Wings."*[25]

Park's view, though expressed with excusable intemperance, is substantially correct. Sholto-Douglas wrote to Portal, then CAS, on 1st October 1941 agreeing to send six squadrons of fighters to the Middle East as long as they were replaced by the spring. However, he added, he did 'feel very anxious about the rumour which reaches me that you are proposing to send Spitfires to the Middle East.' Spitfire production, Douglas wrote, was barely enough to keep up the flow of replacements needed by the 69 squadrons he would have left out of the current 75. (Leigh-Mallory was indeed losing large numbers of Spitfires – and their pilots – over France.) In any case, Spitfires might not be able to stand up to the rigours of the desert as well as Hurricanes. Above all, Douglas feared that Portal would turn on a 'tap' which would put Fighter Command into 'a parlous condition'. If Russia, already in receipt of Hurricanes, and still reeling from the first blows of the German invasion, were to go under during the winter, Britain could be open to 'a mortal blow next spring'. Four days later, Portal sent Douglas a soothing reply, suggesting that he was being 'unduly pessimistic', that plenty of Spitfires were rolling off the production lines and that the Germans could not invade Britain against as few as sixty squadrons of them even if Russia did surrender. He added some diplomatic advice about reducing Spitfire wastage in France. There was a further exchange, but in the end, Douglas wrote to Tedder in the Middle East at the beginning of November, telling him that he was to get seven fighter squadrons – though he did not say what type of aircraft they would have. None arrived during the winter, but the cogs in the Air Ministry ground away to the extent that a worried Douglas was moved to write to Portal's deputy, Freeman, on 7th February 1942 asking that the number of Spitfires sent to the Middle East be restricted to 20 a month.[26]

The first few Spitfires got to Malta in March 1942, where they finally blunted the Luftwaffe's offensive. In July, Park arrived and with Spitfires at his disposal and a new interception policy stopped the bombing of the island within three weeks. But the Desert Air Force had to wait till late May, when 145 Squadron got Spitfire Vs. In September the Luftwaffe's fighter force in the desert, JG 27, lost 16 pilots, including three of its top scorers, Steinhausen, Stahlschmidt and Marseille, and were withdrawn to re-fit, totally demoralised. By then the Desert Air Force had just three squadrons of Spitfires but between them they certainly accounted for a third, and maybe as many as half of JG 27's losses. They established air superiority in the desert just in time for Alamein and never lost it.

In 1940 the main effort was the defence of the home base. Dowding understood that. In 1941-2 the main effort should have been establishing air superiority where the British Army was fighting – in the Mediterranean and the Far East. Douglas did not understand that. It is ironic that in writing to Portal Douglas actually used Dowding's image of a tap. His failure to shift main effort delayed the attainment of Allied air superiority in the key theatres and cost an unknown number of lives both in the air and on the ground. Such is the sobering responsibility of command.

Perspectives: Command or Control?

In his seminal work *Command in War*, Martin van Creveld suggests that outstanding command systems have five characteristics. They set decision thresholds as low as possible and have self-contained units at low-level to enable this. They complement formal information-transmission systems which work top-down and bottom-up with an active search for information by headquarters and have an informal as well as formal network of communications inside the organisation.[27] The Dowding–Park system exhibited all of those characteristics.

Dowding exercised command in three main ways; by building and maintaining organisational capability, developing a strategy and allocating resources. He was effective as long as his approach was aligned with political intent. As long as he was able to exercise command effectively, he did not need to exercise much control. However, there lay his weakness. If we follow John Adair in seeing leadership in terms of the three circles of task, team and individual, Dowding was outstanding at the task, but had a flawed team because he failed to control one individual – Leigh-Mallory. He has admitted the mistake.[28] That failure led to a lack of alignment at the top. As a result, interceptions failed and raids got through. It was a failure of leadership which comes down not just to disagreements about substance, but to bad personal relationships and a consequent failure of trust. The quality of personal relationships between its top leaders has an impact on the effectiveness of a whole organisation.

The trust Dowding displayed towards Park was not misplaced. Park passed the trust on to his organisation. The resulting performance was outstanding, for in 11 Group too, effective command obviated the need for close control. Park controlled performance through metrics analysed by his staff. He exercised command personally through active, visible leadership. He won hearts and minds. That got him commitment. As a result he did not need to force compliance. Commitment beats compliance every time. In warfare it may be the only way. Achieving it is a subtle and very human thing. It is the oldest, most enduring and most difficult challenge of leadership.

Stephen Bungay's book, *The Most Dangerous Enemy – A History of the Battle of Britain* is published by Aurum Press

Endnotes

1. *Ack-Ack*, Pile. Harrap 1949.
2. *Battle of Britain Despatch*, Dowding, in AIR 8/863.

3. *The Narrow Margin*, Derek Wood and Derek Dempster. Tri-Service Press 1990.
4. *Wilfred Freeman*, Anthony furse. Spellmount 2000.
5. Wood and Dempster, op, cit.
6. Furse, op. cit.
7. *Air Defence*, Major General E.B. Ashmore. Longmans Green & Co. 1929.
8. AIR 16/677.
9. Flint, op. cit.
10. AIR 24/526.
11. AIR 2/3034.
12. AIR 16/903 and AIR 20/2759.
13. *Years of Command*, Lord Douglas of Kirtleside and Robert Wright. Collins 1966.
14. *The Battle of Britain – New perspectives*, John Ray. Arms and Armour Press 1994, pp. 139.
15. *ibid.*
16. *The Night Blitz 1940-41*, John Ray. Arms and Armour Press 1996.
17. *ibid, pp. 239.*
18. AIR 16/735.
19. *ibid.*
20. *ibid.*
21. Park Report, 7th November 1940. AIR 2/5246, pp. 14.
22. Orange, op. cit., pp. 151-2.
23. *ibid, pp. 138.*
24. *The Right of the Line*, John Terraine. Hodder & Stoughton 1985, pp. 282-8.
25. Park, unpublished letter to Derek Dempster, 18th May 1960.
26. PRO AIR 16/623.
27. *Command in War*, Martin van Creveld. Harvard 1985, pp.270.
28. *Dowding and the Battle of Britain*, Robert Wright. Macdonald 1979, pp. 197, 199-209.

CHAPTER SEVEN

LEADERSHIP THROUGHOUT THE RAF

EXPOSED LEADERSHIP!

Sergeant 'Tomi' Tomiczek and Corporal Brendan McGarrity

During Operation TELIC I was the Commander of a small Bomb Disposal Team detached from 5131 Bomb Disposal (BD) Squadron to work with the Army. What follows is a brief account of my experiences as a leader, working in a fairly non-standard operational environment.

I will begin by outlining the work of 5131 (BD) Squadron (Sqn). In terms of manpower, the squadron is around the size of the ground crew element of a Tornado Sqn; that is, about 105 men. Our traditional role has been tied closely to the main operating bases, as we are responsible for keeping airfields clear and operable. For that purpose we are equipped with armoured Spartan vehicles. Since the RAF Regiment lost their armoured capability a few years ago we are now the only armoured unit within the Royal Air Force. Although I am trained as an armoured vehicle commander, it is a far cry from that of a tank commander.

When Op TELIC loomed, there was a realisation amongst the Army that they did not have the appropriate Explosive Ordnance Disposal (EOD) assets to address the lessons and issues learnt from the first Gulf War. It had been evident then that the Iraqis were more than willing to destroy oil installations, refineries and pipelines and there was no reason to expect that they would not do the same again second time around. It was therefore imperative that appropriate assets were positioned forward of the frontline as early as possible in order to deal with this threat. Our part in proceedings was therefore dictated by this need. In fact, RAF bomb disposal teams made up 60% of the EOD teams that deployed into theatre in support of Op TELIC.

About 2 weeks before we were due to enter Iraq from Kuwait we were attached to the 5th and 7th Regimental Combat Troops of the American Marines. Unfortunately there was very little time to train with these units, coming down, in the end to just a couple of days. We crossed the border with the American Marines at H+20 minutes and made straight for the Gas and Oil Separation Plants (GOSPs). Intelligence had indicated that the Iraqi military had protected the installations, therefore, we had to assume that, at best, these had been set for demolition, at worst, that they would be either defended or booby trapped; it turned out to be a combination of both. Firstly we were tasked to clear GOSP Manchester. As we approached the first installation, which was fiercely alight and shrouded by a thick, acrid, black smoke, we were surrounded by troops engaged in sporadic contact and to our west four helicopter gunships were battering an Iraqi convoy. It was at this point it was all too apparent that we were at war and seemingly, very alone.

Our task amidst this completely alien environment was to ensure the safe capture of the installation. This was essential to the regeneration of the country post war. The ability of the country to produce oil and sell it on the world markets would expedite the stability of the country. Working in extremely stressful conditions, the team set about its search to clear a safe route to enable trained personnel to shut the GOSP down. It was a task that would take the whole day.

Shortly after this initial action we were detached in support of 16 Air Assault Brigade as a small (3 man) BD team. We were now completely on our own in terms of RAF Command; fully assimilated into the Brigade's chain of command and procedures (of which I had no prior knowledge or training). Detached with us were 2 Royal Engineer teams and 1 Royal Logistics team and, apart from a few RAF Forward Air Controllers who worked for Brigade Headquarters we were the only light blue element in the Brigade. We worked directly for an SO3 Royal Engineer who, although he did his best for us, was not in a position to give us the sort of command we would normally get from a Flight Commander or Troop Commander. This did have its advantages because it meant we were able to make the most of some opportunities, as no one really understood how we worked! For all tasking in the next 7 weeks I became the troop commander to my team of 3 and our vehicle.

Each evening at around 2100 hours we would get into the vehicle and go down to Brigade HQ where I was given a list of grid references or place names for the next day's tasking. On a good working day we would get 6 or 7 jobs, but if only 1 appeared on the list we knew it would be a long or more dangerous task. The briefing system that the Brigade used was critical in keeping everyone informed and getting all the appropriate information disseminated to all levels. I would be briefed by my SO3 who had already been briefed by the Brigade Commander. I was then expected to go back and brief both my lads in our vehicle with the same information. It meant that there was a great deal of clarity throughout the task and everybody was fully informed. I believe it was crucial to our success that everyone understood not only what we had to do, but why we had to do it and how it fitted into the bigger picture. In fact this kind of briefing system is perhaps something that is missing at our level within the RAF.

There was one particular task that we had to go to on a bridge, North of Ramayla on one of the main supply routes. It was like a scene from the film "The Longest Day". The whole bridge had been heavily mined, but the Royal Engineers had managed to clear most of it. In the area leading up to the bridge, a very thick minefield ran out to about 300 metres. American Marine Combat Units had blown their way through to the road but there was only just enough room for one vehicle to pass at a time. The Royal Irish, Army Air Corps Battle Group and Parachute Regiment had already gone across the bridge, supported from the other side by AS90s, large pieces of self-propelled Army artillery. The limited dimensions of the cleared area, along with the fact that the supply route was running very close to the edge of the minefield meant that there were doubts about moving the AS90s across the bridge itself.

Along with the Royal Engineer team, we were tasked with expanding the cleared area to a few metres either side of the road, in order for armoured vehicles to pass through safely. We agreed to take one side of the road each, as that seemed fair, and began our work. On a normal task we arrive at an incident control point (ICP), hopefully with an evacuation plan already set up for us; we walk in and do what we have to do. However, with the time constraints dictated by the situation we found ourselves in here, we were the forward edge of a combat zone. The task was possibly strictly more of a Royal Engineer Combat Engineer task but we were the ones who were responsible for completing it.

Despite having a raft of sophisticated mine clearing equipment on board the Spartan, we found that as we couldn't discount the presence of wooden or plastic mines, the only way to achieve the aim in this case was to resort to more traditional methods. I can say that we have progressed a little further than simply using a bayonet; we've got a pointed spike to use instead, but the basic principle remains the same in that you basically get down on your belly and prod.

When you come into a career in EOD the one thing you learn is that every risk is the operator's risk. We work on a one man principle and we have to make sure, for the sake of all those who follow us, that the area is clear. The actual job was not hard, but it was physically draining. It involved an immense amount of concentration on the metre or so in front. This meant that I couldn't do it all myself and this was a real command crisis moment for me in many ways because I realised that I had to ask one of my troops (my number 2 and man 3) to come and take my risk. I should explain here that the role of the number 2 within the team is to coordinate the task and to look after the dynamics of how it is run. The number 2 sends the operator forward to take his risk while he ensures the force protection is in place. It is the number 2 who ensures the operator maintains his concentration by bringing him out for breaks.

Back to our task in the Gulf, at the point when I decided I could no longer complete the task, the number 2's focus shifted from the task itself to the small metre in front of him. That changed everything he did and everything he thought about, although his mind did try to wander back to how the task was running. Over the next couple of days we took it in turns to do the job and to drive the vehicle. The emotion felt by all the team in handing over the task to each other was something I never expected to experience in my life.

Moving on from that experience I'd now like to talk a little about another incident which outlines the leadership challenges we faced during our time with

16 Air Assault Brigade. The important thing to point out here is that during training build-up where we train to work on Deployed Operating Bases, we are always protected by support from the RAF Regiment, and as part of Joint Force EOD we were told that we would always have access to Force Protection. However, when we joined 16 Air Assault Brigade we realised that, being at the sharp edge of Army operations, we had suddenly become the Force itself.

To be honest, for this example I still can't remember what we were tasked to do that day. What I can say is that it was right on the edge of our sphere of influence, before we reached the American Forces area. We were travelling through the desert on our way to the task at about 40 mph and suddenly we heard simultaneous screams of "STOP". The braking nearly threw me out of the vehicle and once we'd settled we realised that we were about 150 metres into an American bomblet field left over from Gulf War 1. Obviously we had been sent several miles in the wrong direction and were now facing a very interesting leadership problem!

Once the moment where everyone stands still and waits for a bang was over, we contemplated the Standard Operating Procedure (SOP) for finding a vehicle in a bomblet field: **Call a Bomb Disposal Team**! Obviously, this was a bit ironic but even if we'd wanted to, there was nobody on the other end of the radio; we were completely on our own. The only feasible way out of the situation was for me to get out of the vehicle, walk ahead by a few yards and basically guide the vehicle to safety. We started off well and had managed to get to within 30 yards of the perceived edge of the field before I saw the first Lynx, which was hovering 300 metres to our right. Now, one thing we discovered quickly about Army Air Corps Lynx is that if you see one, there are inevitably 3 more not far behind. Sure enough, a few seconds later a second dome appeared ahead, keeping their beady eye on us. So, now relying on the recognition skills of the Army, I was forced to make yet another command decision; do I tell the rest of my team of this new development or not? I decided that it was best to keep it to myself as I probably wouldn't even make it back to the vehicle if the Lynx crew made the wrong decision, and because we couldn't have got out the way in time anyway, still being in the middle of the bomblet field. I have to say that being sat in a tank in the middle of a bomblet field, hunted by Army helicopters was not a situation I expected to face when I joined the RAF. Anyway, thankfully the Army made the correct decision and we got out of it all in the end. What's more, I don't think we ever did finish that task.

The final situation I would like to talk about is one that happened to me when I was working quite late one night. A Land Rover pulled up outside and took me to Brigade HQ where I was faced with a circle of people waiting eagerly for the Bomb Disposal Officer to arrive. As the Commander of my team that meant me. There was an Armoured Commander from the Royal Horse Artillery Armoured Screen; a Paratroops Commander who was ready to provide a blocking force; an American specialist decontamination unit; one of our own joint NBC Commanders; an in-theatre weapons intelligence person and my SO3. The Brigade Commander was apparently arriving 10 minutes later. Now, I was a bit confused by the expectant looks on their faces but apparently it is Army tradition that the task is always Bomb Disposal led. So, at that moment everyone in the room was expecting me to put together the task. The Army Commander wanted to know where to push the armoured screen, the Paratrooper really wanted the blocking force in place and the intelligence people wanted to know how I was going to get the information back to them. This was quite a stirring moment because I had no idea what to do with an armoured screen, or how to carry out blocking. After a quick run down of what I needed to know I managed to find my way through a plan. It must have been sound because, despite the screen coming under fire, the task was carried out smoothly.

Unfortunately, things went wrong for us just one day later when we were leaving the area. We were travelling south, excited to be going towards home when there was a loud bang and my vehicle went over. The following 24 hours were to challenge the whole team in many ways. Post casualty evacuation, the team were to spend their first night apart for nine weeks, during which, all had been placed in situations for which we were untrained; yet, we had met those challenges head on and won. Leadership has many guises, yet without the team it means nothing. We had become an unbreakable team with an indestructible bond.

So, that basically concludes the discussion of our experiences of an Operational Theatre at NCO level. We've tried to restrict the content to the events themselves in order to allow the actual leadership lessons learnt to be considered by the audience. Personally, having faced many challenging command situations, the resounding success of my war was that, not only had I made it back in one piece, but that my whole team had also returned safely.

© Keith Grint 2005

FOLLOWERSHIP: THE ANVIL OF LEADERSHIP [1]

Professor Keith Grint

This chapter takes its starting point from the approach to leadership that perceives it to be a consequence of a person; an individual human who embodies and demonstrates personal characteristics traditionally associated with leaders. However, the first part suggests that this reduction of leadership to the individual human constitutes an analytically inadequate explanatory foundation and this is illustrated by reference to the importance of followers and especially their commitment to 'sense-making', to their community, and to independence from their leader. Hence the sub-title: the anvil of leadership – I suggest that it is the followers that make or break leadership not the leaders. I go on to suggest that leadership might be better configured as a function of the community; 'the god of small things,' rather than the result of superhuman individuals.

Leadership, Followership, Commitment and Independence

When listing the traits required by formal leaders it is usual for a class to come up with any number of characteristics: charisma, energy, vision, confidence, tolerance, communication skills, 'presence', the ability to multitask, listening skills, decisiveness, team building, 'distance', strategic skills and so on and so forth. No two lists constructed by leadership students or leaders ever seems to be the same and no consensus exists as to which traits or characteristics or competences are essential or optional. Indeed, the most interesting aspect of list-making is that by the time the list is complete the only plausible description of the owner of such a skill base is 'god'. Irrespective of whether the traits are contradictory it is usually impossible for anyone to name leaders who have all these traits, at least to any significant degree; yet it seems clear that all these traits are necessary to a successful organization. Thus we are left with a paradox: the leaders who have all of these – the omniscient leaders – do not exist but we seem to need them. Indeed, complaints about leaders and calls for more or better leadership occur on such a regular basis that one would be forgiven for assuming that there was a time when good leaders were ubiquitous. Sadly a trawl through the leadership archives reveals no golden past but nevertheless a pervasive yearning for such an era. An urban myth like this 'Romance of Leadership' – the era when heroic leaders were allegedly plentiful and solved all our problems – is not only misconceived but positively counter-productive because it sets up a model of leadership that few, if any of us, can ever match and thus it inhibits the development of leadership, warts and all. It should be no surprise, then, to see, for example, the continuous re-advertising of vacancies for head teachers when the possibilities of success are either beyond the control of individuals or so clearly defined by comparative reference to Superman and Wonder woman that only those who can walk on water need apply: not for these leaders Seneca the Elder's warning: *nemo sine vitio est* (no-one is without fault).

The traditional solution to this kind of recruitment problem, or the perceived weakness of contemporary business chief executives or directors of public services or not-for-profit organizations, is to demand better recruitment criteria so that the 'weak' are selected out, leaving the 'strong' to save the day. But this is to reproduce the problem not to solve it. An alternative approach might be to start from where we are, not where we would like to be: with all leaders – because they are human – as flawed individuals, not all leaders as the embodiments of all that we merely mortal and imperfect followers would like them to be: perfect. The former approach resembles a White Elephant – in both dictionary definitions: as a mythical beast that is itself a deity, and as an expensive and foolhardy endeavour. Indeed, in Thai history the King would give a White Elephant to an unfavoured noble because the special dietary and religious requirements would ruin the noble.

The White Elephant is also a manifestation of Plato's approach to leadership, for to him the most important question was 'Who should lead us?' The answer, of course, was the wisest amongst us: the individual with the greatest knowledge, skill, power, resources of all kinds. This kind of approach echoes our current search criteria for omniscient leaders and leads us unerringly to select charismatic, larger than life characters and personalities whose magnetic charm, astute vision and personal forcefulness will displace all the bland and miserable failures that we have previously recruited to that position – though strangely enough using precisely the same selection criteria. Unless the new leaders are indeed Platonic Philosopher-Kings, endowed with extraordinary wisdom, they will surely fail sooner or later and then the whole circus will start again, probably with the same result.

Of course for Plato it was more than likely that the leaders would be men, after all Greek women were not even citizens of their own city states, though he did admit that it was theoretically possible that a woman might have all the natural requirements of leadership. Since Plato's time, assumptions about the role of gender in leadership have varied enormously, even if the presence of women as leaders has proved remarkably limited and remarkably stable. It is well known that the proportion of women declines rapidly as they rise through the organizational hierarchies (see Bratton, Grint and Nelson, 2004: 180-99) but the explanation for this often reproduces the person-based criteria for defining leadership. For example, Goldberg (1993) and Browne (2002) insists that the chemical hormones, especially testosterone, generate behavioural patterns that leave men 'naturally' more suited to positions of dominance and leadership than women who are 'naturally' less aggressive. Whether aggression is necessarily and essentially linked to leadership is, of course, a moot point; aggressive men may bully their subordinates into compliance but this does not necessarily equate with effective leadership, especially in the long run. Thus even if we could select for aggression we cannot determine whether this particular 'trait' is advantageous for leadership.

An alternative approach is to start from the inherent weakness of leaders and work to inhibit and restrain this, rather than to assume it will not occur. Karl Popper provides a firmer foundation for this in his assumption that just as we can only disprove rather than prove scientific theories, so we should adopt mechanisms that inhibit leaders rather than surrender ourselves to them. For Popper, democracy was an institutional mechanism for deselecting leaders, rather than a benefit in and of itself, and, even though there are precious few democratic systems operating within non-political organizations, similar processes ought to be replicable elsewhere. Otherwise, although omniscient leaders are a figment of irresponsible followers' minds and utopian recruiters' fervid imagination, when subordinates question their leader's direction or skill these (in)subordinates are usually replaced by those 'more aligned with the current strategic thinking' – otherwise known as Yes People. In turn, such subordinates become transformed into Irresponsible Followers whose advice to their leader is often limited to Destructive Consent: they may know that their leader is wrong but there are all kinds of reasons not to say as much, hence they consent to the destruction of their own leader and possibly their own organization too.

Popper's warnings about leaders, however, suggest that it is the responsibility of followers to inhibit leader's errors and to remain as Constructive Dissenters, helping the organization achieve its goals but not allowing any leaders to undermine this. Thus Constructive Dissenters attribute the assumptions of Socratic Ignorance rather than Platonic Knowledge to their leaders: they know that nobody is omniscient and act accordingly.

Of course, for this to work subordinates need to remain committed to the goals of the community or organization while simultaneously retaining their spirit of independence from the whims of their leaders, and it is this paradoxical combination of commitment and independence that provides the most fertile ground for Responsible Followers. Figure 1, over the page outlines the possible combinations of this mix of commitment and independence. But note that this is for illustrative purposes and generates a series of Weberian 'ideal types' that are neither 'ideal' in any normative sense nor 'typical' in any universal sense. On the contrary, these types are for heuristic purposes, designed to flag up and magnify the extreme consequences of theoretically polar positions.

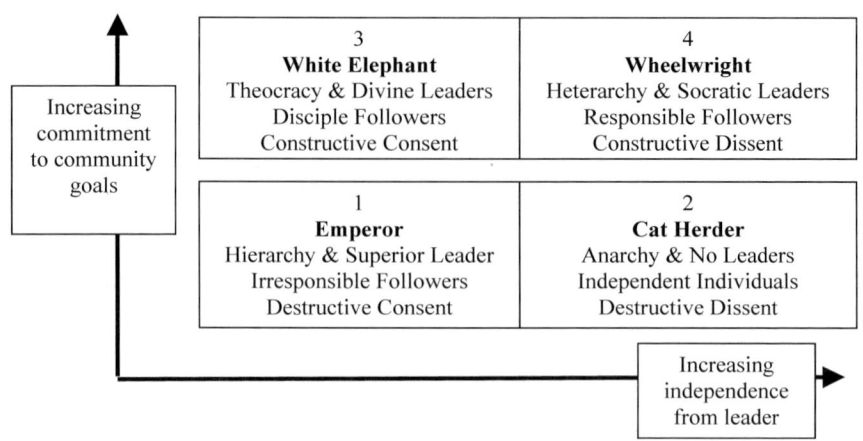

Figure 1: Leadership, Followership, Commitment & Independence.

Despite these reservations, Box 1 – the hierarchy – probably contains the most typical form of relationship between leaders and followers wherein a conventional hierarchy functions under a leader deemed to be superior to his or her followers by dint of superior *personal* qualities of intelligence, vision, charisma and so on and so forth, and thus to be responsible for solving all the problems of the organization. Such imperial ambitions resonate with the label for this form of leader: the emperor. In turn, that generates followers who are only marginally committed to the organization's goals – often because these are reduced to the personal goals of the leader – and hence the followers remain literally 'irresponsible' through the Destructive Consent that is associated with the absence of responsibility.

Box 2 is rooted in a similar level of disinterest in the community but, combined with an increase in the level of independence from the leader, the consequence is a formal 'anarchy' – without leadership – and without the community that supporters of anarchism suggest would automatically flow from the absence of individual leaders. The result is a leader that resembles a Herder of Cats – an impossible task.

Box 3 – the theocracy – generates that community spirit in buckets but only because the leader is deemed to be a deity, a divine leader whose disciples are compelled to obey through religious requirement: the White Elephant described above. That consent remains constructive if – and only if – the leader is indeed divine, a god who omniscience and omnipotence are unquestionably present. However, it is clear that although many charismatics generate cults that would ostensibly sit within this category the consent is destructive because the leader is in fact a false god, misleading rather than leading his or her disciples.

The final category, box 4 – the heterarchy – denotes an organization where the leaders recognize their own limitations, in the fashion of Socrates, and thus leadership is distributed according to the perceived requirements of space and time (a rowing squad is a good example of a heterarchy in which the leadership switches between the cox, the captain, the stroke and the coach depending on the situation; the English rugby team that won the World Cup in 2003 operated on the same basis with a formal captain (Martin Johnson), plus 'captains' of the forwards, the backs, the line out and the scrum (Catt, 2003). That recognition of the limits of any individual leader generates a requirement for Responsible Followers to compensate for these limits which is best served through Constructive Dissent, in which followers are willing to dissent from their leader if the latter is deemed to be acting against the interests of the community.

Perhaps an ancient Chinese story, retold by Phil Jackson (1995: 149-51), coach of the phenomenally successful Chicago Bulls basketball team, makes this point rather more emphatically. In the 3rd century BC the Chinese Emperor Liu Bang celebrated his consolidation of China with a banquet where he sat surrounded by his nobles and military and political experts. Since Liu Bang was neither noble by birth nor an expert in military or political affairs some of the guests asked one of the military experts, Chen Cen, why Liu Bang was the Emperor. In a contemporary setting the question would probably have been: 'what added value does Liu Bang bring to the party?' Chen Cen's response was to ask the questioner a question in return: 'What determines the strength of a wheel?' One guest suggested the strength of the spokes' but Chen Cen countered that two sets of spokes of identical strength did not necessarily make wheels of identical strength. On the contrary, the strength was also affected by the spaces between the spokes, and determining the spaces was the true art of the wheelwright. Thus while the spokes represent the collective resources necessary to an organization's success – and the resources that the leader lacks – the spaces represent the autonomy for followers to grow into leaders themselves.

In sum, holding together the diversity of talents necessary for organizational success is what distinguishes a successful from an unsuccessful leader: leaders don't need to be perfect but, on the contrary, they do have to recognize that the limits of their knowledge and power will ultimately doom them to failure unless they rely upon their subordinate leaders and followers to compensate for their own ignorance and impotence. Real White Elephants – albinos – do exist, but they are so rare as to be irrelevant for those who are looking for them to drag us out of the organizational mud; far better to find a good wheelwright and start the organizational wheel moving. In effect, leadership is the property and consequence of a community rather than the property and consequence of an individual leader.

Moreover, whereas White Elephants are born, wheelwrights are made. In fact the analogy is useful in distinguishing between the learning pedagogies of both, for while those who believe themselves born to rule need no teachers or advisers, but merely supplicant followers, those who are wheelwrights have to serve an apprenticeship in which they are taught how to make the wheel and in which trial and error play a significant role.

The attribution of god-like qualities by irresponsible followers to allegedly omniscient leaders also generates an equivalent assumption about the power of leaders. While Plato's leaders rest like mythical Greek Gods on Mount Olympus manipulating the lives of mortals at will and with irresistible power, Popper's leaders should be resisted for precisely this reason. Yet it should also be self-evident that an individual can have virtually no control over anything or anybody – as an *individual*. Indeed, we have known for a long time that leaders spend most of their time talking – not actually 'doing' anything else. In effect, leaders might pretend to be omnipotent, to have the future of their organizations and its members in their hands, but this can only ever be a symbolic or metaphorical control because leaders only get things done through others. In short, the power of leaders is a consequence of the actions of followers rather than a cause of it. If this were not so then no parents would ever be resisted by their children, no CEO would ever face a defeat by the board of directors, no general would suffer a mutiny, and no strikes would ever occur. That they do should lead us to conclude that no leader is omnipotent and that the kind of leadership is a consequence of the kind of followership, rather than a cause of it. Thus while Plato's leaders might construct formal hierarchies for subordinates to execute their perfect orders, Popper's leaders work through networks and relationships because that's where power is actually generated: it is essentially distributed like a wheel not concentrated in what is actually a White Elephant.

None of this is new: Helmuth von Motlke, Chief of the Prussian General Staff from 1857-1888, understood Clausewitz's dictum that the local concentration of force was critical for military success and recognized that the nascent system of decentralized leadership already present in the Prussian army was crucial to achieving this. After all, a central commander in Berlin, or even 5 miles behind the battle had no way of understanding, let alone controlling, what was happening in each and every sector of the battle. The result was a system of leadership rooted in Mission Command – *Auftragstaktiker* or general directives, not specific orders, strategic aims not operational requirements, thereby enabling decentralized control that facilitated distributed leadership and the ability of local ground commanders to seize the initiative rather than await orders. [2]

Leadership as the god of small things

Another resolution of this paradox is that the focus should be shifted from the leader to leader*ship* – such that as a social phenomenon the leadership characteristics may well be present within the leadership team or the followers even if no individual possesses them all. Thus it is the crew of the metaphorical 'ship' not the literal ship's 'captain' that has the requirements to construct and maintain an organization; hence the need to put the 'ship' back into 'the leadership'. In other words, rather than leadership being restricted to the Gods it might instead be associated with the opposite. As Arundhati remarks about her own novel, "To me the god of small things is the inversion of God. God's a big thing and God's in control. The god of small things ..." [3] Here I want to suggest that leadership is better configured as *The God of Small Things*.

The Big Idea, then, is that there isn't one; there are only lots of small actions taken by followers that combine to make a difference. This is not the same as saying that small actions operate as 'Tipping Points' (Gladwell, 2002), though they might, but rather that big things are the consequence of an accumulation of small things. An organization is not an oil tanker which goes where the captain steers it but a living and disparate organism, a network of individuals – its direction and speed is thus a consequence of many small decisions and acts (Barabási, 2003; Kilduff, 2003). Or, as William Lowndes (1652-1724) [Auditor of the Land Revenue under Queen Anne] suggested, 'Take care of the pence and the pounds will take care of themselves.' This has been liberally translated as 'Take care of the small things and the big things will take care of themselves,' but the important thing here is to note the shift from individual heroes to multiple heroics. This doesn't mean that CEOs, Head Teachers, Chief Constables, Generals and Air Chief Marshals etc are irrelevant; their role is critical but limited and dependent upon the actions of subordinates, and indeed their own preparation for the 'big' decision that may derive from the accumulation of many small acts and decisions. In the words of Lord Naoshige, a samurai war lord (1538-1618), 'Matters of great concern should be treated lightly' (Tsunemoto, 2000: 27).

Another way of putting this is that the traditional focus of many leadership studies – the decision-making actions of individual leaders – is better configured as the consequence of 'sense-making' activities by organizational members. As Weick (1993) suggests, what counts as 'reality' is a collective and ongoing accomplishment as people try to make sense of the 'mess of potage' that surrounds them, rather than the consequence of rational decision-making by individual leaders. That is not to say that sense-making is a democratic activity because there are always some people more involved in sense-making than others and these 'leaders' are those 'bricoleurs' – people who make sense from variegated materials that they are faced with, and manage to construct a novel solution to a specific problem from this assembly of materials.

Because of this, success and failure are often dependent upon small decisions and small acts – both by leaders and 'followers' who also 'lead'. This implies that we should abandon Plato's question: 'Who should rule us?' and focus instead on Popper's question: 'How can we stop our rulers ruining us?' [4] In effect, we cannot secure omniscient leaders but because we concentrate on the selection mechanism those that become formal leaders often assume they are omniscient and are therefore very likely to make mistakes that may affect all of us mere followers and undermine our organizations.

Take, for example, Sir Clowdisley Shovell (1650-1707) a British Admiral who, returning home from an attack on Toulon in 1707, in his flagship 'Association', allegedly hanged a sailor who had the temerity to insist that the fleet was heading for the rocks off the Isles of Scilly. The fleet was subsequently lost on the aforementioned non-existent rocks with between 800 and 2000 dead from all 4 ships [5] or the equally infamous Vice-Admiral Sir George Tryon whose actions on 22 June 1893 caused the loss of his own flagship, the *Victoria*, after he insisted that the fleet, then split into two columns, turn towards each other in insufficient space. Despite being warned by several subordinates that the operation was impossible Tryon insisted on its execution and 358 sailors were drowned – including Tryon. At the subsequent courts martial of Rear Admiral Markham on the *Camperdown* that rammed the *Victoria*, he was asked, if he knew it was wrong why did he comply? 'I thought' responded Markham, 'Admiral Tryon must have some trick up his sleeve.' The court found Tryon to blame but accepted that it 'would be fatal for the Navy to encourage subordinates to question superordinates.' [6] Thus, to misquote Burke, it only takes the good follower to do nothing for leadership to fail. [7]

Nor are attributions of omniscience limited to national military or political leaders alone. For instance, when the Air Florida 90 ('Palm 90'), flight crashed on 13 January 1982 in poor weather conditions it is apparent from the conversation between Captain Larry Wheaton and the 1st Officer Roger Pettit that the latter was unconvinced that the plane was ready for lift off, yet his failure to stop Wheaton from going ahead inadvertently led to the crash. [8] Precisely the same thing occurred in the Tenerife air crash where the co-pilot thought that there was a problem but failed to prevent the pilot from taking off in a dangerous situation because his warnings were too 'mitigated' (another plane was taking off directly in front of them and, unbeknown to the co-pilot, his own pilot did not have permission to take off) (O'Hare and Roscoe, 1990: 219).

A similar level of 'inappropriate subordination' or 'irresponsible followers' seems to have occurred in Marks and Spencer. According to Judy Bevan, Richard Greenbury, having achieved significant successes, became more and more isolated from his subordinate board members to the point where they only engaged in destructive consent and not constructive dissent. She remarks about one of the final board meetings through the words of a board member:

> The thing about Rick is that he never understood the impact he had on people – people were just too scared to say what they thought. I remember one meeting we had to discuss a new policy and two or three directors got me on one side beforehand and said they were really unhappy about it. Then Rick made his presentation and asked for views. There was total silence until one said, "Chairman we are all 100% behind you on this one." And that was the end of the meeting (Bevan, 2002: 3).

Alfred Sloan, according to Drucker (2001: 254) faced a similar problem with his board but was able to recognize the manifestations of Destructive Consent, 'Gentlemen, I take it we are all in complete agreement on the decision here?' [Consensus of nodding heads.] 'Then I propose we postpone further discussion of this matter until our next meeting to give ourselves time to develop disagreement and perhaps gain some understanding of what the decision is all about.' Three hundred years earlier Yamamoto Tsunetomo (2000: 37) relates a Japanese equivalent:

> Last year at a great conference there was a certain man who explained his dissenting opinion and said that he was resolved to kill the conference leader if it was not accepted. This motion was passed. After the procedures were over the man said, "Their assent came quickly. I think that they are too weak and unreliable to be counsellors to the master."

This problem persists across all areas; take the case of Wayne Jowett who was erroneously injected with Vincristine, by the intrathecal (spinal) route on 4th January 2001, under the supervision of the Specialist Registrar Dr Mulhem, by Dr Morton, a Senior House Officer at the Queen's Medical Centre Nottingham (QMC). [9] Such a procedure almost always results in death but the issue here is not that a mistake was made. According to the BBC version of events:

> Dr Mulhem read out the name and dose of the drug, but he did not say how it should be administered and said that when he saw the Vincristine that he was thinking of another drug which is administered spinally. Dr Morton asked whether the Vincristine should be given spinally and said Dr Mulhem had told him yes. *He said he was surprised by this, but had not felt he could challenge a superior* (my emphasis). [10]

Note here how that the subordinate is, once again, concerned about the veracity of the decision made by the superordinate but feels unable or unwilling to challenge that decision.

Unfortunately, not only are all leaders flawed – and thus incompetent to some degree or other – but most people are actually unable to recognize their own levels and areas of incompetence: to put it another way we don't know what we don't know (Kruger and Dunning, 1999).

Nor are the problems of knowledge and competence limited to individuals. In September 1998 Long Term Capital Management (LTCM), a Hedge Fund, was in debt to the tune of $4.6 billion and was only bailed out by the intervention of the US Federal Reserve organized by Greenspan. [11] LTCM included 2 Nobel Economics Prize winners and an ex-VC of the American Federal Reserve. It used complex math formulas to spread risk across a range of stocks, bonds etc and its sophistication encouraged Robert Merton (one of the Nobel Prize winners) to claim that the model 'would provide the perfect hedge'; it obviously did not (Stein, 2003: HR 56:5).

What can be done about this problem? Clearly the provision of honest and timely advice to leaders – Constructive Dissent – provides an appropriate solution but it is equally clear, first that leaders tend to discourage this by recruiting and appointing subordinates that are 'more aligned with the official line' – that usually means sycophants and 'Yes people' who provide Destructive Consent. Moreover, leaders' unwillingness to admit to mistakes reinforces followers' attribution of omniscience. Historically only the royal 'Fool' or court jester could provide Constructive Dissent – and survive, primarily because the advice was wrapped up in humour and therefore could be publicly dismissed by the monarch, even if privately he or she could then reconsider it rather more carefully. There is, perhaps, no better example of the difficulty and importance of this role than the Fool in Shakespeare's *King Lear*.

Lear, having given away his kingdom to his daughters in a show of bravado and omniscience, is warned first by his loyal follower, Kent, that the action is foolhardy but Kent is exiled for his honesty. Then the Fool attempts the same advice but does so through a series of riddles that, unfortunately Lear only begins to understand when it is too late:

> Fool: That lord that counsell'd thee
> To give away thy land,
> Come place him here by me,
> Do thou for him stand:
> The sweet and bitter fool
> Will presently appear;
> The one in motley here,
> The other out there
> Lear: Dost thou call me fool, boy?
> Fool: All thy other titles thou hast given away; that thou wast born with.
> *King Lear*, Act 1 Scene 1, 154-65.

It is possible to recreate the role of honest advisor played by Shakespeare's Fool without the 'motley' clothes and perhaps with more success, either by leaders relying on one or more individuals whose position cannot be threatened by the advice proffered, and it may also be possible to institutionalize the role by requiring all members of a decision-making body to enact the role of Devil's Advocate in turn. In this way the advice is required by the role and not derived from the individual and hence should provide some degree of protection from leaders annoyed by the 'helpful' but perhaps embarrassing advice of their subordinates.

Alternatively, in some cases the consequences of decisions by leaders are so critical that procedures may be developed to inhibit individual error – of the kind exemplified in *Dr Strangelove* – subtitled *'Or how I learned to stop worrying and love the bomb.'* In Stanley Kubrick's 1964 movie, an impotent US Air Force Commander single-handedly initiates World War Three, aided and abetted by equally incompetent political and military leaders (several played by Peter Sellers). The notoriously dark humour of the film however, underlines the dangers of allowing individuals with limited knowledge to take critical decisions.

Ironically, and probably unknown to the film makers, two years before the film's release such a situation was almost enacted during the Cuban Missile Crisis in 1962. On Saturday 27 October that year, as the US and the USSR brought the world ever-closer to a nuclear stand off over the deployment of Soviet nuclear missiles in Cuba, an American U-2 spy plane was shot down over Cuba at 1341 hrs. At 1600 hrs the American Joint Chiefs of Staff recommended an invasion of the island by Monday 29 October at the latest. Half an hour after this recommendation was made the American Navy destroyer, the USS Beale (DD 471), made sonar contact with an unknown submarine. At 1659 hrs the Beale dropped 5 signalling depth charges on what turned out to be the Soviet submarine B-59. These depth charges are very small explosives designed to force the submarine to identify itself, rather than designed to destroy the submarine. Half an hour later, with no response from the submarine, the USS Cony dropped 5 more signalling depth charges on the B-59 which then tried to evade its American pursuers for four hours. However, technical problems on the submarine led to increased temperatures on the submarine (100F), oxygen deterioration, and the beginnings of health problems amongst the soviet crew. According to the Soviet captain's (Valentin Savitsky) account, at this point the B-59 was then rocked by 'something bigger than signalling depth charge.' Savitsky then ordered the crew to prepare for firing a nuclear torpedo at their 'attackers.' As he apparently stated: 'Maybe the war has already started up there, while we were doing somersaults here. We're going to blast them now! We will die but we will sink them all – we will not disgrace our navy.' Fortunately, the Soviet Navy's Rules of Engagement at the time required the agreement of three officers: the Captain plus the two deputy commanders. The first deputy commander agreed, but the second – Vasili Arkhipov – refused and the Captain was unable to fire the torpedo; instead the B-59 surfaced at 2050 hours. Understandably, Vasili Arkhipov was later lauded as 'the man who saved the world' but it is also important to note that the fail-safe procedures were critical to inhibiting the intention of the captain (Blanton, 2002).

Perhaps the thing to note from these examples is that attributing god-like qualities to leaders does not result in god-like qualities – but it might encourage us to think of leaders as gods and take 'appropriate action'. For example, during the 2002 Football World Cup I asked my MBA class what kind of leader the

English coach, Sven Goran Erikson, was? The immediate answer from one English student was that since England had just beaten Argentina 'Sven must be a God!' But when I then asked what would happen if England lost their next game against Brazil the same student responded, 'We will crucify him!' Here is an intriguing dialogue for it exposes the attributions of saint and sinner, saviour and scapegoat, that hoists leaders onto pedestals that cannot support them and then ensures those same leaders are hoist by their own petard. What this also reveals is the consequence of attributing omnipotence to leaders – we, the followers, are rendered irresponsible by our own action, for when the gods of leadership fail their impossible task – as fail they must eventually – we followers have a scapegoat to take all the blame for what is, in reality, our own failure to accept responsibility.[12]

Nevertheless this unresolved the yearning for perfection in leaders perhaps also reflects our collective dissatisfaction with the lives of unacknowledged followers – the gods of small things. As Albert Schweitzer in his autobiography *Out of My Life and Thought* remarked:

> Of all the will toward the ideal in mankind only a small part can manifest itself in public action. All the rest of this force must be content with small and obscure deeds. The sum of these, however, is a thousand times stronger than the acts of those who receive wide public recognition. The latter, compared to the former, are like the foam on the waves of a deep ocean.

This is a critical assault upon the idea that leadership can be reduced to the personality and behaviour of the individual leader and implies that we should recognize that organizational achievements are just that – achievements of the entire organization rather than merely the consequence of a single heroic leader. Yet although it is collective leaders and collective followers that move the wheel of history along it is often their formal or more Machiavellian individual leaders who claim the responsibility, leaving most people to sink unacknowledged by history, nameless but not pointless. George Eliot (1965: 896) makes this poignantly clear at the end of her novel *Middlemarch* in her description of Dorothea:

> Her full nature, like that river of which Cyrus broke the strength, spent itself in channels which had no great name on the earth. But the effect of her being on those around her was incalculably diffusive: for the growing good of the world is partly dependent on unhistoric acts; and that things are not so ill with you and me as they might have been, is half owing to the number who lived faithfully a hidden life, and rest in unvisited tombs.

This does not mean that individual leaders play no role, but it does suggest that their role is often quite limited. Leaders may be important – but there are whole rafts of other elements that are also important and it is often these that make the difference between success and failure. Perhaps the least understood or evaluated of these other elements is the role of the followers, without whom leaders cannot exist. A useful way to consider the all too easily overlooked role of followers in the construction of a leader's power is to envisage the difference between a domino-run and a Mexican wave. In the former all the power resides in the first movement that stimulates the dominoes to fall in sequence, generating a 'run'. Thus power lies with the pusher, the leader. But a Mexican wave that runs around a sports stadium does not depend on an individual leader to make it work – it works without apparent leadership and it 'dies' when the collective decide not to engage in further 'waves.'

In effect, power is a consequence as much as a cause of followership: if – and only if – followers follow then leaders become powerful, but that act remains contingent not determined, and certainly not determined by any future imaginings because acts are quintessentially indeterminate: followers always have the choice not to act, and though they may pay the consequences of not acting the point is that no leader or situation can guarantee followership – leaders are neither omnipotent nor omniscient – but irresponsible followers can make them appear both. Worse, irresponsible followers allow irresponsible leaders to take us to their private and unachievable utopias via three-easy-steps that usually include (1) blaming someone else for everything; (2) leaving all decisions in the hands of the leader and ceasing to take personal responsibility for actions taken in their name; and (3) taking on trust the leader's version of the 'truth'. Responsible followers may not be able to lead us to utopia but they can prevent us from ending up in the dystopia that irresponsible leaders usually end up in, and perhaps that pragmatic foundation is the best way forward.

Conclusion

This chapter has suggested that followership – a much maligned and often ignored element of leadership – is actually critical to its success, operating as an anvil upon which leadership is either made or destroyed. The first part of the chapter traced out the connections between leadership, followership, commitment and independence to construct a hypothetical schema of four ideal types of leadership: the 'white elephant', to represent the leader who is born a god, who is omnipotent, omniscient and as rare as an albino elephant; the 'cat herder', where leadership proved impossible in the face of individually-oriented and independently minded 'followers'; the 'emperor', where an assumed superiority acted to generate irresponsible followers; and the 'wheelwright', founded upon the acceptance by the leader of his or her limitations, his or her need to learn how to lead through an apprenticeship, and rooted in a dependence upon the advice and support of responsible followers who were both committed to the community but retained their independence of judgement from the leader. The role of the last type was then explored in some detail through various examples where the role of the followers – responsible or otherwise – supported or undermined the success of their leaders through an accumulation of small acts. Indeed, it was suggested the leadership was better understood as the god of small things because of the importance of this relationship between leaders and followers.

Endnotes

1. An earlier version of this chapter appeared in Grint, K. *Leadership: Limits and Possibilities*. Palgrave/Macmillan 2005.
2. Mission Command – which has long played a role in some aspects of the British Army – has recently become a critical aspect of the British military's Defence Leadership Centre doctrine. See Watters 2004.
3. http://www.eng.fju.edu.tw/worldlit/lecture/Roy.ppt.
4. Thanks to Jack Nasher-Awakemian for reminding me of this distinction.
5. http://www.geocities.com/Athens/3682/clowdisley.html
6. http://www.odyssey.dircon.co.uk/Victoria.htm. It is to inhibit the powerful influence of rank that contemporary British Courts Martial precede the final verdict with a discussion of individual conclusions by the most junior officer first, and the senior officer last (thanks to Group Captain Graham Evans for pointing this one out to me).
7. Edmund Burke (1729-97) is alleged to have said that "all that is necessary for the triumph of evil is for good men to do nothing."
8. http://pw1.netcom.com/~asapilot/p90.html. In 1994 Boeing published research into airline safety that used Hofstede's cultural categories to examine the link between culture and air crashes. That research suggested that those countries deemed to be high on power-distance and low on individualism (specifically Panama, Colombia, Venezuela, China, Korea, Pakistan, Thailand) had an accident rate 2.6 times the average. Phillips, D. Building a Cultural Index to World Airline Safety. Washington Post 21 August 1994, p.8. (thanks to Adrian Wilkinson for alerting me to this research).

9. "Provided Vincristine is administered intravenously (IV), it is a powerful and useful drug in the fight against Leukaemia. However, if the drug is administered, in error, through an intrathecal injection (IT) the result is usually the death of the patient, or if the patient does survive, they typically suffer from severe neurological trauma." External Inquiry into the adverse incident that occurred at Queen's Medical Centre, Nottingham, 4th January 2001 by professor Brian Toft. http://www.doh.gov.uk/qmcinquiry/.
10. http://news.bbc.co.uk/1/hi/health/1284244.stm
11. Hedge Funds (started with LTCM in 1994) are Ltd Partnerships, max 99 partners, almost unregulated, 4000 exist only very wealthy institutions and individuals, very high leverage/gearing [debt to equity/capital at LTCM 50/250-1(most @ 2-1)].
12. Heifetz 1994 on the issue of follower responsibility.

Bibliography

Barabási, A.L. *Linked: How Everything is Connected to Everything Else and What it Means for Business, Science and Everyday Life.* London: Plume, 2003.

Bevan, J. *The Rise and Fall of Marks and Spencer.* London: Profile Books, 2002.

Blanton, T.S. '*The Cuban Missile Crisis: 40 Years Later.*' Washington Post, 16 Oct 2002.

Bratton, J; Grint, K and Nelson, D. *Organisational Leadership.* Mason: Southwester/Thompson, 2005.

Browne, K.R. *Biology at Work: Rethinking Sexual Equality.* New Haven, CT: Yale University Press, 2002.

Drucker, H. *The Essential Drucker.* London: Harper-Collins 2001.

Gladwell, M. *The Tipping Point.* London: Abacus 2002.

Goldberg, S. *Why Men Rule: A Theory of Male Dominance.* Chicago: Open Court, 1993.

Heifetz, R. *Leadership Without Easy Answers.* Cambridge, Mass: Harvard University Press, 1994.

Jackson, P. *Sacred Hoops.* New York: Hyperion, 1995.

Kilduff, M. *Social Networks and Organisations.* London: Sage, 2003.

Kruger, J and Dunning,D. *Unskilled and Unaware of it: How Difficulties in recognising One's Own Competence Lead to Inflated Self-Assessments.* Journal of Personality and Social Psychology 77. 1121-1134.

O'Hare, D and Roscoe, S. *Flightdeck Performance: The Human Factor.* Ames, IA: Iowa State University Press,1990.

Stein, M. *Unbounded Irrationality: Risk and Organisational Narcissism at Long Term Capital Management.* Human Relations, 2003. Vol 56. No. 5. pp 523-40.

Tsunetomo, Y. Hagakure: *The Book of the Samurai*. London: Kodansha International, 2000.
Watters, B. *Mission Command: Auftragstaktik*. Paper delivered at the Leadership Symposium, RAF Cranwell, 13 May 2004.
Weick, K.E. *Sensemaking in Organisations*. London: Sage, 1995.

CHAPTER EIGHT

TRANSFORMATIONAL LEADERSHIP

LEADERSHIP:
WHAT HELPS AND WHAT HURTS

Air Commodore Steve Abbott

This presentation aims to identify what helps and what hurts in the exercise of leadership in a Royal Air Force career spanning some 28 years. In arriving at these conclusions I have drawn upon the shared experience of colleagues to complement my own.28 I do so guided by the dictum of the Israeli Air Force that, after the experience of combat operations, the vicarious experience of others is a good substitute. Although we are experiencing a high operational tempo at present we are not all fighting every day or leading on operations all of the time. During the 2 days of this conference we have been exposed to a great deal of the theories of leadership. I intend to pull together what this means for me in particular and what has guided my thought processes and my actions in what the Commander-in-Chief Strike Command calls 'the steep and scary places of the world'. I have had the privilege of command at every rank from Pilot Officer to Group Captain. My specialist experience is that of an RAF Regiment officer but I am, first and foremost, an airman; understanding the concept of air power and the means to employ it is at the heart of my profession.

I observe that developing as a leader also includes large doses of being a follower too; although I learned this particular lesson relatively slowly. In the early stages of my professional development it is true that 'when I was a child I thought as a child; my knowledge of leadership was limited but my arrogance as a graduate of the Royal Air Force College Cranwell was unbounded. I believed that if I willed something then it would happen; the 'Star Trek' model of leadership. Captain Kirk is on the bridge of the Starship Enterprise and it is all going wrong. Scotty, the engineer, is saying that "the dilithium crystals will not take it" Spock, unemotional, is analysing the situation and Lieutenant Sulu is banging away on the computer. Captain Kirk listens to their inputs, waves his hand and says, "Make it so!" He goes back, sits in his swivel chair and pretends that it is a problem solved – if only it were so simple.

In common with the product of most officer training academies I have always been able to make decisions. As a younger man, I thought that when I

---

[28] I acknowledge in particular the contribution of Air Commodore Graham Stacey who has freely shared his experience and thoughts in this respect.

came to these Star Trek moments, had listened to my team (because Cranwell had taught me to do that) and pronounced my decision that the desired sequence of events would then occur, leading inexorably to success, tea and medals. I was also, of course, a caring officer. I have inspected 28 pairs of feet up on the bedsteads in a tin hut in Belize checking for the things that young airmen are prone to after 2 or 3 weeks in the jungle without taking their boots off. It was a formative experience! I believed that if I made sure their boots fitted and that they got their mail, that I was caring for them. I was to learn much later that this was a long way short of connecting with them emotionally.

As I reached adolescence and I moved away from the front line for short periods I learnt a new lexicon: that of outputs and outcomes. My bed fellows became control and measurement. I offered ideas and I interpreted vision and strategy; I defined clear objectives and the processes needed to achieve them. I embraced the mantra of continuous improvement and data and information became, for me, the breakfast of champions. I learnt the necessity of documenting, sharing and archiving information and I learnt to shape my battle space because I was mindful of the Air Secretary's dictum that "officers shape their environment, they are not shaped by it." I defined clear boundaries between role and function, I limited my span of control and I complied with and demanded compliance with mutually defined operational guidelines. I treated any deviation from these as a problem to be overcome in pursuit of uniform predictable outcomes. Quite simply I strove to impose order upon chaos; in short, I had become a staff officer; even worse, I had learned the transactional approach to leadership and management.

Finally though I became a man and I put away childish things assisted by a process of training and education. In fact, the Air Force trained me extremely well through Staff College and University which developed my intellect and through exposure to the work of others, expanded my experience. This process helped and encouraged a more intuitive approach to leadership and problem solving as opposed to the mechanistic process of the estimate and derived courses of action. Although we now acknowledge that intuition is simply analysis via a different route.

This cumulative experience led me to identify some tenets of leadership that I have found useful on operations and elsewhere; some help and some hurt:

What Helps

Inspiring Individuals. Firstly, I believe firmly that leadership is about inspiring individuals. However, I was privileged to command an airbase during Operation FINGAL in Afghanistan in 2002 and it was quickly apparent that for an overwhelming majority of the time, our people are self motivating to an extraordinary degree. The trick lies in spotting the moment when intervention is required to bolster confidence and boost self confidence in the face of ambiguity and uncertainty. This is borne out by the fact that I can barely remember having to give a direct order to get something done and on that occasion the order was for a unit to take rest and stop working rather than to drive men forward.

Treating Regulations as Tools. Regulations are necessary but they remain merely tools. The adage that they are for the guidance of wise men and the obedience of fools is more than just a truism. Recent command of the RAF Force Protection hub at RAF Honington revealed the extent of the growth of statutory regulation affecting the Armed Forces. Much of this regulation is quite necessary, we are not in the business of damaging our people unnecessarily but there is a tendency for a risk averse mentality to carry over into the preparation for operations and worse, the operational environment proper. In these situations it is important to understand risk and to accept risk as a commander at every level. The bottom line is clear, for any level of command and leadership it is crucial to take ownership of a problem to own the decisions made in solving these problems.

Avoiding the Pursuit of Popularity. Popularity is not important. It does not hurt if it emerges naturally but it does not need to be chased and should not be.

Moral Courage. Moral courage is the ability to say "no" when it is required. It is also the ability to insist on the right course of action often in the face of stark and compelling incentives to adopt less onerous solutions. Personal standards are a related issue in this respect. They must be of the highest order. As a leader, you are under constant scrutiny and observation. All your words and actions are observed by those whom you have the privilege to lead. If you let your petticoat show, someone will see and remember. Equally integral to the moral courage issue is that of 'truth'. Field Marshal Slim told young officers at Sandhurst that they should never hide things from their men, that they should always know the full, most awful truth. However, there is a balance to be struck here. There will be occasions when it will not aid our people to know certain things. This is not to encourage deceit but it is necessary to be able to recognise those moments when they have all they can bear at that single moment and it is not in their interest to overload them with things they are powerless to affect.

Confidence. In all things and at all times leaders must display a natural self confidence, including the confidence to stand apart, if necessary. We often hear that it is wisest to remain the 'grey man' but to be effective as a leader you must be distinctive enough to be remembered. There are countless examples of those leaders who have achieved this in relatively simple ways: Keith Park had his own personal Hurricane, OK1 and a trademark white flying suit; Montgomery adopted 2 cap badges on his beret and Field Marshal Slim wore the Australian style slouch hat rather than a General's hat in the Middle East. On the other hand, TE Lawrence[29] described officers who 'came in a roll which was laid out and chopped off at uniform intervals'. This is definitely not what we should be striving for.

What Hurts

People who Set Limits to their Responsibilities. There should be no limits to the limits we set on our personal responsibilities. I have encountered some people who, even in operational situations, required things set in stone and boundaries to be defined. We all need to accept that sometimes there can be no terms of reference – we do what is necessary when it is necessary and how it is necessary; there are no limits to our responsibilities. It is also important to take on responsibility for those decisions made above you. Units and people are less effective when they are told to do something "because the boss says so." Decisions should be presented in a united fashion at every level of leadership.

Leaders Who Accept Praise but Not Blame. Closely allied to accepting responsibility is the idea that a leader should not absorb all the praise for his unit's work without also accepting blame for any mistakes. Most of the people who have been formally acknowledged for their successes are acutely humble and very mindful of the fact that it was the team behind them which drove them forward. Nevertheless, the analogy of a partridge and its chicks is useful in reminding us of the need to act as a shield: when a predator bears down on a partridge with its chicks, the bird will spread its wings and all the chicks run underneath; come what may the partridge will die before exposing the chicks to harm. We must as leaders inculcate the trust in our people that whatever approbation comes down, we will stand in the firing line.

To achieve this trust on a daily basis and to encourage the adoption of full responsibility by every individual, the principles of Mission Command are crucial. Mission Command does not entail delegating responsibility without authority and the resources necessary to achieve the task. Equally, it is not a case of delegating responsibility and then simply expecting things to happen. The proper exercise of Mission Command is one of the hardest things to achieve. It begins with conveying a clear indication of intent and that is not something that other people can be relied upon to articulate accurately for you. Staff can help but there comes a stage when the leader must articulate what it is he wants to happen in a concise and pithy and personal way. Constraints must be set and a main effort identified to focus activity. If this is achieved then it is reasonable to expect the team to work out the 'how'. Mission Command still requires intervention – it requires us to check and monitor, close enough to the action to be able put a gentle hand on the tiller at the right moment. The beauty of mission command when applied, practiced and understood is that when the

---

[29] Lawrence, TE, (1986), <u>Revolt in the Desert</u>, (London, the Folio Society).

leader is elsewhere and unable to intervene, the team has the courage and understanding to carry the intent forward.

The Expectation of Perfection in Leadership. I do not know a perfect leader and that includes every single person I have ever met in the course of my 28 years of military service. Unfortunately, when we start analysing leadership, defining traits and characteristics, we tend to favour some characteristics over others. We must resist that temptation and look at the overall effect people achieve, allowing some mistakes and establishing a blame free culture. But how can we accept mistakes when on operations and we need to win? Nearly all military people are intensely competitive – it is a by product of being in a winning Air Force and this makes it difficult to accept the mistakes of others if these impact on what you are trying to achieve. I can only state that it takes courage, but in my experience, accepting the mistakes of others does more to engender trust than perhaps any other single thing. A related observation is that in our relatively small Air Force with precious few incompetents there are very few who cannot or will not perform. It is a characteristic of the best leaders that they get the best from a diverse set of people. Seeking to pick and choose teams runs the risk of creating teams in which constructive dissent is absent. Those who repeatedly remove and replace team members should question their own leadership skills for a moment before damning those working for them. Finally, in reflecting on the quest for perfection, and in demanding that leaders lead at all times and in all places, I have learnt that at any given time in any given place, any decision is better than no decision at all.

Conclusion

These are my personal observations distilled from 28 years of Service in the Royal Air Force on a series interesting operations at every rank. I am well aware that they are not unique to me; indeed I am somewhat relieved that they are not. I started off with a very shallow understanding of what was required to make people work for me and, if honest, probably relied more on the fact that it was their duty to do as I said more than anything else. In the middle years I believed that I could impose order on chaos, process was a panacea. Latterly, by rationalising my own experience and assimilating that of others, I have come to understand the values of a transformational approach. That is taking the initiative in establishing and making a commitment to relationships with those I have been given the privilege to lead. Two way communication and the free exchange of information and ideas are at the heart of this approach. The process raises the level of performance of leaders and followers alike.

© Alan Hooper 2005

TRANSFORMATIONAL LEADERSHIP: UNLOCKING HUMAN POTENTIAL

Professor Alan Hooper

In days gone by, running an organisation seemed akin to conducting a symphony orchestra. Nowadays, I think it is more like leading a jazz ensemble. There's more improvisation."

This quote from Warren Bennis (Hooper & Potter, 2000) goes to the heart of the current debate about Leadership and explains, in part, why so many people are discovering that it is difficult to be an effective leader today.

Chris Bones, the principal of Henley Management College, has provided some interesting observations in a recent interview with The Times (10 May 2005): "Running an organisation is 10 percent strategy and 90 percent execution, but we give all our attention to the first and none to the second." In the same interview he points his finger at the "blame culture" as one of the reasons why many people do not take responsibility which, in turn, means that no one is learning from their mistakes "…. Dealing with 'smart failure' positively." Bones believes that the key to success is values: "Managers need to understand what their values are both as an individual and as an organisation, and hold to those values."

Both Bennis and Bones have tried to articulate what lies behind the realities of leadership in today's fast-changing and confused world. Antonio Marturano has argued that the concepts of Transactional Leadership (which is built on reciprocity) and Transformational Leadership (concerned with hearts and minds) are "ambiguous and ill constructed" (Marturano, 2004). His view is supported by Ciulla (1998) who pointed out that Burns would find it difficult to accept Hitler as a leader because his theory of transformational leadership is "…. clearly a prescriptive one about the nature of morally good leadership." (Ciulla, 1998). In contrast, if one considers Bass (1985) definition of transformational leadership, Hitler clearly qualifies. So, given the disagreement between the theorists it is hardly surprising that those who are exercised with the practicalities of transformational leadership are finding it difficult.

In attempting to unravel all this, I intend to cover the relevant ideas and models related to Transformational Leadership by exploring the second part of my title "Unlocking Human Potential" for I believe this is the key to unpicking this issue. But first, let us be clear by what we mean by Transformational Leadership. According to Philip Saddler it is "the process of engaging the commitment of employees in the context of shared values and shared vision." (Saddler, 1997) This is linked strongly to trust and, according to Bass and Avolio (1990), it has four components:

1. Idealised influence (having a clear vision and sense of purpose).
2. Individual consideration (paying attention to people's needs)
3. Intellectual stimulation (acquiring new ideas)
4. Inspiration.

In a later publication they claimed that "the goal of transformational leadership is to transform people in the literal sense – to change them in mind and heart." (Bass & Avolio, 1994).

For Burns, who was the first person to propose the idea of "transforming leadership", this concept "is a relationship of mutual stimulation and elevation that converts followers into leaders and may convert leaders into moral agents" (Burns, 1978).

These definitions are related to the "soft issues" of managing people and contain words which have strong emotional connotations (vision, values, trust) which is essential if the leadership wants to transform people and organisations. However, in order to be effective, these words really have to mean something, with the leaders setting a transparent example, which sets the tone for the culture. A company that has achieved this is the car manufacturer, Honda. They established their culture from the "Honda Philosophy" (a concise pamphlet produced in 1992 by Nobuhiko Kawamoto, then the President and CEO of the company). This philosophy starts with "Fundamental beliefs (which commences with "Respect for the Individual" – based on initiative, equality and trust). It contains words that are not usually associated with management, such as: 'joy', 'dreams' and 'a challenging spirit'. Significantly, throughout the eleven-page document, there is no mention of the word 'car' or 'engine'. The significance of this philosophy is that, in a highly competitive and over-crowded market, Honda is bucking the trend. For example, their European operating profit increased by 60% in 2004 when many of their competitors have been struggling (and Rover, once their partner, has gone out of business).

Another company which has unlocked the potential of their people is John Lewis Partnership. When the author interviewed Sir Stuart Hampson, the Chair, in 1988 he said "ownership has to mean something .... Happiness is a fundamental objective of management. People need a sense of fulfilment, a feeling of satisfaction. If they are happy at work, then they are more likely to give of their best." (Hooper & Potter, 2000). John Lewis has consistently headed the UK unquoted companies league table and in 2003 the bonus award to the group's 59,000 staff (or 'partners') was £87 million (the equivalent of six week's pay – for every individual). Significantly, the ideas expressed in that interview are now incorporated into the purpose of the company:

> "The John Lewis Partnership is owned in trust for its members and its ultimate purpose is the happiness of all its members, through their worthwhile and satisfying employment in a successful business." (The Sunday Times, 10 October 2004)

So, it is quite clear, that such inspirational words which lead to aspirational action, result in very impressive achievements. This has been borne out by the research carried out by Hooper & Potter for their book Intelligent Leadership. They interviewed some 25 effective "change leaders" against a model centred on 'beliefs and values' to discover whether value-based leadership really did lead to good bottom-line performance. It did. The model they used, which is based on Neuro Linguistic Programming, see Figure 1 below, indicates that the identity of an organisation is fundamentally based on its beliefs and values. An organisation with a clear understanding of its values, which are believed and lived by everyone, will have a strong identity and a 'sense of higher purpose.'

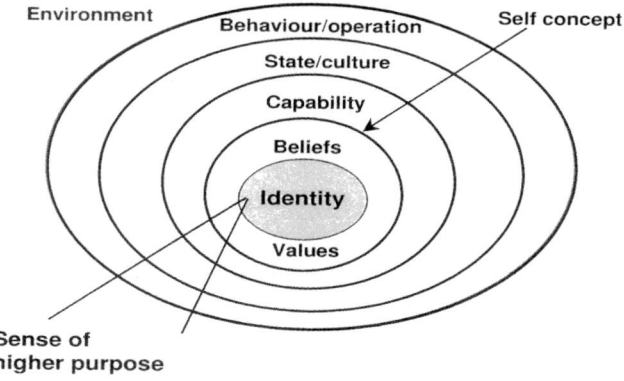

Figure 1: Organisation identity based upon beliefs and values (Hooper & Potter).

In contrast, any organisation which does not have such a culture is unlikely to be confident about its identity. Interestingly, there may be periods when an organisation goes through a period when it is less confident due to the changing nature of its business. This is a normal process for companies who are good at managing change as they accept this as part of today's uncertainty. They are usually led by transformational leaders (such as Sir Richard Branson at Virgin and Lord Browne at BP).

This emphasis on integrity is endorsed by Warren Bennis who has continuously sought to understand the essence of leadership, drawing on his own practical experience as a very young infantry company commander in Europe during World War II and, subsequently, as President (Vice-Chancellor) of the University of Cincinnati. His research has included significant observations about the behaviour of effective leaders. Firstly, they are good listeners:

"Deep listeners abandon their egos to the talents of others"
(Bennis at Exeter University Leadership Forum 1999)

Listening is the most important aspect of communication – and the lack of ego is something that the author notes in his own research (Hooper & Potter, 2000). Secondly, such individuals develop a trust with their people, based on the following model at Figure 2 (presented by Bennis at the same forum).

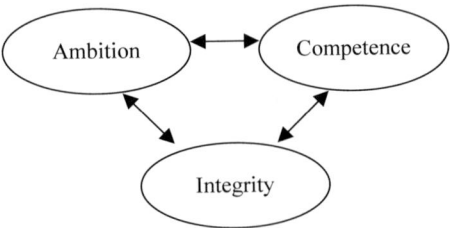

Notes: 1. Integrity is the "moral compass."
         2. Good leaders keep the three ingredients in balance.

Figure 2: The Tripod of trust (Bennis).

Competence and ambition are important ingredients of leadership, but real trust will not be confirmed until people are sure about the integrity of their leaders. This provides the moral compass for leaders – and the good ones keep these three ingredients in balance.

So, in trying to understand how transformational leaders unlock human potential, we are painting a picture which so far includes the following words:

   Happiness
   Beliefs
   Values
   Deep Listening
   Trust
   Integrity
   Comfortable with Ambiguity.

It would be interesting at this point for the reader to consider "leaders whom they have known" to see how well they match up!

A brief review of other authors who have written about transformational leadership, either directly or indirectly, provides supporting evidence. In their impressive research about inspirational leaders, Goffee and Jones came up with four characteristics which an individual needs to be really inspirational (one or two qualities on their own are insufficient):

- They selectively show their weaknesses
- They rely on intuition
- They manage with Tough Empathy
- They reveal their differences.

(Harvard Business Review 2000)

The research revealed that inspirational leaders were sufficiently self-confident to behave in ways that others would not (most of us hide out weaknesses, not reveal them). In particular, the notion of "tough empathy" (a leader being able to empathise with their people so well that when they have to take tough decisions, even when it will adversely affect their employees, they retain their support) lies at the heart of transformational leadership. No leader will be able to transform an organisation unless they are able to reach the hearts and minds of their people. This can be achieved in many ways and through different styles and behaviour, but the litmus test is whether they can really touch their people. So strong is that emotional link that often leaders do not know whether they have reached that depth until they face a crisis. Such a moment occurred when Greg Dyke's offer to resign as Director General of the BBC on 30 January 2004, in the wake of the Gilligan-Kelly incident, was, unexpectedly, accepted by the Board of Governors. The outpouring of emotion from the staff of the BBC as Dyke said goodbye to his people has never been seen before in the long history of that organisation. Some 3000 people gathered outside BBC Television Centre to see him go, many still in shock at losing such an inspirational leader.

Greg Dyke is a good example of someone with a fine sense of Emotional Intelligence, the five main components of which are self-awareness, self-regulation, motivation, empathy and social skills (Goleman 1998). Such leaders are self-confident, trustworthy, comfortable with ambiguity, have a strong drive to achieve, good at building teams, persuasive and effective change leaders.

One almost gets a sense of the extrovert from such hallmarks, but that would be misleading. In his research into what makes a good company truly great, Jim Collins (2001) identified the paradox of transformational leaders: a mixture of personal humility and professional will. On the journey to create extraordinary results with an unwavering determination "to do what must be done" they displayed modesty, kept out of the limelight, were ambitious for the company (not for self) and acted with quiet determination. Such an individual is Sir Terry Leahy who has transformed Tesco since he was appointed the chief executive in 1997. The company is so successful that £1 out of every £8 spent in UK passes through Tesco's tills. He has achieved this with a style of leadership which is understated, inclusive, with an ability to identify strengths in others and a philosophy which is based on maintaining a happy workforce. He is also a very good listener.

A recent piece of research from Phil Hodgson (2004) from Ashridge into top leadership identified some other characteristics that are germane to this topic. Interestingly, his research was inspired in part by listening to a charismatic US business leader speaking at a conference in 2001. His speech went down very well and he was cited as a role model for effective top leadership. His name is Ken Lay and he was then the chairman of Enron. Within four years his reputation and that of his company lay in tatters. Hodgson's survey of 40 CEOs revealed the importance of credibility, developing potential, creating an effective top team, continuous learning and energy – both for themselves and for the organisation.

In the end, it all depends on what leaders do, and how they behave, that will decide whether they can transform organisations. A decade ago Kouzes and Posner (1995) identified five behaviours for effective leadership which contained interesting words:

> Challenge the Process
> Inspire a Shared Vision
> Enable Others to Act
> Model the Way
> Encourage the Heart

These words leap off the page and encourage the reader to discover more about the special ingredients which enable individuals to "transform" their people.

There is a theme running through all of this work, which may help to clarify the realities of transformational leadership. However, before we proceed to that, we need to be aware of "the health warning". Narcissistic leaders. These are the type of people who throughout history have shaped the destiny of countries and organisations by their vision and their ability to inspire people. These are the leaders people talk about – and they fascinate us because they are not particularly likeable and tend to be egotistical, self-promotional, with larger-than-life personalities. The strengths of such individuals are well documented, but the weaknesses are less so. According to Maccoby (2004) these include being sensitive to criticism, being poor listeners, lacking in empathy, distaste for mentoring and an intense desire to compete. "All in all unattractive characteristics – especially as narcissistic leaders can self-destruct." (Hooper, 2006).

Maccoby has indicated succinctly the difference between narcissistic and transformational leadership – and it is the difference between the latter and other forms of leadership which provide us with the clues to understanding what really unlocks human potential.

Let us finish with consideration of what Transformational Leadership actually looks like. This list is not definitive, however, drawing together the key points from various sources it would appear to consist of the following:

Integrity	Tough Empathy	Self-Confidence
Personal Example	Listening	Energy
Trust	Beliefs and Values	Willpower
Encourage the Heart	Talent spotter & developer	Humility
Continuous Learning	Comfortable with Ambiguity	Teambuilder
Alignment	Inspiring a Shared Vision	Persuasive
Creating Happiness		

The styles of transformational leaders will vary but they all share the ability to change their organisations by releasing the talent of their people so that, together, they achieve extra-ordinary results – and it is the results that matter. Furthermore, such leaders set new standards in their fields (for example, Sir Clive Woodward coaching the England rugby team to winning the World Cup in 2004, Sir Terry Leahy's leadership of Tesco and Tim Schmidt's inspiration, the Eden Project). It is only when an individual has achieved all this that they can truly earn the accolade of Transformational Leader.

Bibliography

Bass, B. & Avolio, B. *Developing transformational leadership – 1992 and beyond.* Journal of European Industrial Training, 1990 Vol 14, No 5, pp21-7.
Bass, B.M. & Avolio, B.J. *Improving Organisational Effectiveness through Transformational Leadership.* Thousand Oaks CA: Sage Publications, 1994.
Bass, B.M. *Leadership and Performance Beyond Expectations.* New York: Free Press, 1985.
Burns, J.M. *Leadership.* New York: Harper Row, 1978.
Ciulla, J.B. (ed.) *Ethics: the Heart of Leadership.* Westport, CT: Quorum, 1998.
Collins, J. *Level 5 Leadership.* Harvard Business Review, Jan 2001.
Goffee, R & Jones, G *Why should anyone be led by you?* Harvard Business Review, Sept-Oct 2000.

Goleman, D. *What makes a Leader?* Harvard Business Review, Nov-Dec 1998.
Hodgson, P. *Working Where the Buck Stops*. The Ashridge Journal, Autumn 2004.
Hooper, A. & Potter, J. *Intelligent Leadership*. London: Random House, 2000.
Hooper, A. (ed.) *Leadership Perspectives*. Aldershot: Dartmouth, 2006.
Kouzes, J. & Posner, B. *The Leadership Challenge*. London: Jossey-Bass, 1999.
Maccoby, M. *The Power of Transference* Harvard Business Review, Sept 2004.
Marturano, A. *Transformational and Transactional Leadership: A Critique* Studying Leadership: 3rd International Workshop held at University of Exeter, Dec 2004.

Newspapers

The Times   10 May 2005
The Sunday Times 10 Oct 2004

CHAPTER NINE

CLOSING ADDRESS

CLOSING ADDRESS

Air Chief Marshal Sir Brian Burridge

Introduction

We hear much about the great changes that are taking place in the Royal Air Force at the moment and there is much posturing on the subject of change management. But, if we focus on the strategic level change and cast our minds back to earlier presentations, we can see that, in comparison to the scale of change faced by Sykes, Trenchard and Tedder, today's challenge is not that great. By 2015 our fast jet squadrons will reduce in number only by one, from 17 to 16, Air Transport and Air Refuelling have reduced from 9 squadrons to 8, ISTAR squadrons will reduce from 7 to 6, yet the RAF Regiment Field Squadrons will increase in number from 5 to 6. The overall structure of the RAF is therefore not changing so very much. Inevitably, in a large dynamic organisation, change affects different parts at different rates and at different times. Equally, perspectives are different. The reaction of individuals, sections and units, tends to be predicated on what they predict will be the impact for them, the future viability of their role, trade or even station. Hence, in assessing the impact of change, much depends on where you sit.

The Place of the Individual

In general, people's concerns come down to three questions: "have I got a job?", "will I have to move?", and "what's my new role in this new expeditionary Air Force?" What they are reflecting is not uncertainty in the face of a vast amount of strategic change. Nor are they reflecting a concern for the shape of the future Royal Air Force. Rather, they are reflecting short-term personal uncertainties to which they don't know the answers; this is a natural reaction to change in an organisation like ours.

Unlocking Creativity

I believe we can all, from SAC to Air Chief Marshal, identify three aspects of common ground that play to this: trust, communication and culture. Culture, which may be wrapped up in ethos, reflects on both trust and communication. For me, the dilemma is how to use these three aspects of common ground to unlock the creativity which surely exists at all levels whilst still remaining in the bounds of our necessarily hierarchical organisation. This dilemma confronted me relatively recently. I could see that the reason we have made so much progress in logistics transformation and 'leaning' was due to the ingenuity and experience of our junior personnel. We created the conditions for them to design future logistics processes on the shop-floor that was based on their experience and understanding of actually doing the job. Of course, they know what really works on the ground and it is the corporate arrogance inherent in large hierarchical organisations that tends to suppress that knowledge. We have managed to overcome that arrogance, at least temporarily. The challenge now is to find a way to continue to keep that creativity unlocked without breaking the hierarchical model on which we have to rely as a military force when we go on operations. In other words, we need to increase a sense of empowerment at lower levels without undermining the authority relationships that are fundamental to a military system. If we can achieve this in peacetime then we will truly become an agile and adaptable Air Force. The key in doing so will be to rely on those three aspects that I mentioned earlier: trust, communication and culture.

Taking the Bumps Out of the Ride – Trust

I want to set the context for what we face in the Royal Air Force amongst what is happening within society generally. The following is an extract from a recent paper of mine entitled: 'The Roller Coaster Ride of the Strategic Leader' and it addresses one of those aspects – trust:

According to a MORI poll in the UK, 8 people in 10 do not believe that "Directors of large companies can be trusted to tell the truth." Research from the Committee on Standards in Public Life conducted in September 2004 revealed a widespread lack of trust in holders of public office. Conversely, a recent YouGov poll shows that, in spite of the damning verdict for the BBC of the Hutton report on the lead up to the war in Iraq, the BBC is still the most trusted news network, showing a five fold advantage over its rivals. Clearly, populations have a capricious view on trust but, in the UK, there is a danger that we have entered a downward spiral within which it is not easy to judge cause and effect. There seem to be three variables in this unstable equation. The first is the level of general scepticism or even cynicism that public bodies and some professions are not to be trusted. As a result, and this is the second variable, there is a move towards other measures to ensure accountability, which is aimed at placating an ever-increasing array of stakeholders. Stringent professional codes, regulatory bodies, granular and detailed performance targets, and league tables that name and shame. As for the third variable, against these metrics there are bound to be imperfections and failures. These in turn are reported – and sometimes hyped – by the media and what trust remains is further eroded so starting the cycle again.

So, we are faced with a context beset with scepticism. Organisations tend to respond to that by exercising power manifested through performance indicators, followed-up with the long screwdriver. In other words, we have undermined trust by centralising control to the extent that empowerment is merely a hollow word. It is this trend that we are currently trying to reverse. Strike Command is no different to any other organisation facing this challenge.

Empowerment and Risk

Historically in the Royal Air Force we have a lot in our favour. Sir Michael Howard wrote about the Royal Air Force and its formative days thus:

> *The development of warfare itself...called for a system of command which...increasingly demanded a degree of technical, administrative and professional expertise that was not necessarily to be found among the traditional officer producing classes. Further, it demanded among all ranks a degree of intelligent co-operation and devolution of authority, very different from the instant unquestioning obedience, which the old hierarchy had expected and largely got. The new Royal Air Force, in particular, with its increasing dependence on technology, very quickly found that a structure of command based on rigid distinctions between officers and other ranks simply did not work.*

So, historically we have a culture that will certainly assist us in generating empowerment and unlocking creativity because we do not have artificial barriers in quite the same way as the other Services do. But there *are* some significant barriers. Our biggest barrier to transformation is our innate sense that we want to hang on to process.

Process is the touch stone that most people reach out for in 'steep and scary places' yet much of our process is out of date. In benign hierarchies, there is also an expectation that change and its associated management will be neatly served up, almost like an airline meal, from the top and handed down as a *fait accompli*. Well, we simply do not have the wisdom and detailed experience at the top to manage in that way. But neither have we created the degree of empowerment to generate the necessary buy-in so that everybody realises that they have a part to play in all of this. There is nothing optional about it. Everybody has a part to play in our transformation. Some of the reluctance to participate stems from an innate risk aversion that ultimately would lead to cultural paralysis. People are cautious of taking risks in case they fail and are blamed for mistakes or suffer some adverse comment on their annual report. There is therefore still much to do to tackle these root issues which, once set straight, will provide a solid foundation on which to base our leadership of change at all levels.

Dispensing with Outdated Process

In the not too distant future, the introduction of new technology will offer great opportunities to change fundamentally the way we do things. We can throw out old processes and open our minds to new methods. In logistics, new ways of working have already allowed us to change people's minds about the old processes. Although the need for change was imposed from the top down, and although the pace may initially have been unpopular, it has presented the opportunity to rethink the way tasks are approached. In so doing, it has allowed us collectively to address the frustrations that inevitably arise when we cling to outmoded process. But it has taken investment. The need to invest to save became self-evident in the end. Overall, it really has been a demonstration of the idea that "innovation is a gas that bubbles up from the bottom."

Communications in Turbulence: P Prune versus U-Need-to-Know

This brings me to the crucial need for us to communicate clearly and constantly during this period of change. In my visits to stations, I hear much about a lack of communication and I meet people who simply do not know what is going on. This is a worry as we must ensure that information cascades down right through the command chains so that all are well informed. Lord Bell and his organisation have carried out some research into the changes in the nature and structure of society over the last 50 years. This research offers up some useful pointers as to why our people find themselves in a radically different environment now, and why our methods of communication may not be best suited to our environment anymore.

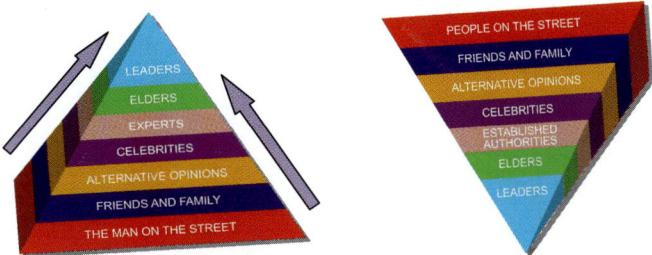

Figure 1 – From Deference to reference. © *Chime Communications*

There are really 3 key factors to these changes in society: the first is the decline of deference and trust in society; the second is the notion of the empowered consumer; and the third addresses technology and the huge developments that have occurred in the last 50 years. I am dealing here with society at large and factors that affect individuals' outlooks as part of that society. People's attitudes are configured across the spectrum of their lives. Judgements over what influences their expectations in the consumer environment to which they are exposed every day can be read across to their working lives. So, the way they behave and respond to communication outside of work can be extremely helpful in informing us of the expectations they will have of their employer and the working environment.

From a commercial point of view, Lord Bell's analysis concluded that; "Clients are spending communication budgets inefficiently because much of the thinking behind communications is still based within the medium of mass communication." Now I wonder if this true of us in the Royal Air Force? With mass produced bulletins from Commanders-in-Chief and websites that no-one consults or only do so on a selective basis. Maybe getting the big messages across requires a different approach.

Figure 1 shows the hierarchy from which people gain their values and their views. In a deferential society, there are certain communications sources which are important. We now need to recognise that we live in a referential society so that the familiar hierarchy is turned on its head. In the late1950s, we were a nation emerging from the Second World War and many in the population were conditioned by their military experience in highly stressful times or by their experience in civil society living under the pressures of a war of national survival. Britain in the1950s was very austere; there was not much spare of anything and society was segmented according to class which aligned precisely with prosperity. Those at the top of society called the shots and ran the show.

At some point all this changed and turned on its head. Some social historians believe it was a comparatively modern phenomenon coinciding with the explosion in information technology. Some believe it stems from the development of New Labour and the premise of the rights of the individual taking precedence; others say it is earlier, first appearing during the Thatcher era. I believe that its roots lie in the 1960s which represented the watershed in terms of emerging from post war austerity and in a growing demand for self determination; it was a period of great social change.

In the consumer world, communication has evolved from being that of 'blind transmission': "this is what we need and therefore must buy" to realising that being selective in the way you targeted the same message to different groups was more effective. 'Relationship branding' was the result with great emphasis being placed on targeting individuals with specific messages. It has also been recognised that it is necessary to target people using a variety of sources. In addition, informal communication also takes place within groups which is greatly magnified with the explosion of new technology. Figure 2 describes this evolution. All this applies to the workplace with informal methods (the rumour networks or grapevine) of drawing information becoming markedly more important. This means that of all the communication that takes place within and about an organisation, the organisation itself only controls a tiny proportion of it.

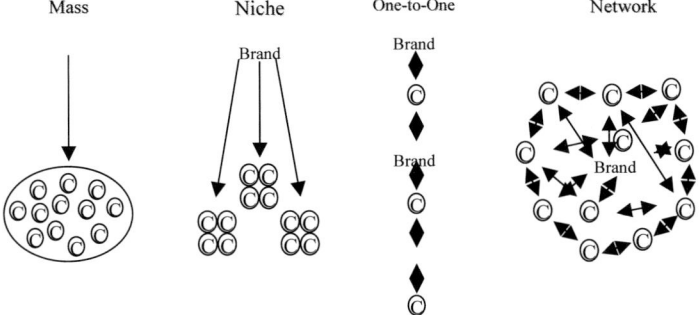

Figure 2 – Networks of Communication © Chime Communications

I would like you to consider all this in the context of your own organisation. Ask yourselves how communication really works and consider how you can capitalise on it.

Conclusion

So how do I draw all of these points together? First, we must move towards an ethos of greater empowerment. This must be backed by action and not just become a hollow promise. We are attempting to move positively towards greater empowerment but a cultural change of this nature will not happen overnight: it will be some time before those at the coalface see enduring effect.

Secondly, and a related point, we need to shift the emphasis towards people having a greater degree of control over their own lives. In a low-level structural sense, 'Pay-As-You-Dine' and the Joint Personal Administration project will see a shift in culture in this direction. But a bigger change will result if we become adept at unlocking the creativity that exists at junior levels just as we did in the Defence Logistics Transformation process. By stimulating analysis among those who actually do the work at the coal face, and really listening to what they have to say, we will greatly improve our effectiveness as well as generating buy-in from those most affected by change. The more that we are seen to do this, the more relatively junior people will feel that they have an element of control over their own lives.

Thirdly, we must stop hiding behind process – each and every one of us – because process is getting in the way of trust. We must understand that the move from a deferential to a referential society and the role that communications plays in creating trust means that high levels of empathy are required from leaders at all levels. You have to understand the way in which the current environment and context for defence impacts on people in terms of their uncertainties, their aspirations and the limits to their understanding. Only then will you generate the necessary empathy with your people such that suspicion and scepticism will be replaced by openness and trust.

The historical norm has been the need for the human touch; Harris and Dowding in their different ways cared about people. Dowding, 'Stuffy' though he was by name and by nature, reminds us that early in the Battle of Britain Churchill wrote to him in affectionate raillery and referred to the fighter pilots of the day as his "chicks", Dowding said "he could not have paid me a greater compliment; every one was needed before the end." His step-daughter, who worked for him at the headquarters at Bentley Priory, said that in the evenings he felt each loss personally, that he felt each one of these pilots was his son. This is not a side to Dowding that comes readily to the fore. Harris too fought hard to reduce the risk to his crews in bomber command. A master of technology, he continually pressed the scientific community to come up with answers to seemingly intractable problems.

So where does this take us in the development of tomorrow's leaders and commanders? The need to develop flexible commanders who show the agility to cope in today's and tomorrow's ambiguous environment relies on their gaining early experience through empowerment. Andrew Gordon's book 'Rules of the Game' describes a period in the history of the Royal Navy when intuitive leadership had been replaced by rigid adherence to the Signals Book. This approach led to the development, from the 1880s, of a mindset of rigid left brain thinking. Gordon describes the resulting tension as "Regulators versus Rat Catchers". In other words, regulators were left brain, rule-bound operators who were constrained by the processes laid out in the Signals Book. The culture discouraged the creative, right brain thinking that leads to the intuitive approach of the rat catcher. In this modern and changing Air Force I don't need many regulators: I need lots of rat catchers. The only system of command that will work for us in future is one that allows rat catchers to flourish; in other words Mission Command.

Finally, we must unleash the passion that resides in everyone about what we do. We must unlock it from individuals and harness it collectively for the common good then use it to our advantage to transform the organisation. People must be confident to do things their way; if you take nothing else away from this conference then let it be that we, as leaders, must all take ownership of problems – no one is going to give you all the answers – you must find your own way.

Bibliography

Howard, M. *The Armed Forces and the Community.* RUSI Journal, Aug 1996.
Mugford, S. *"If you do what you've always done...Leadership Challenges in a Downsizing RAAF"* Air Force Leadership: Beyond Command, Jul 2005.

BIOGRAPHIES

Air Chief Marshal Sir Jock Stirrup

GCB AFC ADC DSc FRAeS FCMI RAF

Air Chief Marshal Sir Jock Stirrup was commissioned in 1970. After a tour as a Qualified Flying Instructor he served on loan with the Sultan of Oman's Air Force, flying Strikemasters in the Dhofar War. Returning to the United Kingdom in 1975 he was posted to No 41(F) Squadron, flying Jaguars in the Reconnaissance role, before taking up an exchange appointment on RF-4C Phantoms in the United States. He then spent two years at RAF Lossiemouth as a flight commander on the Jaguar Operational Conversion Unit, and subsequently attended the Joint Service Defence College in 1984.

He commanded No II (AC) Squadron, flying Reconnaissance Jaguars from Royal Air Force Laarbruch, until 1987 when he took up the post of Personal Staff Officer to the Chief of the Air Staff. He assumed command of Royal Air Force Marham in 1990, in time for Operation GRANBY; following this in 1993 he attended the Royal College of Defence Studies. He completed the Higher Command and Staff Course at Camberley prior to becoming the Director of Air Force Plans and Programmes in 1994.

He became Air Officer Commanding No 1 Group in April 1997 and was appointed Assistant Chief of the Air Staff in August 1998. He took up the appointment of Deputy Commander-in-Chief Strike Command in 2000 and at the same time he assumed the additional roles of Commander of NATO's Combined Air Operations Centre 9 and Director of the European Air Group. He spent the last few months of his tour as UK National Contingent Commander and Senior British Military Advisor to CINCUSCENTCOM for Operation VERITAS, the UK's contribution to the United States led Operation ENDURING FREEDOM in Afghanistan.

Air Chief Marshal Stirrup was appointed KCB in the New Year Honours List 2002 and became Deputy Chief of the Defence Staff (Equipment Capability) in March 2002. He became Chief of the Air Staff, on promotion, on 1 August 2003, and was appointed GCB in The Queen's Birthday Honours List 2005.

Professor Keith Grint

Keith Grint is Professor of Leadership Studies and Director of the Lancaster Leadership Centre at Lancaster University Management School. He was previously Director of Research at the Saïd Business School and Fellow in

Organizational Behaviour, Templeton College, University of Oxford. Keith spent 10 years in industry before switching to an academic career.

As well as being a founding editor (with David Collinson) of the new journal *Leadership,* he is also founding co-organizer of the International Conference in Leadership Research. He wrote the literature review for 'Strengthening Leadership in the Public Sector' 2000, a project of the Performance and Innovation Unit (Cabinet Office). His books include *The Sociology of Work* Polity Press 3rd edition 2005; *The Gender-Technology Relation,* (edited with Ros Gill) Taylor & Francis 1995; *Management,* Polity Press 1995; *The Machine at Work* (with Steve Woolgar) Polity Press 1997; *Leadership* (ed.) Oxford University Press 1997; *Fuzzy Management* Oxford University Press 1997; *The Arts of Leadership* Oxford University Press 2000; and *Work and Society* (ed.) Polity Press 2000; *Organizational Leadership* (with John Bratton and Debra Nelson) Southwestern /Thompson Press; and *Leadership: Limits and Possibilities* Palgrave/Macmillan, 2005

Professor Stephen Mugford

Stephen Mugford is Adjunct Professor in Social Work at the Australian Catholic University in Canberra and Managing Director of Qualitative & Quantitative Social Research. He has an honours degree in Sociology from the University of London (1968) and a PhD from the University of Bristol (1974). The work upon which this paper is based was undertaken in the latter role working as a paid consultant to the Royal Australian Air Force (RAAF).

Wing Commander Robert Rogers RAAF

Wing Commander Bob Rodgers is a serving RAAF officer. For several years he occupied a key position as the head of the Air Force Cultural Alignment Team (as it is now called) where he worked very closely with Professor Stephen Mugford.

Air Vice-Marshal Peter Dye OBE BSc (Eng) CEng ACGI MRAeS RAF

Air Vice-Marshal Peter Dye was commissioned in 1972. His career has largely comprised aircraft-related engineering appointments, including responsibility for the deployment and support of the Jaguar force in the Gulf during 1990/1. He was subsequently awarded the OBE for his work at Royal Air Force Coltishall as Officer Commanding Engineering and Supply Wing and then served as the Personal Staff Officer to three successive Commanders-in-Chief at Headquarters Support Command.

After a tour as Director of the Department of Specialist Ground Training at Royal Air Force College Cranwell, he attended the Royal College of Defence Studies. In April 1998, he was appointed the Senior Engineering Officer at

Royal Air Force St. Athan and subsequently the Deputy Chief Executive, Defence Aviation Repair Agency and Air Officer Wales. In August 2001, he was posted to the Training Group Defence Agency, where he undertook successive tours as Director Corporate Development and Air Commodore Ground Training.

He assumed the appointment of Deputy Commander-in-Chief Personnel and Training Command and Chief of Staff to the Air Member for Personnel on promotion to Air Vice-Marshal in March 2005.

Group Captain Malcolm K Crayford OBE MA RAF

Group Captain 'Ginge' Crayford was commissioned into the Fighter Control Branch of the Royal Air Force (RAF) in 1981. He is qualified as a Weapons Controller, Fighter Allocator and Master Controller and has served at a number of Air Surveillance and Control Systems (ASACS) stations throughout the UK and overseas including Belize, Cyprus and three tours in the Falkland Islands. Promoted to squadron leader in 1992 and following a further operational tour he assumed command of the ASACS Examining Team (STANEVAL). Staff tours at Headquarters 11/18 Group followed and in 1997/98 he was the Personal Staff Officer to the 2* Air Officer Commanding.

Promoted to Wing Commander in 1998, he worked on a study into the future of the UK's Air Command and Control capability prior to attending the Advanced Command and Staff Course at the Joint Services Command and Staff College. In July 2000, he assumed command of No 1 Air Control Centre (1 ACC) at RAF Boulmer during which he commanded deployments to Norway, Cyprus, Oman and Kazakhstan. A staff tour at HQ 2 Gp and subsequently 3 Gp followed in July 2002 where he was responsible for the operational effectiveness of the UK's ASACS organisation (both static and deployable), the Ballistic Missile Early Warning System Site III at RAF Fylingdales and the UK Missile Warning Centre at RAF High Wycombe. Promoted to Group Captain in January 2004, he assumed command of RAF Boulmer on 20 August 2004.

Group Captain Crayford gained a Master of Arts Degree in Defence Studies from King's College London in 2000 and was appointed as an officer to the Order of the British Empire in the Queen's Birthday Honours List in 2003.

Brian Howieson

Brian Howieson was a regular Officer in the Royal Air Force for 18 years. As a Navigator, he amassed 4000 hrs on the Nimrod R1 and MR2 aircraft and saw active service in the Gulf War, Kosovo War and United Nations Air Operations in Northern and Southern Iraq. A Defence Fellow (2002), he has BSc, MBA and MPhil Degrees and is due to complete his PhD in Leadership from the University of Edinburgh in 2006. He is now Head of Education and Professional Development for the Royal College of Physicians and Surgeons.

Professor John Benington

Following fifteen years prior experience of management in the public services John Benington moved into the academic world in 1985, lecturing in policy analysis and management at the School of Public Policy, Birmingham University. He joined Warwick Business School in 1988 to develop its work on public management and policy. He was Founding Director of the Local Government Centre within Warwick Business School for 12 years from its inception. In 2000 he moved on to become Founding Director of the new Institute of Governance and Public Management (IGPM) which was set up by Warwick Business School to provide a focal point for multi-disciplinary research, development and teaching on public management and policy. John was instrumental in the design and setting up of the Warwick MPA (a public sector MBA) and three related post-graduate diploma programmes for public policymakers and practitioners. Since January 2005 John has concentrated on teaching, research and development work within IGPM and WBS, focusing on public value, public leadership, and networked governance. He has a degree in English Literature from Cambridge University and a Diploma in Advanced Economic and Social Studies from Manchester University.

Assistant Chief Constable Irwin Turbitt

Irwin Turbitt is a serving PSNI (Police Service of Northern Ireland) officer seconded to the Police Standards Unit (PSU) in the Home Office where he is currently Deputy Director. He was previously the District Commander in charge of policing for the Craigavon District Command Unit (DCU) in Northern Ireland. Immediately prior to taking over in Craigavon, Irwin was involved in policing the 'Holy Cross' school dispute in North Belfast.

For almost two years prior to September 2001 Irwin was seconded to the Home Office National Police Training College at Bramshill in Hampshire. There he was the head of the Performance Development Unit.

Irwin is a judge for the Northern Ireland Quality Award, has been a senior assessor for the UK Excellence Award and has been involved in training award assessors in Northern Ireland. He has also assisted a number of organisations successfully with award applications and self-assessment. He currently leads in PSU on national projects and is deeply involved in violent crime, its reduction rather than its commission, and also in finding ways to improve police performance in armed, organised and serious violent crime prevention and detection.

A keen student of theory as well as practice Irwin has a first degree in Business Studies, a post graduate diploma in Risk Management and a Master of Public Administration (MPA) from the Warwick Business School. He now teaches on the MPA programme and on a variety of other programmes at Warwick, Lancaster, Harvard and a number of other institutions.

Group Captain John A Jupp OBE MA BA RAF

Group Captain John Jupp joined the Royal Air Force in 1979 as a pilot on completion of his degree in Philosophy and Mathematics at Kings College, London. He flew the Phantom and Tornado F3 in many parts of the world in operations and on exercise becoming an instrument rating examiner and weapons instructor eventually commanding 111(F) Squadron. On the ground, he investigated aircraft accidents, was part of the team developing Typhoon avionics and the operational fleet manager for the Tornado F3. He was also responsible for the preparation and deployment of all RAF operations during the fireman's strike and the second Gulf War before being promoted to Group Captain and setting up the RAF Leadership Centre. He attended Staff College with the Royal Navy and has a MA in Defence Studies.

Squadron Leader Harvey Smyth DFC RAF

Squadron Leader Harvey Smyth was commissioned in the Royal Air Force in 1991. Following flying training he was posted to the Harrier completing tours at RAF Cottesmore, RAF Laarbruch and RAF Wittering. During this time he became a qualified weapons instructor and was also a flight commander. Sqn Ldr Smyth has been involved in many operations including those in the Balkans, Iraq, Kosovo and Afghanistan. For his services Sqn Ldr Smyth was awarded the Distinguished Flying Cross.

Sqn Ldr Smyth spent two years at the Air Warfare Centre, RAF Waddington before being promoted to Wing Commander and posted to the Joint Service Command & Staff College, Shrivenham in late 2005.

Mr Sebastian Cox

Sebastian Cox holds a BA in History from the University of Warwick and an MA in War Studies from Kings College London. He was Curator of Documents at the RAF Museum before joining the MoD's Air Historical Branch (RAF). He has been with the Air Historical Branch (RAF) for two decades, and was appointed as Head of AHB (RAF) on an open competition in 1996. He has written widely on air power history and doctrine and lectured to military and civilian audiences in North America, Australasia and Europe.

Major General Stephen M Goldfein

Major General Stephen Goldfein is Commander, Air Warfare Centre, Nellis Air Force Base, Nevada. The centre conducts operational test and evaluation programs as directed by Headquarters Air Combat Command, and develops tactics for employment of fighter, bomber and unmanned aerial vehicle systems. The general is also responsible for the operations of the 53rd and 57th wings;

99th Air Base Wing; 98th Range Wing; 505th Command and Control Wing; U.S. Air Force Weapons School; Exercises Red Flag and Air Warrior; the Unmanned Aerial Vehicle and Air Expeditionary Force battle labs; and U.S. Air Force Air Demonstration Squadron, the Thunderbirds.

General Goldfein was commissioned in 1978 following graduation from the U.S. Air Force Academy, Colorado Springs, Colorado. His assignments include flying duties as a T-38 and F-15 instructor pilot and flight examiner, U.S. Senate liaison officer, Joint Director for Operations, executive officer to the Air Force Chief of Staff, and Deputy Director of Joint War Fighting Capability Assessments on the Joint Staff. The general also commanded a fighter squadron, operations group and fighter wing. Prior to his current assignment, he was Director of Operational Capability Requirements, Deputy Chief of Staff for Air and Space Operations, Headquarters U.S. Air Force.

During his career General Goldfein has been awarded the following decorations: Defence Superior Service Medal with oak leaf cluster; Legion of Merit with two oak leaf clusters; Meritorious Service Medal with three oak leaf clusters; Air Force Achievement Medal; Combat Readiness Medal with oak leaf cluster.

Doctor Stephen Bungay

Stephen Bungay was educated at St Catherine's College, Oxford, where he received an MA with First Class Honours. He studied for his doctorate at St Catherine's and the University of Tübingen, West Germany.

Stephen worked in the London and Munich offices of The Boston Consulting Group for a total of seventeen years, eight of them as Vice President and Director. On leaving BCG, he became CEO of the Commercial Division of a Lloyds-based insurance company before subsequently joining the Ashridge Strategic Management Centre.

He published his first book on military history, *The Most Dangerous Enemy – A History of the Battle of Britain*, in 2000, and a second, *Alamein*, appeared in 2002. He also works as an independent consultant and teacher and was a consultant to a recent BBC 2 series on leadership. He has made several television appearances, notably as the principal historian on the Channel 4 series 'Spitfire Ace' and 'Bomber Crew'.

Sergeant J F Tomiczek

Sergeant 'Tomi' Tomiczek joined the Royal Air Force in December 1980 as a Weapons Mechanic and served on the Tri-National Tornado Training Establishment at RAF Cottesmore in Rutland, working on the Tornado GR1 aircraft. 'Tomi' also served at RAF Brüggen in Germany. On promotion he was sent to RAF Marham in Norfolk before returning again in 1987 to RAF Brüggen during which time he served in the Falkland Islands and in Saudi Arabia during the first Gulf War. On return to the UK he served at RAF Lossiemouth in Scotland still working on the Tornado GR1/GR4 and completed numerous operational tours to Dhahran, Incirlik (Turkey), Al Kharj (Saudi Arabia) and Ali-al-Salem (Kuwait). He took up his present posting with 5131 (Bomb Disposal) Squadron in January 2002 and it was in this capacity that he served in the second Gulf War. In the course of his duties Sergeant Tomiczek has received the following campaign medals and commendations: Gulf 1990/91, Saudi Liberation of Kuwait, Kuwait Liberation, Long Service & Good Conduct, General Service Medal (Air Operations Iraq), Iraq 2003, the Joint Commander Desert Region Commendation and the Air Officer Commanding No2 Gp Commendation.

Corporal B. McGarrity

Corporal Brendan McGarrity joined the Royal Air Force in September 1987 as a Weapons Mechanic. He served at RAF Leeming in North Yorkshire, RAF Wildenrath in Germany and RAF Wittering near Stamford working on air weapons. In 1994 Brendan was posted to Gibraltar and worked within the Armament Engineering Flight before returning the following year, again to RAF Wittering this time to work as a member of 5131 Bomb Disposal (BD) Squadron. Following promotion, he spent the next 3 years within the Armament Engineering Flight supporting RAF Wittering and Cottesmore. In June 2000 he was posted once again to 5131 (BD) Squadron and whilst there served in the second Gulf War. Brendan was promoted to the rank of Corporal in September 2002 and attended the Junior Management and Leadership Course in early 2004, he is still a member of 5131 (Bomb Disposal) Squadron.

Air Commodore S. Abbott CBE RAF

Air Commodore Stephen Abbott joined the RAF in 1974 as a University Cadet. He gained a BA Honours degree at the University of East Anglia in 1977. He joined 37 Sqn RAF Regiment as a Rapier Flight Commander in 1978 and completed the Long Gunnery Staff course at Larkhill in 1981, followed by tours at RAF Leuchars and RAF Brize Norton. During this period, he completed 5 operational tours in Belize. He also completed tours as a Station Regiment Officer and on Ground Based Air Defence at RAF Coningsby and RAF Gütersloh and completed an operational tour in the Falkland Islands eventually commanding 20 Sqn RAF Regiment.

Air Commodore Abbott's staff officer duties have included being responsible for the all the UK Ground Based Air Defence systems, as Military Advisor to Commander British Forces Hong Kong and being responsible for RAF Nuclear Biological and Chemical Defence policy. In August 1997, he took up an appointment in the MOD Directorate of Air Plans. He commanded the newly formed No 3 RAF Force Protection HQ and deployed immediately to Ali-al-Salem on Operation BOLTON for a 7 month tour. He completed a further tour in Kuwait before returning to be Deputy Assistant Chief of Staff A3 Regiment & Survive to Operate at HQ Strike Command. In December 2001 he was appointed to command the Air Point of Disembarkation at Kabul airport in support of the International Security Assistance Force remaining in Kabul until May 2002. On his return he became Group Captain Force Protection Plans and Force Development for Air Officer Regiment. He commanded RAF Honington from June 03 to May 05 and was promoted to Air Commodore in March 05. He took up the post of Assistant COS Training/COS TG in May 05.

Air Commodore Abbott has attended Joint Service Defence College Greenwich, is a graduate of the Joint Higher Command and Staff Course and has completed a MPhil in International Relations at Downing College, Cambridge. He was awarded the Queens Commendation for Valuable Service in November 2000 and appointed CBE in January 2003.

Professor Alan Hooper DL MA FRSA

Alan Hooper is the Founder and Fellow of the Centre for Leadership Studies, University of Exeter. He is also a Visiting Professor at Bristol Business School. His first career was in the Royal Marines and he retired at the rank of Brigadier. He now consults widely on leadership and change-management with a particular focus on helping people to realise their leadership potential. He is also the author/co-author of four books.

Air Chief Marshal Sir Brian Burridge KCB CBE ADC RAF

Air Chief Marshal Sir Brian Burridge joined the Royal Air Force as a University Cadet in 1967. A pilot, his operational background is in the Maritime Patrol role, serving on No. 206 and 120 Squadrons. He commanded the Nimrod Operational Conversion Unit from 1986-88 and RAF Kinloss from 1990-92. He has also completed a number of tours as a flying instructor, which included command of Cambridge University Air Squadron.

His first staff tour was as Personal Staff Officer to the Air Officer Commanding-in-Chief Strike Command. From 1992-97, he served in MOD, initially as Deputy Director of Force Doctrine (RAF), later becoming the Director of Force Development in the Central Staff before spending almost 3 years as the Principal Staff Officer to the Chief of the Defence Staff.

Promoted to Air Vice-Marshal in 1998, he was appointed Air Officer Commanding No 11/18 Group with operational command of the RAF's air defence, maritime, and search and rescue forces. In this appointment, he was double-hatted in the NATO post of COMMAIREASTLANT. He became Commandant of the Joint Services Command and Staff College in January 2000, subsequently moving the College into a Public Private Partnership at Shrivenham. He was appointed Deputy Commander-in-Chief Strike Command in February 2002, and also assumed the role of Commander of NATO's

Combined Air Operations Centre 9, based at RAF High Wycombe. In October 2002, he was detached from his duties at Strike Command to become the UK's National Contingent Commander for operations against Iraq. Operating alongside US Central Command in Qatar, he commanded the 43,000-strong UK Joint Force during deployment, the combat phase and the early weeks of the aftermath, recovering to the UK in May 2003. He was subsequently appointed as a Knight Commander of the Order of the Bath in the Iraq Operational Honours List.

He has a degree in Physics (1970), an MBA from the Open University Business School (1999) and was a Defence Fellow at King's College, London (1997). He went to the Royal Naval Staff College (1986) and has attended both the Higher Command and Staff Course (1998) and the Cabinet Office Top Management Programme (1997). Air Chief Marshal Burridge speaks extensively in the UK and abroad on command and leadership. In 2003, he delivered, the Windsor Leadership Annual Lecture entitled High Stakes Strategic Leadership in Ambiguity and Chaos, the Open University Business School Annual Lecture entitled, Trust me, I'm a leader! – Orthodoxy or Oxymoron and an address to the CBI entitled, War and Business: synonymous or separate? In 2004 he gave the St George's House lecture on The Principles and Practice of Military Intervention in the Post-Modern World and in 2005 he delivered the Trenchard Memorial Lecture at RUSI.